# LATIN PHRASE BOOK

# LATIN PHRASE BOOK

## C. MEISSNER

Translated from the sixth German edition with the
addition of supplementary phrases and references

BY

## H. W. AUDEN

DUCKWORTH

This impression 2002

Gerald Duckworth & Co. Ltd.
61 Frith Street, London W1D 3JL
Tel: 020 7434 4242
Fax: 020 7434 4420
inquiries@duckworth-publishers.co.uk
www.ducknet.co.uk

A catalogue record for this book is available
from the British Library

ISBN 0 7156 1470 3

Printed in Great Britain by
Antony Rowe Ltd, Eastbourne

# PREFACE

ALTHOUGH, ideally speaking, a phrase-book should always be compiled by the pupil himself from his own individual observation, yet in these days, when an extended curriculum tends to curtail considerably the amount of Latin read, it seems to me that anything which may help boys to some knowledge of Latinity in a short time is not wholly useless. Hence this translation. The use of such books as *Meissner's Phraseologie* involves no new and untried principles, witness the excellent results obtained in Germany, where the book has passed through six editions. It has also been translated into French (the translation is now in its third edition) and Italian.

My best thanks are due to Professor Meissner for his courtesy in allowing me to make this translation, also to Professor Pascal of Reims, to whose admirable translation I am much indebted.

H. W. AUDEN.

FETTES COLLEGE, EDINBURGH,
1894.

# CONTENTS

# I. THE WORLD AND NATURE

## 1. THE WORLD—CREATION

*rerum* or *mundi universitas*—the universe.

*rerum natura* or simply *natura*—creation ; nature.

*haec omnia, quae videmus*—the visible world.

*totius mundi convenientia et consensus*—the perfect harmony of the universe.

*deus mundum aedificavit, fabricatus est, effecit* (not *creavit*) [1]—God made the world.

*deus est mundi procreator* (not *creator*), *aedificator, fabricator, opifex rerum*—God is the Creator of the world.

*elementa ; initia* or *principia rerum*—the elements.

*elementa et tamquam semina rerum*—the elements and first beginnings.

*nutus et pondus* or simply *nutus* ($\dot{\rho}o\pi\dot{\eta}$)—gravity.

---

[1] *Creare* is usually employed in the sense of producing, originating, causing, e.g. *similitudo creat errorem ; periculum alicui creare*. It has, however, occasionally the meaning to create, e.g. De Fin. *rerum quas creat natura*.

## 2. THE EARTH AND ITS SURFACE

*orbis terrae, terrarum* [1]—the earth ; the globe.

*(terra) continens* (B. G. 5. 8. 2)—the continent.

*terra (regio) mediterranea*—an inland region; the interior.

*interior Asia ; interiora Asiae*—the interior of Asia.

*sinus urbis* (Sall. Cat. 52. 35)—the heart of the city.

*in ipsam* or *intimam Graeciam penetrare*—to penetrate into the heart of Greece.

*terra effert* (more rarely *fert*,[2] but not *profert*) *fruges*—the earth brings forth fruit, crops.

*terra fundit fruges*—the earth brings forth fruit abundantly.

*animata (animalia) inanimaque* (not *inanimata*)—animate and inanimate nature.

*ea, quae terra gignit*
*ea, quae e terra gignuntur*
*ea, quae a terra stirpibus continentur*
*ea quorum stirpes terra continentur*
    (N. D. 2. 10. 26)
*arbores stirpesque, herbae stirpesque*
    (De Fin. 5. 11. 33)
} the vegetable kingdom.

*radices agere* (De Off. 2. 12. 73)—to take root.

*gemmas agere*—to bud, blossom.

*gemmae proveniunt*—the trees are budding.

*arbores frondescunt*—the trees are coming into leaf.

*rami late diffunduntur*—the twigs are shooting out, spreading.

---

[1] To the Romans *orbis terrarum* (more rarely *orbis terrae*) meant all those countries which made up the Roman Empire.

[2] *ferre* is also used metaphorically, to produce, e.g. *haec aetas perfectum oratorem tulit* (Brut. 12. 45).

*montes vestiti silvis*—wooded hills.

*summus mons*—the top of a mountain.

*culmina Alpium*—the summits of the Alps.

*sub radicibus montis, in infimo monte, sub monte*—at the foot of the mountain.

*superare Alpes, Pyrenaeum, Apenninum* [1] (both always in the sing.)—to cross the Alps, Pyrenees, Apennines.

*altissimis montibus undique contineri*—to be shut in on all sides by very high mountains.

*prospectus est ad aliquid*—one has a view over . . . ; one is able to see as far as . . .

*collis leniter ab infimo acclivis* (opp. *leniter a summo declivis*)—a gentle ascent.

*ad extremum tumulum*—on the edge of the hill.

*loca edita, superiora*—heights, high ground.

*loca aspera et montuosa* (Planc. 9. 22)—rough and hilly ground.

*loca plana* or simply *plana*—level country; plains

*saxa praerupta*—steep rocks.

*loca inculta*—uncultivated districts.

*loca deserta* (opp. *frequentia*)—deserts.

*loca amoena, amoenitas locorum*—pleasant districts; charming surroundings.

## 3. WATER—RIVERS—SEA

*summa aqua*—the surface of the water.

*ex aqua exstare*—to stand out of the water.

*aqua est umbilico tenus*—the water reaches to the waist.

*aqua pectus aequat, superat*—the water is up to, is above, the chest.

---

[1] But *Pyrenaei montes, saltus* occur (B. G. 1. 1. 7 ; B. C. 1. 37. 1).

*(se) ex aqua emergere* [1]—to come to the surface.

*aquam ex flumine derivare*—to draw off water from a river.

*aquam ducere per hortum*—to bring a stream of water through the garden.

*aquae ductus* (plur. *aquarum ductus*) [2]—a conduit ; an aqueduct.

*agros irrigare*—to irrigate fields.

*aqua viva, profluens* (opp. *stagnum*)—running water.

*aqua iugis, perennis*—a perpetual spring.

*frigidā, calidā lavari* (Plin. Ep. 3. 5. 11)—to take a cold, warm, bath.

*aquae, aquarum inops*—ill-watered.

*fluctuare* or *fluctuari*—driven by the waves.

*fluctibus iactari*—tossed hither and thither by the waves.

*fluctibus (undis) obrui,* [3] *submergi*—to be engulfed.

*gurgitibus hauriri*—to be drowned in the eddies.

*flumen citatum fertur*—the river flows with a rapid current.

*flumen imbribus auctum*—a river swollen by the rain.

*flumen super ripas effunditur* ⎱ the river is over its banks,
*flumen extra ripas diffluit* ⎰ is in flood.

*flumen agros inundat* [4]—the river floods the fields.

*flumen vado transire*—to wade across, to ford a river.

---

[1] Also used metaphorically, e.g. *(se) emergere ex malis* (Nep. Att. 11. 1) to recover from misfortune. So *emergere e fluctibus servitutis* (Harusp. Resp. 23. 48).

[2] *aquae ductio*=the action, process of drawing off the water ; *canalis*=the water-pipe, channel, conduit.

[3] So metaphorically, *aere alieno obrŭtum esse*, to be over head and ears in debt ; *nomen alicuius obruere perpetua oblivione*, to drown a person's name in oblivion.

[4] Inundation=*eluvio*, not *inundatio* which is post-classical.

*flumine secundo*—with the stream ; downstream.

*flumine adverso*—against the stream ; upstream.

*Rhenus oritur* or *profluit ex Alpibus*—the Rhine rises in the Alps.

*accessus et recessus aestuum*—ebb and flow (of tide).

*decessus aestus*—the ebb.

*aestus maritimi mutuo accedentes et recedentes* (N. D. 2. 53. 132)—the alternation of tides.

*aestus ex alto se incitat* (B. G. 3. 12)—the tide is coming in.

*aestu rursus minuente*—when the tide begins to go down.

*mare ventorum vi agitatur et turbatur*—there is a storm at sea.

*mare medium* or *internum* [1]—the Mediterranean Sea.

## 4. FIRE

*ignem facere, accendere*—to light, make a fire.

*ignem tectis inferre, subicere*—to set fire to houses.

*ignem concipere, comprehendere*—to take fire.

*ignem excitare* (pro Mur. 25. 51)—to make up, stir up a fire.

*ignem alere*—to keep up a fire.

*accendere, incendere aedificia*—to set buildings on fire.

*inflammare urbem*—to set fire to a city.

*flammis corrĭpi*—to be devoured by the flames.

*incendio flagrare*, or simply *conflagrare, ardere* (Liv. 30. 7) —to be on fire, in flames.

*incendio deleri, absūmi*—to be burned to ashes.

*igni cremari, necari*—to perish in the flames.

---

[1] The Romans called it *mare nostrum* (B. G. 5. 1). Similarly *mare Oceanus* (B. G. 3. 7), the Atlantic ; *mare superum*, the Adriatic (Att. 8. 16. 1) ; *mare inferum*, the Etruscan Sea (Att. 8. 3. 5).

*ignem conclamare*—to raise an alarm of fire.

*ventus ignem distulit* (B. G. 5. 43)—the wind spread
the conflagration.

## 5. AIR—SKY—CLIMATE—HEAVENLY BODIES

*aër terrae circumiectus* or
  *circumfusus*
*aër qui est terrae proximus* } the atmosphere.

*suspicere*[1] (*in*) *caelum*
*oculos tollere, attollere ad* } to raise the eyes to heaven ;
  *caelum* } to look up to the sky.

*sub divo*—in the open air.

*orbis finiens* (Div. 2. 44. 92)—the horizon.

*caelum* or *natura caeli*—climate.

*caelum salūbre, salubritas caeli* (opp. *grave, gravitas*)—
healthy climate.

*caeli temperatio*
*aër calore et frigore temperatus* } temperate climate.

*caeli asperitas*—rough climate.

*caeli varietas*—variable climate.

*caelestia*—(1) the heavenly bodies, (2) celestial pheno-
mena.

*sol oritur, occĭdit*—the sun rises, sets.

*ortus, occasus solis*—sunrise ; sunset.

*sol*[2] (*luna*) *deficit, obscuratur*—the sun, moon, is eclipsed.

*solis defectio*—an eclipse of the sun.

*luna crescit ; decrescit, senescit*—the moon waxes, wanes.

---

[1] *suspicere* is also used figuratively, to look up to, esteem, honour,
e.g. *viros, honores.* Similarly *despicere.*

[2] For an account of an eclipse *vid.* Liv. 44. 37.

*motus stellarum constantes et răti*—the regular courses of the stars.

*cursum conficere in caelo*—to run its course in the sky.

*caelum astris distinctum et ornatum*—the star-lit sky ; the firmament.

*nox sideribus illustris*—a star-light night.

*stellae errantes, vagae*—the planets.

*stellae inerrantes* (**N. D. 2.**

  2 1. 54) ⎫
*sidera certis locis infixa* ⎬ the fixed stars.
  ⎭

*orbis lacteus*—the milky way.

*orbis signifer*—the zodiac.

*vertex caeli, axis caeli, cardo caeli*—the pole.

*orbis, pars (terrae), cingulus*—a zone.

*orbis medius*—the temperate zone.


## 6. NATURAL PHENOMENA

*vocis imago,* or simply *imago* [1]—an echo.

*saxa voci respondent* or *resŏnant*—the rocks re-echo.

*ventus remittit* (opp. *increbrescit*)—the wind is falling.

*ventus cadit, cessat*—the wind dies down, is at rest.

*ventis secundis, adversis uti*—to have favourable, contrary, winds.

*ventus se vertit in Africum*—the wind is turning to the south-west.

*tempestas cooritur*—a storm is rising.

*imber tenet* (Liv. 23. 44. 6)—the rain continues.

*imbres repente effusi*—a sudden shower.

*tempestatem idoneam, bonam nancisci*—to meet with good weather.

---

[1] Also metaphorically, e.g. *gloria virtuti resonat tamquam imago* (Tusc. **3. 3**), glory is as it were the echo of virtue.

*calor se frangit* (opp. *increscit*)—the heat is abating.

*sol ardet, urit*—the sun burns, scorches.

*ardore solis torreri*—to be dried up by the sun's heat.

*tanta vis frigoris insecuta est, ut*—the frost set in so severely that . . .

*frigore (gelu) rigere, torpere*—to be numb with cold.

*frigore confici*—to freeze to death.

*aestus et frigoris patientem esse*—to be able to bear heat and cold.

*tempestas cum magno fragore (caeli) tonitribusque* (Liv. 1. 16) — a storm accompanied by heavy claps of thunder.

*caelum tonitru contremit*—the heavens are shaken by the thunder.

*fulmina* [1] *micant*—the lightning flashes.

*fulmen locum tetigit* — the lightning has struck somewhere.

*fulmine tangi, ici*  
*de caelo tangi, percŭti* } to be struck by lightning.

*fulmine ictus*—struck by lightning.

*eruptiones ignium Aetnaeorum*—an eruption of Etna.

*Vesuvius evŏmit* (more strongly *eructat*) *ignes*—Vesuvius is discharging flame.

*venti ab ortu solis flant*—the east winds are blowing.

---

[1] Used sometimes figuratively, e.g. *fulmen verborum, fulmina eloquentiae, fulmina fortunae* (Tusc. 2. 27), *fulmina imperii* (Balb. 15. 34).

## II. SPACE AND TIME

### 1. POINTS OF THE COMPASS—SITUATION

*spectare in (vergere ad) orientem (solem), occidentem* [1] *(solem), ad meridiem, in septentriones*—to lie to the east, west, south, north.

*spectare inter occasum solis et septentriones*—to be situate to the north-west.

*Germania quae* or *Germaniae ea pars quae, ad orientem, occidentem vergit*—eastern, western Germany.

*est a septentrionibus collis*—a hill lies to the north.

*situs loci*—the situation of a place.

*natura loci*—the natural position of a place.

*opportunitas loci* (B. G. 3. 14)—the advantageous situation of a place.

*opportuno loco situm* or *positum esse*—to be favourably situated.

*urbs situ ad aspectum praeclara est*—the city is very beautifully situated.

*oppidum mari adiăcet*—the town lies near the sea.

*villa tangit viam*—the country-house stands near the road.

*oppidum colli impositum est*—the town stands on rising ground.

*oppidum monti subiectum est*—the town lies at the foot of a mountain.

*promunturium in mare procurrit*—a promontory juts out into the sea.

---

[1] "The east" and "the west"=*orientis, occidentis (solis) terrae, partes, regiones, gentes.* The adjectives *orientalis, occidentalis* are not used in good Latin. The north, i.e. northern countries, is represented by *terrae septentrionibus subiectae ;* the south by *terra australis.*

*paeninsula in mare excurrit, procurrit*—a peninsula pro-
    jects into the sea.
*promunturium superare*—to double a cape.
*urbs in sinu sita est*—the city is situate on a bay.


## 2. BOUNDARY—TERRITORY—DISTANCE

*tangere, attingere terram* } to   be   contiguous,   adjacent
*finitimum* [1] *esse terrae*     }     to a country.
*continentem esse terrae* or *cum terra* (Fam. 15. 2. 2)—
    to have the same boundaries; to be coterminous.
*Gallia Rhodano continetur* (*vid.* p. 46, note)—Gaul is
    bounded by the Rhine.
*Rhodanus Sequănos ab Helvetiis dividit*—the Rhine is the
    frontier between the Helvetii and the Sequani.
*fines (imperii) propagare, extendere, (longius) proferre*—to
    enlarge the boundaries of a kingdom.
*(ex) finibus excedere*—to evacuate territory.
*in Sequanis*—in the country of the Sequani.
*in Sequanos proficisci*—to invade the territory of the
    Sequani.
*porrigi ad septentriones*—to stretch northwards.
*haec gens pertinet usque ad Rhenum*—the territory of this
    race extends as far as the Rhine.
*in latitudinem, in longitudinem patere*—to extend in
    breadth, in length.
*late patere* [2] (also metaphorically *vid.* p. 138)—to have a
    wide extent.

---

[1] *vicinum esse,* to be neighbouring; used of houses, gardens, etc.
[2] *patere* denotes extension in its widest sense; *pertinere,* extension
from one point to another, e.g. *ars et late patet et ad multos pertinet*
(De Or. 1. 55. 235); *ex eo oppido pars ad Helvetios pertinet* (B. G.
1. 6. 3).

*imperium orbis terrarum terminis definitur*—the empire
　　reaches to the ends of the world.
*longe, procul abesse ab urbe*—to be far from town.
*prope (propius, proxime) abesse*—to be not far away.
*paribus intervallis distare*—to be equidistant.
*tantundem viae est*—the road is the same length.
*longo spatio, intervallo interiecto*—at a great distance.
*intervallo locorum et temporum disiunctum esse*—to be
　　separated by an immense interval of space and time.
*a mille passibus*—a mile away.
*e longinquo*—from a distance.
*loca longinqua*—distant places.
*ultimae terrae* ⎱ the most distant countries, the
*extremae terrae partes* ⎰ 　world's end.
*longinquae nationes*—distant tribes.

## 3. ROAD—TRAVEL

*viam sternere (silice, saxo)*—to pave a road.
*substruere viam glarea* (Liv. 41. 27)—to make a gravel path.
*via strata*—a street, a made road.
*via trita* [1]—a well-trodden, much-frequented way.
*viam munire* [2]—to make a road.
*viam patefacere, aperire*—to open a route.
*ferro viam facere (per confertos hostes)*—to cut one's way
　　(through the enemies' ranks).
*viam intercludere* ⎱
*iter obstruere* ⎰ to obstruct a road ; to close a route.

---

[1] *tritus* is also used figuratively, e.g. *proverbium (sermone)
tritum* (De Off. I. 10. 33), *vocabulum latino sermone non tritum*
(Acad. I. 7. 27).

[2] Cf. in metaphorical sense, *viam ad honores alicui munire*
(Mur. 10. 23).

*via fert, ducit aliquo*—a road leads somewhere.

*in viam se dare* ⎫
*viae se committere* ⎭ to set out on a journey.

*viam ingredi, inire* (also metaphorically)—to enter upon a route; to take a road.

*rectā (viā)*—straight on.

*de via declinare, deflectere* (also metaphorically)—to turn aside from the right way; to deviate.

*(de via) decedere alicui*—make way for any one.

*Appia via proficisci*—to set out by the Appian road.

*erranti viam monstrare*—to direct a person who has lost his way.

*errores Ulixis*—the wanderings of Ulysses.

*viam persequi* (also metaphorically)—to continue one's journey, pursue one's course.

*longam viam conficere*—to accomplish a long journey.

*fessus de via*—weary with travelling; way-worn.

*Hercules*[1] *in trivio, in bivio, in compĭtis*—Hercules at the cross-roads, between virtue and vice.

*iter facere*—(1) to take a journey, (2) to make, lay down a road (rare).

*una iter facere*—to travel together.

*iter ingredi (pedibus, equo, terra)*—to begin a journey (on foot, on horseback, by land).

*iter aliquo dirigere, intendere* ⎫
*tendere aliquo* ⎭ to journey towards a place.

*longum itineris spatium emetiri*—to finish a very long journey.

*ex itinere redire*[2]—to return from a journey.

---

[1] *vid.* on this subject De Off. 1. 32. 118; Fam. 5. 12. 3.

[2] *reverti* means properly to turn back and retrace one's steps, after giving up one's intention of remaining longer in a place, or continu-

*in itinere* [1]—on a journey ; by the way.

*iter terrestre, pedestre*—travel by land, on foot.

*itinera diurna nocturnaque*—travelling day and night.

*iter unius diei* or simply *diei*—a day's journey.

*iter impeditum*—an impassable road.

*disiunctissimas ultimas terras peragrare* (not *permigrare*) —to travel through the most remote countries.

*peregrinatio*—a foreign journey.

*peregrinari, peregre esse*—to be travelling abroad.

*peregre proficisci*—to go abroad.

*aliquem proficiscentem prosequi*—to accompany any one when starting ; to see a person off.

*aliquem proficiscentem votis ominibusque prosequi* (*vid*. p. 88, note)—to wish any one a prosperous journey.

*rus excurrere*—to make a pleasure-trip into the country.

*ruri vivere, rusticari*—to live in the country.

*vita rustica*—country life (the life of resident farmers, etc.)

*rusticatio, vita rusticana*—country life (of casual, temporary visitors).

## 4. COMING—GOING

*pedibus ire*—to go on foot.

*discedere a, de, ex loco aliquo* }
*egredi loco ;* [2] *excedere ex loco* } to leave a place.

ing one's journey, cf. Div. I. 15. 27, *itaque revertit ex itinere, cum iam progressus esset multorum dierum viam.* Similarly *reditus* = return, *reversio* generally = turning back. Cicero only uses *revenire* in conjunction with *domum.*

[1] *ex itinere* implies that the march was interrupted, thus there is a difference between *in itinere aliquem aggredi* and *ex itinere*, etc. In the same way distinguish *in fuga* and *ex fuga*, e.g. *ex fuga evadere, ex fuga dissipati.*

[2] *relinquere*, e.g. *domum*, properly means to give up, renounce the possession or enjoyment of a place.

*decedere loco, de, ex loco* [1]—to quit a place for ever.

*ingredi, intrare urbem, introire in urbem*—to enter a city.

*portâ ingredi, exire*—to go in at, go out of a gate.

*extra portam egredi*—to go outside the gate.

*commeare ad aliquem*—to go in and out of any one's house ; to visit frequently.

*Romam venire, pervenire*—to come to Rome.

*adventus Romam, in urbem*—arrival in Rome, in town.

*in unum locum convenire, confluere*—to collect together at one spot.

*Romam concurrere* (Mil. 15. 39)—to stream towards Rome.

*obviam ire alicui*—to meet any one.

*obviam venire alicui*—to go to meet some one.

*obvium* or *obviam esse, obviam fieri*—to meet some one by chance.

*incidere in aliquem* } to meet, come across a per-
*offendere, nancisci aliquem* } son ; to meet casually.

*obviam alicui aliquem mittere*—to send to meet a person.


## 5. RIDING—DRIVING

*curru vehi, in rheda* (Mil. 21. 55)—to drive.

*equo vehi*—to ride.

*sternere equum*—to saddle a horse.

*conscendere equum* }
*ascendere in equum* } to mount.


[1] Cf. especially *decedere (ex, de) provincia*, used regularly of a magistrate leaving his province on expiry of his term of office. Similarly, where life is compared to a province, *decedere (de) vita*, or merely *decedere* = to quit this life, die (cf. De Sen. 20. 73).

*descendere ex equo*—to dismount.

*in equo sedere ; equo insidĕre*—to be on horseback.

(*in*) *equo haerere*—to sit a horse well; to have a good seat.

*calcaria subdere equo*
*calcaribus equum concitare*⎱to put spurs to a horse.

*equo citato* or *admisso*—at full gallop.

*freno remisso ; effusis habenis*—with loose reins.

*equum in aliquem concitare*—ride against any one at full speed ; charge a person.

*habenas adducere*—to tighten the reins.

*habenas permittere*—to slacken the reins.

*admittere, permittere equum*
*frenos*[1] *dare equo*⎱to give a horse the reins.

*agitare equum*—to make a horse prance.

*moderari equum*—to manage a horse.

*equi consternantur*—the horses are panic-stricken, run away.

*equos incitatos sustinere*—to bring horses to the halt when at full gallop.

## 6. WALKING—FOOTSTEPS—DIRECTION

*gradum facere*—to take a step.

*gradum addere* (sc. *gradui*) (Liv. 26. 9)—to increase one's pace.

*suspenso gradu*—on tiptoe.

*gradum sensim referre*—to retreat step by step.

---

[1] Cf. *frenos, calcaria alicui adhibere,* used metaphorically.

*vestigia alicuius sequi, per-*
    *sequi,* or *vestigiis aliquem*
    *sequi, persequi*                  ⎫
*vestigiis alicuius insistere,*        ⎬ to follow in any one's steps.
    *ingredi* (also metaph.)           ⎭

*loco* or *vestigio se non movere*—not to stir from one's place.

*recta (regione, via); in directum*—in a straight line.

*in obliquum*—in an oblique direction; sideways.

*obliquo monte decurrere*—to run obliquely down the hill.

*in contrarium; in contrarias partes*—in an opposite direction.

*in transversum, e transverso*—across; transversely.

*quoquo versus; in omnes partes*—in all directions.

*in diversas partes* or simply *diversi abeunt, discedunt*—they disperse in different directions.

*huc (et) illuc*—hither and thither.

*ultro citroque*—on this side and on that; to and fro.

*longe lateque, passim* (e.g. *fluere*)—far and wide; on all sides; everywhere.


## 7. MOVEMENT IN GENERAL

*se conferre in aliquem locum*  ⎫
*petere locum*                   ⎬ to go to a place.

*quo tendis?*—where are you going?

*sublimem* or *sublime* (not *in sublime* or *sublimiter*) *ferri, abire*—to fly aloft; to be carried into the sky.

*praecipitem ire; in praeceps deferri*—to fall down headlong.

*in profundum deici*—to fall down into the abyss.

*se deicere de muro*—to throw oneself from the ramparts.

*deicere aliquem de saxo Tarpeio*—to throw some one down the Tarpeian rock.

*Nilus praecipitat*[1] *ex altissimis montibus*—the Nile rushes down from very high mountains.

*se proripere ex domo*—to rush out of the house.

*humi procumbere*—to fall on the ground.

*humi prosternere aliquem*—to throw any one to the ground.

*in terram cadere, decidere*—to fall to the earth.

*in terram demergi*—to sink into the earth.

*appropinquare urbi*, rarely *ad urbem*—to draw near to a city.

*propius accedere ad urbem* or *urbem*—to advance nearer to the city.

*longius progredi, procedere*—to march further forward.

*Romam versus proficisci*—to advance in the direction of Rome.

*ad Romam proficisci*—to set out for Rome.

*properat, maturat proficisci*—he starts in all haste, precipitately.

*consequi, assequi aliquem*—to catch some one up.

*praecurrere aliquem (celeritate)* ⎫ to overtake and pass
*post se relinquere aliquem* ⎭ some one.

*multitudo circumfunditur alicui*—a crowd throngs around some one.

*per totum corpus diffundi*—to spread over the whole body.


## 8. TIME IN GENERAL

*tempus praeterit, transit*—time passes.

*tempus habere alicui rei*—to have time for a thing.

---

[1] *praecipitare* is also transitive, e.g. *praecipitare aliquem*, to hurl a person down ; *ruere* always intransitive except in poetry.

*tempus mihi deest ad aliquid faciendum*—I have no time to do something.

*tempus consumere in aliqua re*—to pass one's time in doing something.

*tempus terere, conterere (in) aliqua re*—to waste time on something.

*tempus conferre ad aliquid*—to employ one's time in . . .

*tempus tribuere alicui rei*—to devote time to anything.

*tempus non amittere, perdere*—to lose no time.

*nullum tempus intermittere, quin* (also *ab opere*, or *ad opus*) —to devote every spare moment to . . . ; to work without intermission at a thing.

*tempus ducere*—to spend time.

*aliquid in aliud tempus, in posterum differre*—to put off till another time ; to postpone.

*nihil mihi longius est* or *videtur quam dum* or *quam ut*—I cannot wait till . . .

*nihil mihi longius est quam* (c. Inf.)—nothing is more tiresome to me than . . .

*tempus (spatium) deliberandi* or *ad deliberandum postulare, dare, sibi sumere*—to require, give, take time for deliberation.

*paucorum dierum spatium ad deliberandum dare*—to give some one a few days for reflection.

*tempori servire,*[1] *cedere*—to accommodate oneself to circumstances.

*ex quo tempore* or simply *ex quo*—since the time that, since (at the beginning of a sentence).

---

[1] The verb *servire* helps to form several phrases, e.g. *servire valetudini*, to be a valetudinarian ; *iracundiae*, to be unable to restrain one's anger ; *brevitati*, to be concise ; *communi utilitati*, to be devoted to the public good, etc.

*eo ipso tempore, cum ; tum ipsum, cum*—at the same moment that, precisely when.

*incidunt tempora, cum*—occasions arise for . . .

*tempus (ita) fert* (not *secum*)—circumstances demand.

*tempus maximum est, ut*—it is high time that . . .

*haec tempora, nostra haec aetas, memoria*—the present day.

*his temporibus, nostra (hac) aetate, nostra memoria, his* (not *nostris) diebus*—in our time ; in our days.

*nostra aetas multas victorias vidit*—our generation has seen many victories.

*memoria patrum nostrorum*—in our fathers' time.

*aetate (temporibus) Periclis*—in the time of Pericles.

*antiquis* [1] *temporibus*—in old days, in the olden time.

*libera re publica*—in the time of the Republic.

*tempora Caesariana*—the imperial epoch.

*media quae vocatur aetas*—the middle ages.

*Pericles summus vir illius aetatis*  
*Pericles, quo nemo tum fuit clarior*  
*Pericles, vir omnium, qui tum fuerunt, clarissimus*  
} Pericles, the greatest man of his day.

*vir ut temporibus illis doctus*—a man of considerable learning for those times.

*tempore progrediente*—in process of time.

*primo quoque tempore*—at the first opportunity.

*hoc tempore*—at this moment.

*puncto temporis*—in an instant.

---

[1] *antiquitas* = the state of affairs in times gone by, not a division of time ; so *antiquitatis studia*, archaeology ; *veteres* or *antiqui poetae, populi*, the poets, people of antiquity ; *antiqua monumenta*, the relics of antiquity. *antiquitates* plur. is used for the institutions, usages of times gone by.

*momento* [1] *temporis*—at the important moment.

*in ipso discrimine* (*articulo*) *temporis*—just at the critical moment.

*temporis causa*—on the spur of the moment.

*ad tempus* [2] *adesse*—to be there at a given time.

*ad exiguum tempus*
*brevis* or *exigui temporis*⎰for a short time.

*satis longo intervallo*—after a fairly long interval.

*spatio temporis intermisso*—after some time.

*in praesentia, in praesens* (*tempus*)—at present; for the moment.

*in posterum ; in futurum*—for the future.

*in perpetuum*—for ever.

*semel atque iterum ; iterum ac saepius ; identidem ; etiam atque etiam*—more than once; repeatedly.

*futura providere* (not *praevidere*)—to foresee the future.

*futura* or *casus futuros* (*multo ante*) *prospicere*—to foresee the far distant future.

*futura non cogitare, curare*—to take no thought for the future.

*saeculi* [3] *consuetudo* or *ratio atque inclinatio temporis* (*temporum*)—the spirit of the times, the fashion.

*his moribus*—according to the present custom, fashion.

---

[1] *momentum* (i.e. *movimentum*) is properly that which sets in motion, which gives a decisive impulse to things, cf. Luc. iv. 819 *momentumque fuit mutatus Curio rerum.* Livy and later writers employ the word in the sense of a moment of time.

[2] *ad tempus* also means (1) according to the circumstances of the case, e.g. *ad tempus consilium capere*, (2) for a short time, temporarily.

[3] The *spirit* of a thing is usually rendered by such words as *natura, proprietas, ratio atque voluntas*, e.g. the spirit, genius of a language, *natura* or *proprietas sermonis ;* the spirit of the laws, *voluntas et sententia legum.*

## 9. YEAR—SEASONS

*praeterito anno* (not *praeterlapso*)—in the past year.

*superiore, priore anno*—last year.

*proximo anno*—(1) last year, (2) next year.

*insequenti(e) anno* (not *sequente*)—in the following year.

*anno*[1] *peracto, circumacto, interiecto, intermisso*—after a
      year has elapsed.

*anno vertente*—in the course of the year.

*initio anni, ineunte anno*—at the beginning of the year.

*exeunte, extremo anno*—at the end of the year.

*singulis annis, diebus*—year by year; day by day.

*quinto quoque anno*—every fifth year.

*ad annum*—a year from now.

*amplius sunt (quam) viginti anni* or *viginti annis*—it is
      more than twenty years ago.

*viginti anni et amplius, aut plus*—twenty years and more.

*abhinc (ante) viginti annos* or *viginti his annis*—twenty
      years ago.

*quinque anni sunt* or *sextus annus est, cum te non vidi*—I
      have not seen you for five years.

*quinque annos* or *sextum (iam) annum abest*—he has been
      absent five years.

*anno ab urbe condita quinto*—in the fifth year from the
      founding of the city.

*commutationes temporum quadripartitae*—the succession
      of the four seasons.

*verno, aestivo, auctumnali, hiberno tempore*—in spring,
      summer, autumn, winter time.

*ineunte, primo vere*—at the beginning of spring.

---

[1] Unless *one* is emphasised *unus* is left out with the following
words: *annus, mensis, dies, hora,* and *verbum*.

*ver appetit*—spring is approaching.

*suavitas verni temporis*—the charms of spring.

*summa aestate, hieme*—in the height of summer, depth of winter.

*hiems subest*—winter is at hand.

*hiemem tolerare*—to bear the winter.

*anni descriptio*—the division of the year (into months, etc.)

*annus (mensis, dies) intercalaris*—the intercalary year (month, day).

*fasti*—the calendar (list of fasts and festivals).


## 10. DAY—DIVISIONS OF THE DAY

*ante lucem*—before daybreak.

*prima luce*—at daybreak.

*luce (luci)*—in full daylight.

*ubi illuxit, luxit, diluxit*—when it was day.

*lucet*—it is daylight.

*diluculo*—in the morning twilight.

*advesperascit*—evening is drawing on.

*die, caelo vesperascente*—when it is growing dusk; towards evening.

*multus dies* or *multa lux est*—the day is already far advanced.

*ad multam noctem*—till late at night.

*de nocte, de die*—while it is still night, day.

*multa de nocte*—late at night.

*intempesta, concubia nocte*—in the dead of night; at midnight.

*silentio noctis*—in the silence of the night.

*vicissitudines dierum noctiumque*—the succession of day and night.

*noctes diesque, noctes et dies, et dies et noctes, dies noctesque,*
    *diem noctemque*—night and day.

*tempus matutīnum, meridianum, vespertinum, nocturnum,*
    —morning, noon, evening, night.

*tempora matutina*—the morning hours.

*in dies (singulos)*—from day to day.

*in diem vivere*—to live from day to day, from hand
    to mouth.

*alternis diebus*—every other day.

*quattuor dies continui*—four successive days.

*unus et alter dies*—one or two days.

*dies unus, alter, plures intercesserant*—one, two, several
    days had passed, intervened.

*diem proferre* (Att. 13. 14)—to adjourn, delay.

*biduo serius* [1]—two days late.

*horā citius*—an hour too soon.

*postridie qui fuit dies Non. Sept.* (*Nonarum Septembrium*)
    (Att. 4. 1. 5)—on the day after, which was Sep-
    tember 5th.

*hodie qui est dies Non. Sept. ; cras qui dies futurus est
    Non. Sept.*—to-day the 5th of September ; to-
    morrow September the 5th.

*dies hesternus, hodiernus, crastĭnus*—yesterday, to-day, to-
    morrow.

*diem dicere colloquio*—to appoint a date for an interview.

*ad diem constitutam*—at the appointed time.

*diem videre, cum . . .*—to live to see the day when . . .

*dies dolorem mitigabit*—time will assuage his grief.

*quota hora est ?*—what time is it ?

*tertia hora est*—it is the third hour ( = 9 A.M.)

*ad horam compositam*—at the time agreed on.

---

[1] Used absolutely "too late" = *sero ;* if "too late for," "later
than," always *serius (quam)*.

## III. PARTS OF THE HUMAN BODY

*omnibus artubus contremiscere*—to tremble in every limb.

*aures claudere, patefacere* (e.g. *veritati, assentatoribus*)—to turn a deaf ear to, to open one's ears to . . .

*aures praebere alicui*—to listen to a person.

*aures alicuius obtundere* or simply *obtundere* (*aliquem*)—to din a thing into a person's ears.

*in aurem alicui dicere* (*insusurrare*) *aliquid*—to whisper something in a person's ear.

*ad aures alicuius* (not *alicui*) *pervenire, accidere*—to come to some one's ears.

*aures erigere*—to prick up one's ears.

*oratio in aures influit*—his words find an easy hearing, are listened to with pleasure.

*aures elegantes, terĕtes, tritae* (De Or. 9. 27)—a fine, practised ear.

*neque auribus neque oculis satis consto*—I am losing my eyesight and getting deaf.

*caput aperire* (opp. *operire*)—to uncover one's head.

*capite aperto* (opp. *operto*)—bare-headed.

*capite obvoluto*—with head covered.

*caput demittere*—to bow one's head.

*caput praecīdere*—to cut off a man's head.

*caput*[1] *parieti impingere*—to strike one's head against the wall.

---

[1] *caput* has several metaphorical meanings, e.g. *capita coniurationis* (Liv. 9. 26), the leaders of the conspiracy ; *caput Graeciae*, the capital of Greece ; *caput cenae*, the chief dish ; *capita legis*, the headings, clauses of a law ; *id quod caput est*, the main point ; *de capite deducere* (Liv. 6. 15), to subtract from the capital ; *capitis periculum*,

*cervices* (in Cic. only in plur.) *frangere alicui* or *alicuius*—to break a person's neck.

*gladius cervicibus impendet*—a sword hangs over his neck.

*hostis*[1] *in cervicibus alicuius est*—the foe is at our heels, is upon us.

*promittere crinem, barbam* — to grow one's hair, beard long.

*passis crinibus*—with dishevelled hair.

*capilli horrent*—his hair stands on end.

*capilli compti, compositi* (opp. *horridi*)—well-ordered, well-brushed hair.

*extremis digitis aliquid attingere*—to touch with the finger-tips.

*frontem contrahere, adducere* (opp. *explicare*)—to frown.

*frontem ferire, percutere*—to beat one's brow.

*in fronte alicuius inscriptum est*—one can see it in his face.

*ab alicuius latere non discedere*—to be always at a person's side.

*a latere regis esse*—to belong to the king's bodyguard.

*manum (dextram) alicui porrigere*—to give one's hand to some one.

*manum non vertere alicuius rei causa*[2]—to make not the slightest effort ; not to stir a finger.

---

mortal peril ; *capitis deminutio* (*maxima, media, minima*) (Liv. 22. 60), deprivation of civil rights. *caput* is often combined with *fons* = source, origin, e.g. *ille fons et caput Socrates* (Cic. De Or. 1. 42) ; *in aegritudine est fons miseriarum et caput* (Cic.) By metonymy *caput* is used with *liberum* (and *noxium*) (Verr. 2. 32. 79) with the meaning of a free (guilty) person, individual.

[1] Cf. *velut in cervicibus habere hostem* (Liv. 44. 39) ; *bellum ingens in cervicibus est* (Liv. 22. 33. 6).

[2] Cf. *ne digitum quidem porrigere alicuius rei causa.*

*manus inicere, inferre, afferre alicui*—to lay violent hands on a person.

*manus tollere*—to raise one's hands in astonishment.

*manus dare*—to own oneself conquered, surrender.

*manu ducere aliquem*—to lead some one by the hand.

*manu* or *in manu tenere aliquid*—to hold something in one's hand.

*in manibus habere aliquid* (also metaphorically)—to have something in one's hands, on hand.

*de manu in manus* or *per manus tradere aliquid*—to pass a thing from hand to hand.

*ex* or *de manibus alicui* or *alicuius extorquere aliquid*—to wrest from a person's hand.

*e manibus dimittere*—to let go from one's hands.

*in alicuius manus venire, pervenire*—to come into some one's hands.

*in alicuius manus incidere*—to fall unexpectedly into some one's hands.

*in manus (m) sumere aliquid*—to take something into one's hand.

*in manibus*[1] *aliquem gestare*—to carry in one's arms.

*e (de) manibus effugere,*[2] *elābi*—to slip, escape from the hands.

*inter manus auferre aliquem*—to carry some one away in one's arms.

----

[1] Notice too *liberos de parentum complexu avellere* (Verr. 2. 1. 3. 7), to snatch children from their parents' *arms* (not *brachium*), so *in alicuius complexu mori; in alicuius complexu haerere. medium aliquem amplecti,* to take to one's arms, embrace; *libentissimo animo accipere,* to welcome with open arms.

[2] Distinguish *effugere aliquid,* to escape the touch of, e.g. *invidiam, mortem ;* and *effugere ex aliqua re,* to escape from a position one is already in, e.g. *e carcere, e caede, e praelio.* Notice *fugit me,* it escapes my notice.

*compressis manibus sedere* (proverb.) (Liv. 7. 13)—to sit with folded arms ; to be inactive.

*mordicus tenere aliquid*—to hold fast in the teeth (also metaphorically, obstinately).

*oculos conicere in aliquem*—to turn one's gaze on ; to regard.

*oculos circumferre*—to look in every direction.

*in omnes partes aciem (oculorum) intendere*—to gaze intently all around.

*omnium oculos (et ora) ad se convertere*—to draw every one's eyes upon one.

*omnium animos* or *mentes in se convertere*—to attract universal attention.

*conspici, conspicuum esse aliqua re*—to make oneself conspicuous.

*oculos (aures, animum* [1]*) advertere ad aliquid*—to turn one's eyes (ears, attention) towards an object.

*oculi in vultu alicuius habitant*—his eyes are always fixed on some one's face.

*oculos figere in terra* and *in terram*—to keep one's eyes on the ground.

*oculos pascere aliqua re* (also simply *pasci aliqua re*)—to feast one's eyes with the sight of . . .

*oculos deicere, removere ab aliqua re*—to turn one's gaze away from an object.

*oculos operire (morienti)* [2]—to close the eyes of a dying person.

*oculorum aciem alicui praestringere* (also simply *praestringere*)—to dazzle a person.

*oculos, lumina amittere*—to lose one's sight.

---

[1] *animum advertere aliquid = animadvertere aliquid =* to notice a thing ; *animadvertere* in *aliquem =* to punish a person.

[2] To shut one's eyes to a thing, *conivere in aliqua re.*

*oculis privare aliquem* }
*luminibus orbare aliquem* } to deprive a person of his eyes.

*oculis captum esse*[1] (*vid.* p. 36, note)—to be blind.

*ante oculos aliquid versatur*—something presents itself to my vision.

*oculis, ante oculos* (*animo*) *proponere aliquid*—to picture a thing to oneself; to imagine.

*ante oculos vestros* (not *vobis*) *res gestas proponite*—picture to yourselves the circumstances.

*cernere et videre aliquid*—to see clearly, distinctly.

*oculis mentis videre aliquid*—to see with the mind's eye.

*in oculis aliquem ferre* }
*aliquis est mihi in oculis* } to cherish as the apple of one's eye.

*abire ex oculis, e conspectu alicuius*—to go out of sight, disappear.

*venire in conspectum alicuius*—to come in sight.

*se in conspectum dare alicui*—to show oneself to some one.

*fugere alicuius conspectum, aspectum*—to keep out of a person's sight.

*in conspectu omnium* or *omnibus inspectantibus*—before every one, in the sight of the world.

*omnia uno aspectu, conspectu intueri*—to take in everything at a glance.

*non apparere*—to have disappeared.

*pedibus obterere, conculcare*—to trample under foot.

*ad pedes alicuius accidere*—to fall at some one's feet.

*ad pedes alicuius se proicere, se abicere, procumbere, se prosternere*—to throw oneself at some one's feet.

*ad pedes alicuius iacēre, stratum esse* (*stratum iacēre*)—to prostrate oneself before a person.

---

[1] Cf. *caecatus, occaecatus cupiditate, stultitia.*

*quod ante pedes est* or *positum est, non videre*—to fail to see what lies before one.

*sanguine manare, redundare*—to drip blood ; to be deluged with blood.

*vultum fingere*—to dissemble, disguise one's feelings.

*vultus ficti simulatique*—a feigned expression.

*vultum componere ad severitatem*—to put on a stern air.

*vultum non mutare*—to keep one's countenance, remain impassive.

# IV. PROPERTIES OF THE HUMAN BODY

## 1. FEELINGS—SENSATIONS—POWERS

*sensus sani, integri, incorrupti*—sound, unimpaired senses.

*sensibus praeditum esse*—to be endowed with sense.

*sensu audiendi carere*—not to possess the sense of hearing.

*sub sensum* or *sub oculos, sub aspectum cadere* / *sensibus* or *sub sensus subiectum esse*—to come within the sphere of the senses.

*sensibus percipi*—to be perceptible to the senses.

*res sensibus* or *oculis subiectae* (De Fin. 5. 12. 36) / *res quas oculis cernimus* / *res externae*—the world of sense, the visible world.

*sensus movere* (more strongly *pellere*)—to make an impression on the senses.

*aliquid sensus suaviter afficit* / *aliquid sensus iucunditate perfundit*—a thing makes a pleasant impression on the senses.

*pulsu externo, adventicio agitari*—to be affected by some external impulse, by external impressions.

*sevocare mentem a sensibus* (De Nat. D. 3. 8. 21)—to free
  one's mind from the influences of the senses.

*aliquid a sensibus meis abhorret*—something offends my
  instincts, goes against the grain.

*vires corporis* or merely *vires*—bodily strength.

*vires colligere*—to gain strength.

*vires aliquem deficiunt*—to lose strength.

*dum vires suppetunt*—as long as one's strength holds
  out.

*bonis esse viribus*—to be robust, vigorous.

*pro viribus* or *pro mea parte*⎫ as well as I can ; to the
*pro virili parte*[1] (cf. p. 70) ⎭    best of my ability.


## 2. BIRTH—LIFE

*in lucem edi*—to see the light, come into the world.

*ei, propter quos hanc lucem aspeximus*—those to whom we
  owe our being.

*tollere*[2] or *suscipere liberos*—to accept as one's own child ;
  to make oneself responsible for its nurture and
  education.

*aliquem in liberorum loco habere*—to treat as one's own
  child.

*sexus* (not *genus*) *virilis, muliebris*—the male, female sex.

*patre, (e) matre natus*—son of such and such a father,
  mother.

*Cato Uticensis ortus erat a Catone Censorio*—Cato of
  Utica was a direct descendant of Cato the Censor.

---

[1] *pro virili parte* is distinct from the other expressions, as implying
more assurance and confidence on the part of the speaker.

[2] It was the custom for a Roman father to lift up his new-born
child, which was laid on the ground at his feet ; hence the expression
*tollere, suscipere.*

*originem ab aliquo trahere, ducere*—to trace one's descent from some one.

*Romae natus,* (*a*) *Roma oriundus*—a native of Rome.

*cuias es ?*—what country do you come from ?

*natione, genere Anglus*—an Englishman by birth.

*ortus ab Anglis* or *oriundus ex Anglis*—a native of England.

*urbs patria* or simply *patria*—native place.

*animam, spiritum ducere*—to breathe, live.

*aëra spiritu ducere*—to breathe the air.

*animam continere*—to hold one's breath.

*cursu exanimari* (B. G. 2. 23. 1)—to run till one is out of breath.

*spiritum intercludere alicui*—to suffocate a person.

*in vita esse*—to be alive.

*vita* or *hac luce frui*—to enjoy the privilege of living; to be alive.

*vitam beatam* (*miseram*) *degere*—to live a happy (unhappy) life.

*vitam, aetatem* (*omnem aetatem, omne aetatis tempus*) *agere* (*honeste, ruri, in litteris*), *degere, traducere*—to live (all) one's life (honourably, in the country, as a man of learning).

*dum vita suppetit ; dum* (*quoad*) *vivo*—as long as I live.

*si vita mihi suppeditat* [1]
*si vita suppetit* } if I live till then.

*quod reliquum est vitae*—the rest of one's life.

*vitae cursum* or *curriculum* [2] *conficere*—to finish one's career.

---

[1] *suppeditare* (1) transitive, to supply sufficiently ; (2) intrans. to be present in sufficient quantities = *suppetere*.

[2] *vitae* (*vivendi*) *cursus* or *curriculum* = life, career—considering its duration, length. Life = biography is not *curriculum vitae*, but simply *vita, vitae descriptio*.

*Homerus fuit*[1] *multis annis ante Roman conditam*—Homer
lived many years before the foundation of Rome.

### 3. TIME OF LIFE

(The terms for the different ages of man are *infans,
puer, adulescens, iuvenis, senior, senex, grandis natu.*)

*ea aetate, id aetatis esse*—to be of such and such an age.

*a puero* (*is*), *a parvo* (*is*), *a parvulo* (*is*)—from youth up.

*a teneris unguiculis* (ἐξ ἁπαλῶν ὀνύχων) (Fam. 1. 6. 2)
—from one's cradle, from one's earliest childhood.

*ab ineunte* (*prima*) *aetate* (De Or. 1. 21. 97)—from one's
entry into civil life.

*ex pueris excedere*—to leave one's boyhood behind one,
become a man.

*flos aetatis*—the prime of youthful vigour.

*aetate florere, vigere*⎫
*integra aetate esse*⎭ to be in the prime of life.

*adulescentia deferbuit*—the fires of youth have cooled.

*aetate progrediente*—with advancing years.

*aetate ingravescente*—with the weight, weakness of declin-
ing years.

*aetas constans, media, firmata, corroborata* (not *virilis*)—
manhood.

*grandior factus*⎫
*corroborata, firmata aetate*⎭ having reached man's estate.

*sui iuris factum esse*—to have become independent, be
no longer a minor.

*aetate provectum esse* (not *aetate provecta*)—to be advanced in years.

---

[1] To live, speaking chronologically, is *esse*; *vivere* denotes to be
alive, pass one's life, e.g. *laute, in otio.*

*longius aetate provectum esse*—to be more advanced in years.

*grandis natu*—aged.

*aetate affecta esse*—to be infirm through old age.

*vires consenescunt*—to become old and feeble.

*senectute, senio confectum esse*—to be worn out by old age.

*exacta aetate mori*—to die at a good old age.

*ad summam senectutem pervenire*—to live to a very great age.

*senectus nobis obrēpit*—old age creeps on us insensibly.

*admodum adulescens, senex*—still quite a young (old) man.

*extrema aetas* ⎱ the last stage of life, one's last
*extremum tempus aetatis* ⎰　days.

*vita occidens*—the evening of life.

*aequalem esse alicuius*—to be a contemporary of a person.

*maior (natu)*—the elder.

*aetate alicui antecedere, anteire*—to be older than.

*quot annos natus es ?* ⎱ how old are you?
*qua aetate es ?* ⎰

*tredecim annos natus sum*—I am thirteen years old.

*tertium decimum annum ago*—I am in my thirteenth year.

*puer decem annorum*—a boy ten years old.

*decimum aetatis annum ingredi*—to be entering on one's tenth year.

*decem annos vixisse*—to be ten years old.

*decimum annum excessisse, egressum esse*—to be more than ten years old, to have entered on one's eleventh year.

*minorem esse viginti annis*—to be not yet twenty.

*tum habebam decem annos*—I was ten years old at the time.

*centum annos complere* &#125; to reach one's hundredth
*vitam ad annum centesimum* &#125; year, to live to be a
   *perducere.* &#125; hundred.

*accessio paucorum annorum*—the addition of a few years.

*tertiam iam aetatem videre*—to be middle-aged (*i.e.* between thirty and forty).

*in aetatem alicuius, in annum incidere*—to happen during a person's life, year of office.

*omnium suorum* or *omnibus suis superstitem esse*—to outlive, survive all one's kin.

*homines qui nunc sunt* (opp.
   *qui tunc fuerunt*)    our contemporaries; men
*homines huius aetatis, nos-*    of our time.
   *trae memoriae*

*posteri*—posterity.

*scriptores aetate posteriores* or *inferiores*—later writers.

## 4. HUNGER—THIRST

*esurire*—to be hungry.

*fame laborare, premi*—to be tormented by hunger, to be starving.

*famem tolerare, sustentare*—to endure the pangs of hunger.

*inediâ mori* or *vitam finire*—to starve oneself to death.

*fame confici, perire, interire*—to die of starvation.

*fame necari*—to be starved to death (as punishment).

*famem, sitim explere* &#125;
*famem sitimque depellere cibo* &#125; to allay one's hunger, thirst.
   *et potione* &#125;

*siti cruciari, premi*—to suffer agonies of thirst.

*sitim colligere*—to become thirsty.

*sitim haustu gelidae aquae sedare*—to slake one's thirst by a draught of cold water.

*famis et sitis* [1] *patientem esse*—to be able to endure hunger
and thirst.


## 5. LAUGHTER—TEARS

*risum edere, tollere* [2]—to begin to laugh.

*cachinnum tollere, edere*—to burst into a roar of laughter.

*risum movere, concitare*—to raise a laugh.

*risum elicere* (more strongly *excutere*) *alicui*—to make a
person laugh.

*risum captare*—to try and raise a laugh.

*risum tenere vix posse* ⎫ to be scarcely able to restrain
*risum aegre continere posse*⎭ one's laughter.

*aliquid in risum vertere*—to make a thing ridiculous, turn
it into a joke.

*lacrimas, vim lacrimarum effundere, profundere*—to burst
into a flood of tears.

*in lacrimas effundi* or *lacrimis perfundi*—to be bathed in
tears.

*lacrimis obortis*—with tears in one's eyes.

*multis cum lacrimis* ⎫ with many tears.
*magno cum fletu* ⎭

*lacrimas tenere non posse* ⎫
*fletum cohibere non posse* ⎪ to be hardly able to
*vix mihi tempero* ⎱ *quin lacrimem* ⎰ restrain one's tears.
*vix me contineo* ⎰

---

[1] *sitis* is also used metaphorically—e.g. *libertatis sitis* (Rep. 1. 43.
66), so *sitire*—e.g. *honores* (De Fin. 4. 5. 3), *libertatem* (Rep. 1. 43.
66), *sanguinem* (Phil. 2. 7. 20). The participle *sitiens* takes the
Gen. when used of a habit—e.g. *sitiens virtutis* (Planc. 5. 13).

[2] Not *in risum erumpere*, which only occurs in late Latin. However, *risus, vox, fletus erumpit* is classical, similarly *indignatio* (Liv.
4. 50), *furor, cupiditates* (Cael. 12. 28).

*lacrimas* or *fletum alicui movere*—to move to tears.

*prae lacrimis loqui non posse*—to be unable to speak for emotion.

*gaudio lacrimare*—to weep for joy.

*hinc illae lacrimae* (proverb.) (Ter. And. 1. 1. 99 ; Cael. 25. 61) hence these tears ; there's the rub.

*lacrimula* (Planc. 31. 76)⎱
*lacrimae simulatae*　　　　⎰crocodiles' tears.

## 6. HEALTH—SICKNESS

*bona* (*firma, prospera*) *valetudine*[1] *esse* or *uti* (*vid.* p. 84, note)—to enjoy good health.

*valetudini consulere, operam dare*—to take care of one's health.

*firma corporis constitutio* or *affectio*—a good constitution.

*infirma, aegra valetudine esse* or *uti*—to be ill, weakly.

*in morbum incidit*⎱he fell ill.
*aegrotare coepit*　　⎰

*morbo tentari* or *corripi*—to be attacked by disease.

*morbo affligi*—to be laid on a bed of sickness.

*lecto teneri*—to be confined to one's bed.

*vehementer, graviter aegrotare, iacēre*⎫
*gravi morbo affectum esse, conflictari,*⎬to be seriously ill.
　*vexari*　　　　　　　　　　　　　　　⎭

*leviter aegrotare, minus valere*—to be indisposed.

*aestu et febri iactari*—to have a severe attack of fever.

*omnibus membris captum esse*[2]—to be affected by disease in every limb ; to be paralysed.

---

[1] *valetudo* is a neutral term = state of health.　*sanitas* = soundness of mind, reason—e.g. *ad sanitatem reverti*, to recover one's reason.

[2] Note *auribus, oculis, captum esse*, to be deaf, blind ; *mente captum esse*, to be mad.

*ex pedibus laborare, pedibus aegrum esse*—to have the gout.

*pestilentia* (not *pestis*) *in urbem* (*populum*) *invadit*—the plague breaks out in the city.

*animus relinquit aliquem*—a man loses his senses, becomes unconscious.

*morbus ingravescit*[1]—the disease gets worse.

*morbo absūmi* (Sall. Iug. 5. 6)—to be carried off by a disease.

*assidēre aegroto* (Liv. 25. 26)—to watch by a sick man's bedside.

*aegrotum curare*—to treat as a patient (used of a doctor).

*curationes*—method of treatment.

*aegrotum sanare* (not *curare*)—to cure a patient.

*ex morbo convalescere* (not *reconvalescere*)—to recover from a disease.

*e gravi morbo recreari* or *se colligere*—to recruit oneself after a severe illness.

*melius ei factum est*—he feels better.

*valetudinem* (*morbum*) *excusare*[2]
  (Liv. 6. 22. 7), *causari*  } to excuse oneself on the score of health.
*valetudinis excusatione uti*


## 7. SLEEP—DREAMS

*cubitum ire*—to go to bed.

*somno* or *quieti se tradere*—to lay oneself down to sleep.

*somnum capere non posse*—to be unable to sleep.

---

[1] The comparative and superlative of *aeger* and *aegrotus* are not used in this connection, they are replaced by such phrases as *vehementer, graviter aegrotare, morbus ingravescit*, etc.

[2] But *se excusare alicui* or *apud aliquem* (*de* or *in aliqua re*) = to excuse oneself to some one about a thing.

*curae somnum mihi adĭmunt, dormire me non sinunt*—I cannot sleep for anxiety.

*somnum oculis meis non vidi* (Fam. 7. 30)—I haven't had a wink of sleep.

*arte, graviter dormire* (*ex lassitudine*)—to sleep soundly (from fatigue).

*artus somnus aliquem complectitur* (Rep. 6. 10)—to fall fast asleep.

*somno captum, oppressum esse* — to be overcome by sleep.

*sopītum esse*—to be sound asleep.

*in lucem dormire*—to sleep on into the morning.

*somno solvi*—to awake.

(*e*) *somno excitare, dormientem excitare*—to rouse, wake some one.

*e lecto* or *e cubīli surgere* — to rise from one's bed, get up.

*per somnum, in somnis*⎱
*per quietem, in quiete*⎰ in a dream.

*in somnis videre aliquid* or *speciem*—to see something in a dream.

*in somnis visus* (*mihi*) *sum videre*—I dreamed I saw . . .

*species mihi dormienti oblata est*—I saw a vision in my dreams.

*somnium verum evādit* (Div. 2. 53. 108)—my dream is coming true.

*somnium interpretari*—to explain a dream.

*somniorum interpres, coniector*—an interpreter of dreams.

*somniare de aliquo*—to dream of a person.

## 8. DEATH

*(de) vita decedere* or merely *decedere*  
*(ex) vita excedere, ex vita abire*  
*de vita exire, de (ex) vita migrare*  
*mortem (diem supremum) obire*  
    to depart this life.

*supremo vitae die*—on one's last day.

*animam edere* or *efflare*  
*extremum vitae spiritum edere*  
    to give up the ghost.

*animam agere*—to be at one's last gasp.

*mors immatura* or *praematura*—an untimely death.

*mature decedere*—to die young.

*subita morte exstingui*—to be cut off by sudden death.

*necessaria* (opp. *voluntaria*) *morte mori*  
*morbo perire, absūmi, consūmi*  
*debitum naturae reddere* [1] (Nep. Reg. 1)  
    to die a natural death.

*mortem sibi consciscere* [2]—to commit suicide.

*se vita privare*—to take one's own life.

*manus, vim sibi afferre*—to lay hands on oneself.

*vitae finem facere*—to put an end to one's life.

*talem vitae exitum* (not *finem*) *habuit* (Nep. Eum. 13)—  
    such was the end of . . . (used of a violent death).

*mortem oppetere*—to meet death (by violence).

*mortem occumbere pro patria*—to die for one's country.

---

[1] *sua morte defungi* or *mori* is late Latin, cf. Inscr. Orell. 3453 *debitum naturae persolvit.*

[2] *se interficere, se occidere, se necare* are rare. During the classic period, when suicide was not common, *ipse* is often added—e.g. *Crassum se ipsum interemisse* (Cic. Scaur. 2. 16), *Lucretia se ipsa interemit* (Fin. 2. 20. 66); but later, when suicide had become frequent, *se interemit ; nonnulli semet interemerunt* (Suet. Iul. 89), etc., occur commonly.

*sanguinem suum pro patria effundere* or *profundere*—to shed one's blood for one's fatherland.

*vitam profundere pro patria* ⎱ to sacrifice oneself for
*se morti offerre pro salute patriae* ⎰ one's country.

*dare venenum in pane*—to give a person poison in bread.

*venenum sumere, bibere*—to take poison.

*veneno sibi mortem consciscere*—to poison oneself.

*poculum mortis (mortiferum) exhaurire* (Cluent. 11. 31)—to drain the cup of poison.

*potestas vitae necisque*—power over life and death.

*plagam extremam* or *mortiferam infligere*—to inflict a death-blow.

*e* or *de medio tollere*—to remove a person.

*perii ! actum est de me !* (Ter. Ad. 3. 2. 26)—I'm undone ! it's all up with me !

## 9. BURIAL

*funere efferri* or simply *efferri (publice ; publico, suo sumptu)* —to be interred (at the expense of the state, at one's own cost).

*sepultura aliquem afficere*—to bury a person.

*iusta facere, solvere alicui* ⎱ to perform the last rites
*supremo officio in aliquem fungi* ⎰ for a person.

*funus alicui facere, ducere* (Cluent. 9. 28)—to carry out the funeral obsequies.

*funus alicuius exsequi* ⎱ to attend a person's
*exsequias alicuius funeris prosequi* ⎰ funeral.

*supremis officiis aliquem prosequi* (*vid.* p. 88, note) — to perform the last offices of affection.

*mortuum in sepulcro condere*—to entomb a dead body.

*aliquem mortuum* [1] *cremare* (Sen. 23. 84)—to burn a corpse.
*pompa funebris*—a funeral procession.
*funus* or *exsequias celebrare*—to celebrate the obsequies.
*ludos funebres alicui dare* — to give funeral games in
      honour of a person.
*oratio funebris* [2]—a funeral oration.
*sepulturae honore carere* ⎱ to be deprived of the rites of
*iustis exsequiarum carere* ⎰    burial.
*elogium in sepulcro incisum*—the epitaph.
*sepulcro* (Dat.) or *in sepulcro hoc inscriptum est*—this is the
      inscription on his tomb . . .
*hic situs est* . . .—here lies . . .
*aliquem in rogum imponere*—to place on the funeral-pyre.
*proiici inhumatum (in publicum)*—to be cast out unburied.


# V. HUMAN LIFE; ITS VARIOUS RELA-
## TIONS AND CONDITIONS

### 1. CIRCUMSTANCE—SITUATION—
### DIFFICULTY

*res humanae* or simply *res*—human life.
*haec est rerum humanarum* ⎱
   *condicio*       ⎰ that is the way of the world;
                    such is life.
*sic vita hominum est* ⎰
*ita (ea lege, ea condicione) nati sumus*—this is our natural
      tendency, our destiny; nature compels us.

---

[1] "Corpse" usually = *corpus mortui* or simply *corpus*. *cadaver* is a
corpse which has begun to decompose.
[2] For eulogy, panegyric, use *laudatio funebris* or simply *laudatio*,
cf. Mil. 13. 33; Liv. 5. 50.

*res externas* or *humanas despicere*—to despise earthly things.

*res humanas infra se positas arbitrari*—to feel superior to the affairs of this life.

*meliore (deteriore) condicione esse, uti*—to find one's circumstances altered for the better (the worse.)

*condicio ac fortuna hominum infimi generis*—the position of the lower classes.

*res meae meliore loco, in*⎫
*meliore causa sunt*  ⎬ my position is considerably improved; my prospects are brighter.
*meliorem in statum redigor*⎭

*aliquem in antiquum statum, in pristinum restituere*—to restore a man to his former position.

*in tanta rerum (temporum) iniquitate*—under such unfavourable circumstances.

*res dubiae, perditae, afflictae*—a critical position; a hopeless state of affairs.

*in angustias adducere aliquem*—to place some one in an embarrassing position.

*in angustiis, difficultatibus,*⎫
*esse* or *versari*  ⎬ to be in a dilemma; in difficulties.
*angustiis premi, difficultatibus*⎪
*affici*  ⎭

*agitur praeclare, bene cum aliquo*—so-and-so is in a very satisfactory position; prospers.

*res ita est, ita (sic) se habet*—the facts are these; the matter stands thus.

*eadem (longe alia) est huius rei ratio*—the case is exactly similar (entirely different).

*hoc longe aliter, secus est*—this is quite another matter.

*res (ita) fert*—circumstances make this necessary; the exigencies of the case are these.

*pro re (nata), pro tempore*  
*pro tempore et pro re* } according to circumstances.

*res eo* or *in eum locum deducta est, ut . . .*—the matter
has gone so far that . . .; the state of affairs is
such that . . .

*quo loco res tuae sunt?*—how are you getting on?

*eadem est causa mea* or *in eadem causa sum*—my circumstances have not altered.

*si quid (humanitus) mihi accidat* or *acciderit*—if anything
should happen to me; if I die.

*quae cum ita sint*—under such circumstances.

*utcumque res ceciderit*—whatever happens; in any case.


## 2. COMMENCEMENT—END—RESULT

*initium capere; incipere ab aliqua re*—to begin with a
thing.

*initium facere, ducere, sumere (alicuius rei)*—to commence
a thing.

*ab exiguis initiis proficisci*—to start from small beginnings.

*parare* with Inf.  
*aggredi ad aliquid faciendum* } to prepare to do a thing.

*incunabula* [1] *doctrinae* — the origin, first beginnings of
learning.

*finem facere alicuius rei*  
*finem imponere, afferre, consti-*  
   *tuere alicui rei*  
*ad finem aliquid adducere*  
*ad exitum aliquid perducere*  
} to finish, complete, fulfil,
accomplish a thing.

*finem habere*—to come to an end.

---

[1] *incunabula* literally swaddling-clothes. *cunabula*, cradle, is not
used in this metaphorical sense except in post-Augustan Latin.

*aliquid* (*bene, prospere*) *succedit* or *procedit* (opp. *parum procedere, non succedere*)—the matter progresses favourably, succeeds.

*eventum, exitum* (*felicem*) *habere*—to turn out (well); to result (satisfactorily).

*quorsum haec res cadet* or *evadet?*—what will be the issue, end, consequence of the matter?

*ad irritum redigere aliquid*—to frustrate, nullify.

*res aliter cecidit ac putaveram*—the result has surprised me; I was not prepared for this development.

*quid illo fiet?*—what will become of him?

*quid huic homini* (also *hoc homine*) *faciam?*—what am I to do with this fellow?


## 3. CAUSE—MOTIVE—ORIGIN

*causam afferre*—to quote as a reason; give as excuse.

*iustis de* [1] *causis*—for valid reasons.

*magnae* (*graves*) *necessariae causae* — cogent, decisive reasons.

*non sine causa*—on good grounds; reasonably.

*quid causae fuit cur . . . ?*—how came it that . . . ?

*causa posita est in aliqua re*
*causa repetenda est ab aliqua re* (not *quaerenda*) } the motive, cause, is to be found in . . .

*multae causae me impulerunt ad aliquid* or *ut . . .*—I was induced by several considerations to . . .

*causam interponere* or *interserere*—to interpose, put forward an argument, a reason.

---

[1] Notice the order; so regularly *ea* and *qua de causa;* but *ob eam causam* not *eam ob causam.* For the meaning of *iustus* cf. xvi. 5 *bellum iustum* and xvi. 10a *praelium iustum.*

*praetendere, praetexere aliquid*—to make something an excuse, pretext.

*causam idoneam nancisci*—to find a suitable pretext.

*per causam* (with Gen.)—under the pretext, pretence of . . .

*causae rerum et consecutiones*—cause and effect.

*causae extrinsecus allatae* (opp. *in ipsa re positae*)—extraneous causes.

*rerum causae aliae ex aliis nexae*—concatenation, interdependence of causes.

*ex parvis saepe magnarum rerum momenta pendent* —important results are often produced by trivial causes.

*ex aliqua re nasci, manare*  
*ab aliqua re proficisci*  }to originate in, arise from.

*ex aliqua re redundare* (*in* or *ad aliquid*)—to accrue in great abundance.

*utilitas efflorescit ex aliqua re*—untold advantages arise from a thing.

*e fontibus haurire* (opp. *rivulos consectari* or *fontes non videre*)—to draw from the fountain-head.

*haec ex eodem fonte fluunt, manant*—these things have the same origin.

*fons et caput* (*vid.* p. 24, note)—source, origin.


## 4. REGARD—IMPORTANCE—INFLUENCE— POWER—INCLINATION

*rationem habere alicuius rei*  }to have regard for; take  
*respicere* [1] *aliquid*  }  into consideration.

*quo in genere*—from this point of view; similarly.

---

[1] But *respicere ad aliquid* (*aliquem*)=to look round at an object.

*multis rebus* or *locis*—in many respects; in many points.

*in utraque re*—in both cases; whichever way you look at it.

*ceteris rebus* (not *cetera*)—as regards the rest; otherwise.

*omni ex parte; in omni genere; omnibus rebus*—from every point of view; looked at in every light.

*aliqua ex parte*⎫  
*aliquatenus* ⎭ to a certain extent.

*magni (nullius) momenti esse*—to be of great (no) importance.

*momentum afferre ad aliquid*—to determine the issue of; to turn the scale.

*pertinere ad aliquid*—to be essentially important to a thing.

*hoc nihil ad sapientem pertinet*—a wise man is in no way affected by this.

*hoc in sapientem non cadit*—it is incompatible with the nature of a wise man; the wise are superior to such things.

*multum valere ad aliquid*⎫ to contribute much towards  
*multum afferre ad aliquid*⎭ . . .; to affect considerably; to be instrumental in . . .

*magnam vim habere ad aliquid*—to have considerable influence on a question.

*positum, situm esse in aliqua re*⎫  
*contineri aliqua re* [1] ⎪  
*consistere in aliqua re* ⎬ to depend upon a thing.  
*pendēre ex aliqua re* ⎭

*in te omnia sunt*—everything depends on you.

---

[1] *contineri aliqua re* also means (1) to be bounded by . . ., e.g. *oceano*; (2) to be limited, restricted to, e.g. *moenibus*.

*in ea re omnia vertuntur*—all depends on this; this is the decisive point.

*constare ex aliqua re*—to be composed of; to consist of.

*cernitur (in) aliqua re* (not *ex aliqua re*)—it is evident from . . .

*in manu, in potestate alicuius*
　*situm, positum esse*　　　　⎫
*penes aliquem esse*　　　　 ⎬ to be in a person's power.

*res integra* [1] *est*—the matter is still undecided; it is an open question.

*res mihi integra est*—I have not yet committed myself.

*mihi non est integrum, ut* . . .—it is no longer in my power.

*integrum (causam integram) sibi reservare*—to leave the question open; to refuse to commit oneself.

*quantum in me (situm) est*—as far as in me lies; to the best of my ability.

*penes te arbitrium huius rei est*—the decision of the question rests with you.

*arbitrio alicuius omnia permittere*⎫ to put the matter en-
*omnium rerum arbitrium alicui*　 ⎬ tirely in some one's
　*permittere*　　　　　　　 ⎭ hands.

*arbitratu, arbitrio tuo*—just as you wish.


## 5. OPPORTUNITY—POSSIBILITY—OCCASION— CHANCE

*occasio datur, offertur*—a favourable[2] opportunity presents itself.

---

[1] The proper meaning of *integer* (*in-TAG, tango*) is untouched, unsullied.

[2] Not *occasio opportuna, bona, pulchra*, the notion "favourable" being contained in the word itself. We find, however, *occasio praeclara, ampla, tanta*, not unfrequently.

*occasione data, oblata*⎫ when occasion offers ; as oppor-
*per occasionem*　　　⎭ tunity occurs.

*quotienscunque occasio oblata est ; omnibus locis*—on every
　　occasion ; at every opportunity.

*occasionem alicui dare, praebere*⎫
　*alicuius rei* or *ad aliquid*　　　｜
　　*faciendum*　　　　　　　　　　｜ to give a man the
*facultatem alicui dare alicuius*　 ⎬ opportunity of doing
　*rei* or *ut possit* . . .　　　　　 ｜ a thing.
*potestatem,*[1] *copiam alicui dare,*　｜
　*facere* with Gen. gerund.　　　　⎭

*occasionem nancisci*—to get, meet with, a favourable
　　opportunity.

*occasione uti*—to make use of, avail oneself of an oppor-
　　tunity.

*occasionem praetermittere, amittere* (through carelessness),
　　*omittere* (deliberately), *dimittere* (through indiffer-
　　ence)—to lose, let slip an opportunity.

*occasioni deesse*[2]—to neglect an opportunity.

*occasionem arripere*—to seize an opportunity.

*facultatem, potestatem alicui eripere, adimere*—to deprive
　　a man of the chance of doing a thing.

*nulla est facultas alicuius rei*—no opportunity of carrying
　　out an object presents itself.

*locum dare suspicioni*—to give ground for suspicion.

---

[1] Notice *potestatem alicui pugnandi facere,* to offer battle, and
*potestatem sui facere alicui,* (1) to give opportunity of battle, and
also (2) to grant an audience to (cf. *sui conveniendi potestatem
facere*).

[2] In the same way *deesse officio,* to leave one's duties undone ;
*d. muneri,* to neglect the claims of one's vocation ; *d. rei publicae,*
to be careless of state interests, to be unpatriotic ; *d. sibi,* not to
do one's best.

*ansas dare ad reprehendendum, reprehensionis*—to give occasion for blame ; to challenge criticism.

*ansam habere reprehensionis*—to contain, afford matter for criticism.

*adduci aliqua re (ad aliquid* or *ut . . .)*—to be induced by a consideration.

*nescio quo casu* (with Indic.)—by some chance or other.

*temere et fortuito ; forte (et) temere*—quite accidentally, fortuitously.


## 6. SUCCESS—GOOD FORTUNE

*fortuna secunda uti*—to be fortunate, lucky.

*fortunae favore* or *prospero flatu* \
  *fortunae uti (vid.* note, p. 84) } to be favoured by Fortune ; to bask in Fortune's smiles. \
*fortunam fautricem nancisci*

*fortuna caecos homines efficit, animos occaecat*—Fortune makes men shortsighted, infatuates them.

*fortunam tentare, experiri*—to try one's luck.

*fortunam periclitari (periculum facere)*—to run a risk ; to tempt Providence.

*fortunae se committere*—to trust to luck.

*fortunam in manibus habere*—to have success in one's grasp.

*fortunam ex manibus dimittere*—to let success slip through one's fingers.

*fortuna commutatur, se inclinat*—luck is changing, waning.

*ludibrium fortunae*—the plaything of Fortune.

*is, quem fortuna complexa est*—Fortune's favourite.

*a fortuna desertum, derelictum esse*—to be abandoned by good luck.

*fortuna aliquem effert*—Fortune exalts a man, makes him conspicuous.

*rebus secundis efferri*—to be puffed up by success; to be made arrogant by prosperity.

*ad felicitatem (magnus) cumu-*
*lus accedit ex aliqua re* — his crowning happiness is
*aliquid felicitatis cumulum* — produced by a thing;
*affert* — the culminating point of
*aliquid felicitatem magno* — his felicity is . . .
*cumulo auget*

*in rebus prosperis et ad voluntatem fluentibus*—when life runs smoothly.

*beata vita, beate vivere, beatum esse* [1]—happiness, bliss.

*ad bene beateque vivendum*—for a life of perfect happiness.

*peropportune accidit, quod*—it is most fortunate that . . .


## 7. MISFORTUNE—FATE—RUIN

*fortuna adversa*
*res adversae, afflictae, perditae* } misfortune, adversity.

*in calamitatem incidere*—to be overtaken by calamity.

*calamitatem accipere, subire*—to suffer mishap.

*nihil calamitatis (in vita) videre*—to live a life free from all misfortune.

*calamitatem haurire*
*omnes labores exanclare* } to drain the cup of sorrow.[2]

---

[1] *beatitas* and *beatitudo* are used by Cicero in one passage only (De Nat. Deorum, I. 34. 95), but merely as a linguistic experiment.

[2] In Latin metaphor the verb only, as a rule, is sufficient to express the metaphorical meaning—e.g. *amicitiam iungere cum aliquo*, to be bound by the bands of affection to any one; *religionem labefactare*, to undermine the very foundations of belief; *bellum exstinguere*, to extinguish the torch of war; *cuncta bello ardent*, the fires of war are

*calamitatem, pestem inferre alicui*—to bring mishap, ruin on a person.

*calamitatibus affligi*—to be the victim of misfortune.

*calamitatibus obrui*—to be overwhelmed with misfortune.

*calamitatibus defungi*—to come to the end of one's troubles.

*calamitate doctus*—schooled by adversity.

*conflictari (cum) adversa fortuna*—to struggle with adversity.

*in malis iacere*—to be broken down by misfortune.

*malis urgeri*—to be hard pressed by misfortune.

*fortunae vicissitudines*—the vicissitudes of fortune.

*ancipites et varii casus*—the changes and chances of this life.

*sub varios incertosque casus subiectum esse*—to have to submit to the uncertainties of fortune; to be subject to Fortune's caprice.

*multis casibus iactari*—to experience the ups and downs of life.

*ad omnes casus subsidia comparare*—to be prepared for all that may come.

*varia fortuna uti*—to experience the vicissitudes of fortune; to have a chequered career.

*multis iniquitatibus exerceri*[1]—to be severely tried by misfortune.

raging all around; *libido consedit*, the storm of passion has ceased; *animum pellere*, to strike the heart-strings; *vetustas monumenta exederat*, the tooth of time had eaten away the monuments.

[1] The first meaning of *exercere* is to keep in motion, give no rest to. Then, metaphorically, to keep busy, to harass—e.g. *fortuna aliquem vehementer exercet*. Lastly, *exercere* is used to express the main activity in any branch of industry, thus, *exercere agros*, to farm; *metalla*, to carry on a mining industry; *navem*, to fit out ships, be a shipowner; *vectigalia*, to levy, collect taxes, used specially of the *publicani; qui exercet iudicium*, the presiding judge (praetor).

*fortunae telis propositum esse*—to be exposed to the assaults of fate.

*fortunae obiectum esse*—to be abandoned to fate.

*ad iniurias fortunae expositum esse*—to be a victim of the malice of Fortune.

*fortunae cedere*—to acquiesce in one's fate.

*aliquem affligere, perdere, pessumdare, in praeceps dare*—to bring a man to ruin; to destroy.

*praecipitem agi, ire*
*ad exitium vocari*
*ad interitum ruere* ⎫to be ruined, undone.
*in perniciem incurrere*⎭

*pestem alicui (in aliquem) machinari*⎫ to compass, devise a
*perniciem (exitium) alicui afferre,* ⎬ man's overthrow,
  *moliri, parare*⎭ ruin.

*ab exitio, ab interitu aliquem vindicare*—to rescue from destruction.

## 8. DANGER—RISK—SAFETY

*in periculo esse* or *versari*—to be in danger.

*res in summo discrimine versatur*—the position is very critical.

*in vitae discrimine versari*—to be in peril of one's life.

*in pericula incidere, incurrere*—to find oneself in a hazardous position.

*pericula alicui impendent, imminent*—dangers threaten a man.

*pericula in* or *ad aliquem redundant*—many dangers hem a person in; one meets new risks at every turn.

*pericula subire, adire, suscipere*—to incur danger, risk.

*periculis se offerre*—to expose oneself to peril.

*salutem, vitam suam in discrimen offerre* (not *exponere*)—to risk one's life.

*aliquem, aliquid in periculum (discrimen) adducere, vocare*[1]
*alicui periculum creare, conflare*
} to endanger, imperil a person or thing.

*in periculum capitis, in discrimen vitae se inferre*—to recklessly hazard one's life.

*salus, caput, vita alicuius agitur, periclitatur, in discrimine est* or *versatur*—a man's life is at stake, is in very great danger.

*in ipso periculi discrimine*—at the critical moment.

*aliquem ex periculo eripere, servare*—to rescue from peril.

*nullum periculum recusare pro*—to avoid no risk in order to . . .

*periculis perfungi*—to surmount dangers.

*periculum facere alicuius rei*—to make trial of; to risk.

*periculum hostis facere*—to try one's strength with the enemy; to try issue of battle.

*res ad extremum casum perducta est*
*ad extrema perventum est*
} affairs are desperate; we are reduced to extremities.

*in tuto esse*—to be in a position of safety.

*in tuto collocare aliquid*—to ensure the safety of a thing.

---

[1] *vocare* helps to form several phrases—e.g. *in invidiam, in suspicionem, in dubium, ad exitium, in periculum vocare*. It is used in the passive to express periphrastically the passive of verbs which have only an active voice—e.g. *in invidiam vocari*, to become unpopular, be hated, *invideor* not being used. Cf. *in invidiam venire*.

## 9. ASSISTANCE—DELIVERANCE—CON-SOLATION

*auxilium, opem, salutem ferre alicui*—to bring aid to ; to rescue.

*auxilio alicui venire*—to come to assist any one.

*alicuius opem implorare*—to implore a person's help.

*confugere ad aliquem* or *ad opem, ad fidem alicuius*—to fly to some one for refuge.

*ad extremum auxilium descendere* [1]—to be reduced to one's last resource.

*auxilium praesens* [2]—prompt assistance.

*adesse alicui* or *alicuius rebus* (opp. *deesse*)—to assist, stand by a person.

*salutem alicui afferre*—to deliver, rescue a person.

$\left.\begin{array}{l}\textit{saluti suae consulere, prospicere}\\\textit{suis rebus}\text{ or }\textit{sibi consulere}\end{array}\right\}$ to take measures for one's safety ; to look after one's own interests.

*salutem expedire*—to effect a person's deliverance.

*solacium praebere*—to comfort.

*nihil habere consolationis*—to afford no consolation.

*hoc solacio frui, uti*—to solace oneself with the thought . . .

*consolari aliquem de aliqua re*—to comfort a man in a matter ; to condole with him.

*consolari dolorem alicuius*—to soothe grief.

---

[1] Similarly *descendere* is frequently used of consenting unwillingly to a thing, condescending. Cf. vi. 9 ad fin. and xvi. 9.

[2] Notice too *poena praesens*, instant punishment, *pecunia praesens*, ready money, *medicina praesens*, efficacious remedy ; *deus praesens*, a propitious deity ; *in rem praesentem venire*, to go to the very spot to make a closer examination.

*consolari aliquem in miseriis*—to comfort in misfortune.

*hoc (illo) solacio me consōlor*⎫
⎬I console myself with . . .
*haec (illa) res me consolatur*⎭


## 10. RICHES—WANT—POVERTY

*divitiis, copiis abundare*—to be rich, wealthy.

*magnas opes habere*⎫
⎪to be very rich; to be in a
*opibus maxime florere*⎬
⎪  position of affluence.
*omnibus opibus circumfluere*⎭

*fortunis maximis ornatum esse*—to be in the enjoyment of a large fortune.

*in omnium rerum abundantia vivere*—to live in great affluence.

*aliquem ex paupere divitem facere*—to raise a man from poverty to wealth.

*inopia alicuius rei laborare, premi*—to suffer from want of a thing.

*ad egestatem, ad inopiam (summam omnium rerum) redigi* —to be reduced to (abject) poverty.

*vitam inopem sustentare, tolerare*—to earn a precarious livelihood.

*in egestate esse, versari*⎫
⎬to live in poverty, destitution.
*vitam in egestate degere*⎭

*in summa egestate* or *mendicitate esse*—to be entirely destitute; to be a beggar.

*stĭpem colligere*—to beg alms.

*stipem (pecuniam) conferre*—to contribute alms.

## 11. UTILITY—ADVANTAGE—HARM—
## DISADVANTAGE

*usui* or *ex usu esse*—to be of use.

*utilitatem afferre, praebere*—to be serviceable.

*multum* (*nihil*) *ad communem utilitatem afferre*—to considerably (in no way) further the common good.

*aliquid in usum suum conferre*—to employ in the furtherance of one's interests.

*omnia ad suam utilitatem referre*—to consider one's own advantage in everything

*rationibus alicuius prospicere*⎫
　or *consulere* (opp. *officere,*　⎬ to look after, guard a
　*obstare, adversari*)　　　　　⎬ person's interests, wel-
*commodis alicuius servire*　　 ⎬ fare.
*commoda alicuius tueri*　　　　⎭

*meae rationes ita tulerunt*—my interests demanded it.

*fructum* (*uberrimum*) *capere, percipere, consequi ex aliqua re* [1]
　　—to derive (great) profit, advantage from a thing.

*fructus ex hac re redundant in* or *ad me*—(great) advantage accrues to me from this.

*aliquid ad meum fructum redundat*—I am benefited by a thing.

*quid attinet?* with Infin.—what is the use of?

*cui bono?*—who gets the advantage from this? who is the interested party?

---

[1] Also *fructum alicuius rei capere, percipere, ferre, consequi ex aliqua re*—e.g. *virtutis fructus ex re publica* (*magnos, laetos, uberes*) *capere* = to be handsomely rewarded by the state for one's high character.

*damnum* (opp. *lucrum*) *facere*  
*damno affici* } to suffer loss, harm, damage.[1]  
*detrimentum capere, accipere, facere*

*iacturam*[2] *alicuius rei facere*—to throw away, sacrifice.

*damnum inferre, afferre alicui*—to do harm to, injure any one.

*damnum ferre*—to know how to endure calamity.

*incommodo afficere aliquem*—to inconvenience, injure a person.

*incommodis mederi*—to relieve a difficulty.

*damnum* or *detrimentum sarcire* (not *reparare*)—to make good, repair a loss or injury.

*damnum compensare cum aliqua re*—to balance a loss by anything.

*res repetere*—to demand restitution, satisfaction.

*res restituere*—to give restitution, satisfaction.


## 12. GOODWILL—KINDNESS—INCLINATION—FAVOUR

*benevolo animo esse in aliquem* } to be well-disposed  
*benevolentiam habere erga aliquem* } towards . . .

*benevolentiam, favorem, voluntatem alicuius sibi conciliare*

---

[1] Notice too *calamitatem, cladem, incommodum accipere*, to suffer mishap, reverse, inconvenience ; *naufragium facere*, to be shipwrecked.

[2] *damnum* (opp. *lucrum*) = loss, especially of worldly possessions ; *detrimentum* (opp. *emolumentum*) = harm inflicted by others ; *fraus* = deceitful injury ; *iactura* (properly "throwing overboard") = the intentional sacrifice of something valuable in order either to avert injury or to gain some greater advantage. "Harmful" = *inutilis, qui nocet*, etc., not *noxius*, which is only used absolutely—e.g. *homo noxius*, the offender, evildoer.

or *colligere (ex aliqua re)*—to find favour with some one ; to get into their good graces.

benevolentiam alicui praestare,
  in aliquem conferre
benevolentia aliquem complecti
  or prosequi
} to show kindness to . . .

gratiosum esse alicui or apud
  aliquem
in gratia esse apud aliquem
} to be popular with ; to stand well with a person.

multum valere gratia apud
  aliquem
florere gratia alicuius
} to be highly favoured by ; to be influential with . . .

gratiam inire ab aliquo or apud
  aliquem
in gratiam alicuius venire
} to gain a person's esteem, friendship.

gratiam alicuius sibi quaerere, sequi, more strongly *aucupari*
  —to court a person's favour ; to ingratiate oneself
  with . . .

studere, favere alicui
studiosum esse alicuius
propenso animo, studio esse
  or propensa voluntate esse
  in aliquem (opp. averso
  animo esse ab aliquo)
} to look favourably upon ; to support.

*alicui morem gerere, obsequi*—to comply with a person's wishes ; to humour.

*alicuius causa* [1] *velle* or *cupere*—to be favourably disposed towards.

*gratum (gratissimum) alicui facere*—to do any one a (great) favour.

---

[1] Probably originally *omnia alicuius causa velle*=to wish everything (favourable) in some one's behalf.

*se conformare, se accommodare*  
   *ad alicuius voluntatem* } to accommodate oneself to  
*alicuius voluntati morem gerere* } another's wishes.

*se convertere, converti ad alicuius nutum* [1]—to take one's  
   directions from another ; to obey him in everything.

*totum se fingere et accommodare ad alicuius arbitrium et*  
   *nutum*—to be at the beck and call of another ; to be  
   his creature.

*voluntatem* or *animum alicuius a se abalienare, aliquem a se*  
   *abalienare* or *alienare*—to become estranged, alien-  
   ated from some one.

## 13. BENEFIT—GRATITUDE—RECOMPENSE

*beneficium alicui dare, tribuere* } to do any one a service  
*beneficio aliquem afficere, ornare* }    or kindness.

*beneficia in aliquem conferre*—to heap benefits upon . . .

*beneficiis aliquem obstringere, obligare, devincire*—to lay  
   any one under an obligation by kind treatment.

*beneficium remunerari* or *reddere* (*cumulate*)—to (richly)  
   recompense a kindness or service.

*gratus* (opp. *ingratus*) *animus* [2]—gratitude.

*gratiam alicui debere*—to owe gratitude to ; to be under  
   an obligation to a person.

---

[1] But *se convertere ad aliquem* = either (1) to approach with hostile intention, or (2) to turn to some one for sympathy or assistance.

[2] *animus* is used similarly in several periphrases to express abstract qualities—e.g. *animus inexorabilis* = inflexibility, severity ; *animus implacabilis* = implacability ; *animus* (*fides*) *venalis* = venality. Cf. *simplices mores, simplex natura, ratio, genus* = simplicity (*simplicitas* is post-Augustan and usually = frankness, candour). *immemor ingenium* = forgetfulness (*oblivio* in this sense is not classical).

*gratiam alicui habere*—to feel gratitude (in one's heart).

*gratiam alicui referre* (*meritam, debitam*) *pro aliqua re*—to show gratitude (in one's acts).

*gratias alicui agere pro aliqua re*—to thank a person (in words).

*grates agere* (*dis immortalibus*)—to give thanks to heaven.

*gratiam mereri*—to merit thanks ; to do a thankworthy action.

*par pari referre*
*paria paribus respondere*　}to return like for like.

*bonam* (*praeclaram*) *gratiam referre*—to reward amply ; to give manifold recompense for.

*benefacta maleficiis pensare*—to return evil for good.

*maleficia benefactis remunerari*
*pro maleficiis beneficia reddere*　}to return good for evil.


## 14. MERIT—VALUE—REWARD

*bene, praeclare* (*melius, optime*) *mereri*[1] *de aliquo* — to deserve well at some one's hands ; to do a service to . . .

*male mereri de aliquo*—to deserve ill of a person ; to treat badly.

*meritum alicuius in* or *erga aliquem*—what a man merits at another's hands (Cic. Fam. I. I. I).

*nullo meo merito*—I had not deserved it.

*ex, pro merito*—according to a man's deserts.

*multum* (*aliquid*) *alicui rei tribuere*—to consider of importance ; to set much (some) store by a thing.

---

[1] *mereri* is a middle verb, and consequently always has an adverb with it.

*multum alicui tribuere*—to value, esteem a person.

*praemiis (amplissimis, maximis) aliquem afficere*[1] — to remunerate (handsomely).

*meritum praemium alicui persolvere*—to reward a man according to his deserts.

*praemium exponere* or *proponere* — (to encourage) by offering a reward.

*praemium ponere*—to offer a prize (for the winner).

*palmam deferre, dare alicui*—to award the prize to . . .

*palmam ferre, auferre*—to win the prize.

*pacta merces alicuius rei*—the stipulated reward for anything.

*mercede conductum esse*—to be hired, suborned.

## 15. REQUESTS—WISHES—COMMISSIONS— ORDERS

*orare et obsecrare aliquem*
*magno opere, vehementer, etiam* } to entreat earnestly; to make urgent requests.
*atque etiam rogare aliquem*

*precibus aliquem fatigare*—to importune with petitions.

*supplicibus verbis orare*—to crave humbly; to supplicate.

*precibus obsequi*—to grant a request.

*alicui petenti satisfacere, non deesse*—to accede to a man's petitions.

*magnis (infimis) precibus moveri*—to be influenced by, to yield to urgent (abject) entreaty.

---

[1] Notice the numerous phrases of which *afficere* is a part—e.g. *afficere aliquem admiratione, beneficio, exilio, honore, iniuria, laude, poena, supplicio.* Especially important is its passive use—e.g. *affici admiratione,* to admire; *gaudio, voluptate,* to rejoice, be pleased; *dolore,* to be pained, vexed; *poena,* to suffer punishment.

*negare,* more strongly *denegare*
　*alicui aliquid*
*petenti alicui negare aliquid* }to refuse, reject a request.
*repudiare, aspernari preces ali-*
　*cuius.*

*nihil tibi a me postulanti recusabo*—I will refuse you
　nothing.

*aliquid ab aliquo impetrare*—to gain one's point with any
　one.

*optata mihi contingunt*—my wishes are being fulfilled.

*voluntati alicuius satisfacere, obsequi*—to satisfy a person's
　wishes.

*ex sententia*—as one would wish ; to one's mind.

*aliquid optimis ominibus prosequi* (*vid.* p. 88 note)—to wish
　prosperity to an undertaking.

*bene id tibi vertat!*—I wish you all success in the
　matter.

*mandatum, negotium alicui dare* }to entrust a matter to a
*negotium ad aliquem deferre* } 　person; to commission.

*mandatum exsequi, persequi, conficere*—to execute a com-
　mission.

*iussa* (usually only in plur.), *imperata facere*—to carry out
　orders.


## 16. FRIENDSHIP—ENMITY—RECONCILIATION
### (cf. xii. 8).

*amicitiam cum aliquo jungere, facere, inire, contrahere*—to
　form a friendship with any one.

*amicitiam colere*—to keep up, foster a connection.

*uti aliquo amico*—to be friendly with any one.

*est* or *intercedit mihi cum aliquo amicitia*  
*sunt* or *intercedunt mihi cum aliquo inimicitiae*[1] ⎱ I am on good (bad) terms with a person.

*uti aliquo familiariter*—to be on very intimate terms with . . .

*artissimo amicitiae vinculo* or *summa familiaritate cum aliquo coniunctum esse*—to be bound by the closest ties of friendship.

*vetustate amicitiae coniunctum esse* — to be very old friends.

*amicitiam alicuius appetere*—to court a person's friendship.

*in amicitiam alicuius recipi*  
*ad alicuius amicitiam se conferre, se applicare* ⎰ to gain some one's friendship ; to become intimate with.

*aliquem (tertium) ad (in) amicitiam ascribere*—to admit another into the circle of one's intimates.

*amicitiam renuntiare*  
*amicitiam dissuere, dissolvere, praecīdere* ⎰ to renounce, give up a friendship.

*amicissimus meus* or *mihi*—my best friend.

*homo intimus, familiarissimus mihi*—my most intimate acquaintance.

*inimicitias gerere, habere, exercere cum aliquo*—to be at enmity with a man.

*inimicitias cum aliquo suscipere*—to make a person one's enemy.

*inimicitias deponere*—to lay aside one's differences.

*aequi iniqui*—friend and foe.

---

[1] The singular *inimicitia* is only used to express the abstract idea "enmity."

*placare aliquem alicui* or *in*
   *aliquem*
*reconciliare alicuius animum* } to reconcile two people ; to
   or simply *aliquem alicui*   be a mediator.
*in gratiam aliquem cum*
   *aliquo reducere*

*in gratiam cum aliquo redire*
*sibi aliquem, alicuius animum* } to be reconciled ; to make
   *reconciliare* or *reconciliari*   up a quarrel.
   *alicui*

## 17. AUTHORITY—DIGNITY (cf. xiv. 3)

*magna auctoritate esse*
*auctoritate valere* or *florere* } to possess great authority ;
*magna auctoritas est in aliquo*   to be an influential person.

*multum auctoritate valere, posse*
   *apud aliquem*
*magna auctoritas alicuius est* } to have great influence
   *apud aliquem*   with a person ; to have
*alicuius auctoritas multum valet*   considerable weight.
   *apud aliquem*

*auctoritatem* or *dignitatem sibi conciliare, parare*—to gain
   dignity ; to make oneself a person of consequence.

*ad summam auctoritatem pervenire* — to attain to the
   highest eminence.

*auctoritatem alicuius amplificare* (opp. *imminuere, minuere*)
   —to increase a person's dignity.

*auctoritati, dignitati alicuius illudere*—to insult a person's
   dignity.

*dignitas est summa in aliquo* } to be in a dignified posi-
*summa dignitate praeditum esse*   tion.

*aliquid alienum (a) dignitate sua* ⎫
    or merely *a se ducere*        ⎬ to consider a thing
*aliquid infra se ducere* or *infra* ⎪   beneath one's dignity.
    *se positum arbitrari* ⎭

## 18. PRAISE—APPROVAL—BLAME—REPROACH

*laudem tribuere, impertire alicui* ⎫
*laude afficere aliquem*            ⎪
*(maximis, summis) laudibus*  ⎬ to praise, extol, com-
  *efferre aliquem* or *aliquid*     ⎪    mend a person.
*eximia laude ornare aliquem*   ⎭

*omni laude cumulare aliquem* — to overwhelm with
    eulogy.

*laudibus aliquem (aliquid) in caelum ferre, efferre, tollere*—
    to extol, laud to the skies.

*alicuius laudes praedicare*—to spread a person's praises.

*aliquem beatum praedicare*—to consider happy.

*omnium undique laudem colligere* ⎫
*maximam ab omnibus laudem*  ⎬ to win golden opinions
  *adipisci*                   ⎭    from every one.

*aliquid laudi alicui ducere, dare*—to consider a thing
    creditable to a man.

*aliquem coram, in os* or *praesentem laudare* — to praise a
    man to his face.

*recte, bene fecisti quod* . . .—you were right in . . . ; you
    did right to . . .

*res mihi probatur*—a thing meets with my approval.

*res a me probatur*—I express my approval of a thing.

*hoc in te reprehendo* (not *ob eam rem*)—I blame this in
    you ; I censure you for this.

*vituperationem subire*
*in vituperationem, reprehensionem* } to suffer reproof; to
*cadere, incidere, venire* be criticised, blamed.

*exprobrare alicui aliquid*
*aliquid alicui crimini dare,* } to reproach a person with . . .
*vertere*

*conqueri, expostulare cum aliquo de aliqua re*—to expostulate with a person about a thing.

## 19. RUMOUR—GOSSIP—NEWS—MENTION

*rumor, fama, sermo est* or *manat*—report says; people say.

*rumor, fama viget*—a rumour is prevalent.

*fama serpit (per urbem)*—a report is spreading imperceptibly.

*rumor increbrescit*—a report, an impression is gaining ground.

*rumorem spargere* }
*famam dissipare* } to spread a rumour.

*dubii rumores afferuntur ad nos*—vague rumours reach us.

*auditione et fama accepisse aliquid* }
*fando aliquid audivisse* } to know from hearsay.

*ex eo audivi, cum diceret*—I heard him say . . .

*vulgo dicitur, pervulgatum est*—every one says.

*in ore omnium* or *omnibus (ho-*
*minum* or *hominibus,* but } to be in every one's mouth.
only *mihi, tibi,* etc.) *esse*
*per omnium ora ferri*

*in ore habere aliquid* (Fam. 6. 18. 5)—to harp on a thing, be always talking of it.

*efferre* or *edere aliquid in vulgus*—to divulge, make public.

*foras efferri, palam fieri, percrebrescere, divulgari, in medium
    proferri, exire, emanare*—to become known, be-
    come a topic of common conversation (used of
    things).

*in sermonem hominum venire*⎫
*in ora vulgi abire*⎭ to be a subject for gossip.

*fabulam fieri*—to be the talk of the town, a scandal.

*nuntio allato* or *accepto*—on receiving the news.

*Romam nuntiatum est, allatum est*—news reached Rome.

*certiorem facere aliquem (alicuius rei* or *de aliqua re)*—to
    inform a person.

*mentionem facere alicuius rei* or *de aliqua re*[1]—to mention
    a thing.

*mentionem inicere de aliqua re* or⎫
    Acc. c. Inf.             ⎪ to mention a thing in-
*in mentionem alicuius rei incidere*⎪  cidentally, casually.
*mentio alicuius rei incidit*⎭

## 20. FAME—REPUTATION

*gloriam, famam sibi comparare*—to gain distinction.

*gloriam (immortalem) consequi, adipisci*—to win (undying)
    fame.

*gloriae, laudi esse*⎫ to confer distinction on a person ; to
*laudem afferre*  ⎭   redound to his credit.

*gloria, laude florere*—to be very famous, illustrious.

*summa gloria florere*—to have reached the highest pinnacle
    of eminence.

---

[1] Not *commemorare*, the fundamental meaning of which is "to
make a person mindful of . . . ," and implies an emphatic reference
to a definite point.

*clarum fieri, nobilitari, illustrari* ⎫
　　(not the post-classical *cla-* ⎪
　　*rescere* or *inclarescere*) 　 ⎬ to become famous, dis-
*gloriam colligere, in summam* ⎪ 　tinguish oneself.
　　*gloriam venire* ⎭

*aliquem immortali gloria afficere* ⎫ to confer undying fame
*aliquem sempiternae gloriae com-* ⎬ on, immortalise some
　　*mendare* ⎭ one.

*immortalitatem consequi, adipisci, sibi parĕre*—to attain
　　eternal renown.

*gloria duci* ⎫
*laudis studio trahi* ⎬ to be guided by ambition.
*laudem, gloriam quaerere* ⎭

*stimulis gloriae concitari*—to be spurred on by ambition.

*gloriae, laudis cupiditate incensum esse, flagrare*—to be
　　consumed by the fires of ambition.

*de gloria, fama alicuius detrahere* ⎫ to detract from a
*alicuius gloriae* or simply *alicui* ⎪ 　person's reputation,
　　*obtrectare* 　　　　　　　　　 ⎬ 　wilfully underesti-
*alicuius famam, laudem imminuere* ⎭ 　mate a person.

*obscurare alicuius gloriam, laudem, famam* [1] (not *obscurare
　　aliquem*)—to render obscure, eclipse a person.

*famae servire, consulere*—to have regard for one's good
　　name.

*famam ante collectam tueri, conservare*—to live up to one's
　　reputation.

*bene, male audire (ab aliquo)* ⎫ to have a good or bad
*bona, mala existimatio est de* ⎬ reputation, be spoken
　　*aliquo* ⎭ 　well, ill of.

---

[1] In the same way, to improve a man, *alicuius mores corrigere*
(not *aliquem c.*) ; to understand some one, *alicuius orationem* or
*quid dicat intellegere.*

*famam crudelitatis subire* (Catil. 4. 6. 12)—to gain the reputation of cruelty.

*infamiam alicui inferre, aspergere, conflare*
*infamem facere aliquem*
} to damage a person's character, bring him into bad odour.

*magnam sui famam relinquere*—to leave a great reputation behind one.

*opinionem virtutis habere*—to have the reputation of virtue.

*existimatio*[1] *hominum, omnium*—the common opinion, the general idea.

## 21. HONOUR—DISGRACE—IGNOMINY

*esse in honore apud aliquem*—to be honoured, esteemed by some one.

*honorem alicui habere, tribuere*
*aliquem honore afficere, augere,*
*ornare, prosequi (vid.* note, p. 88)
} to honour, show respect for, a person.

*aliquem cupiditate honorum inflammare* (or *aliquem ad cupiditatem honorum inflammare*)—to kindle ambition in some one's mind.

*honores concupiscere* (opp. *aspernari*)—to aspire to dignity, high honours.

*honoris causa aliquem nominare* or *appellare*—to speak of some one respectfully.

*statuam alicui ponere, constituere*—to set up a statue in some one's honour.

---

[1] *existimatio* has two uses : (1) active—opinion held by others, criticism ; (2) passive—reputation, character, usually in a good sense, consequently = good reputation without the addition of *bona, integra,* etc.

*aliquem colere et observare* (Att. 2. 19)—to pay respect to, be courteous to a person.

*aliquem ignominia afficere, notare* ⎫ to inflict an indignity
*alicui ignominiam inurere* ⎭ upon, insult a person.

*infamiam concipere, subire, sibi conflare*—to incur ignominy.

*vitae splendori (em) maculas (is) aspergere*—to sully one's fair fame.

*notam turpitudinis alicui* or *vitae alicuius inurere*—to injure a man's character, tarnish his honour.

*ignominiam non ferre*—to chafe under an indignity, repudiate it.

*maculam (conceptam) delere, eluere*—to blot out a reproach.


## 22. EFFORT—INDUSTRY—LABOUR—EXERTION

*studiose (diligenter, enixe, sedulo, maxime) dare operam, ut . . .*—to take great pains in order to . . .

*egregiam operam (multum, plus* ⎫
  etc. *operae) dare alicui rei* ⎪
*operam alicui rei tribuere, in* ⎬ to expend great labour
  *aliquid conferre* ⎪ on a thing.
*operam (laborem, curam) in* ⎪
  or *ad aliquid impendere* ⎭

*multum operae ac laboris consumere in aliqua re*—to exert oneself very energetically in a matter.

*studium, industriam* (not *diligentiam*) *collocare, ponere in aliqua re*—to apply oneself zealously, diligently to a thing.

*incumbere in (ad) aliquid*—to be energetic about, throw one's heart into a thing.

*opus*[1] *facere* (De Senect. 7. 24)—to do work (especially agricultural).

*opus aggredi* ⎱ to take a task in hand, en-
*ad opus faciendum accedere* ⎰ gage upon it.

*res est multi laboris et sudoris*—the matter involves much labour and fatigue.

*desudare et elaborare in aliqua re* (De Senect. 11. 38)—to exert oneself very considerably in a matter.

*labori, operae non parcere*—to spare no pains.

*laborem non intermittere*—to work without intermission.

*nullum tempus a labore intermittere*—not to leave off work for an instant.

*lucubrare* (Liv. 1. 57)—to work by night, burn the midnight oil.

*inanem laborem suscipere* ⎫
*operam (et oleum) perdere* or ⎬ to lose one's labour.
*frustra consumere* ⎭

*rem actam* or simply *actum agere* (proverb.)—to have all one's trouble for nothing.

*labore supersedēre (itineris)* (Fam. 4. 2. 4)—to spare oneself the trouble of the voyage.

*patiens laboris*—capable of exertion.

*fugiens laboris*—lazy.

*operae pretium est* (c. Inf.), *tanti est*—it is worth while.

*acti labores iucundi* (proverb.)—rest after toil is sweet.

---

[1] *opus* always means the concrete work on which one is engaged; *labor* is the trouble, fatigue, resulting from effort ; *opera* is the voluntary effort, the trouble spent on an object.   Thus *laborare* = not simply to work, but to work energetically, with exertion and consequent fatigue ; *operari*, to be busy with a thing.   Terence thus distinguishes *opus* and *opera : quod in opere faciundo operae consumis tuae.* Cf. Verg. Aen. 1. 455 *operumque laborem miratur* = the trouble which such huge works must have cost.

*contentionem adhibere*—to exert oneself.

| | |
|---|---|
| *omnes nervos*[1] *in aliqua re contendere* | |
| *omnibus viribus* or *nervis contendere, ut* | to strain every nerve, do one's utmost in a matter. |
| *omni ope atque opera* or *omni virium contentione eniti, ut* | |
| *contendere et laborare, ut* | |
| *pro viribus eniti et laborare, ut* | |

## 23. BUSINESS—LEISURE—INACTIVITY—IDLE-NESS

*negotium suscipere*—to undertake an affair.

*negotium obire, exsequi*—to execute, manage a business, undertaking.

*negotium conficere, expedire, transigere*—to arrange, settle a matter.

*negotia agere, gerere*—to be occupied with business, busy.

*multis negotiis implicatum, districtum, distentum, obrŭtum esse*—to be involved in many undertakings; to be much occupied, embarrassed, overwhelmed by business-claims.

*negotiis vacare*—to be free from business.

---

[1] *nervi* properly = sinews, muscles, not nerves the existence of which was unknown to the ancients. Metaphorically *nervi* denotes not only strength in general but also specially—(1) vital power, elasticity, e.g. *omnes nervos virtutis elidere* (Tusc. 2. 11. 27), *incīdere*, to paralyse the strength of virtue; (2) motive power, mainspring, essence, of a thing, e.g. *vectigalia nervi rei publicae sunt* (Imp. Pomp. 7. 17), *nervi belli pecunia* (Phil. 5. 2. 15).

*occupatum esse* in *aliqua re*⎫
*intentum esse alicui rei*   ⎬ to be engaged upon a matter.

*negotium alicui facessere* (Fam. 3. 10. 1)—to give a person trouble, inconvenience him.

*magnum negotium est* c. Inf.—it is a great undertaking to . . .

*nullo negotio*—without any trouble.

*otiosum esse*⎫
*in otio esse* or *vivere*  ⎬ to be at leisure.
*otium habere*         ⎪
*otio frui*             ⎭

*otio abundare*—to have abundance of leisure.

*otium sequi, amplexari*—to be a lover of ease, leisure.

*otiosum tempus consumere in aliqua re*—to spend one's leisure hours on an object.

*otio abūti*[1] or *otium ad suum usum transferre*—to use up, make full use of one's spare time.

(*in*) *otio languere et hebescere*⎫ to grow slack with inactivity,
*otio diffluere*              ⎬     stagnate.

*desidiae et languori se dedere* ⎫ to abandon oneself to in-
*ignaviae*[2] *et socordiae se dare*⎬  activity and apathy.

*per luxum et ignaviam aetatem agere*—to pass one's life in luxury and idleness.

---

[1] *abuti* properly = to consume, make full use of. From this is developed the rarer meaning to use in excess, abuse = *perverse*, *intemperanter*, *immoderate uti*. Abuse, misuse = *pravus usus*, *vitium male utentium*, *insolens mos*. *abusus* is only found in the Jurists, and *abusio* is a technical term of rhetoric = κατάχρησις.

[2] The original meaning of *ignavia* (*in-gnavus*, cf. *navus*, *navare*) is not cowardice but laziness.

## 24.  PLEASURE—RECREATION

*voluptatem ex aliqua re capere* or *percipere*—to derive
  pleasure from a thing.

*voluptate perfundi*—to revel in pleasure, be blissfully
  happy.

*voluptatibus frui* ⎱
*voluptates haurire* ⎰ to take one's fill of enjoyment.

*se totum voluptatibus dedere, tradere*—to devote oneself
  absolutely to the pursuit of pleasure.

*homo voluptarius* (Tusc. 2. 7. 18)—a devotee of pleasure ;
  a self-indulgent man.

*voluptatis illecebris deleniri* ⎫  to be led astray, corrupted
*voluptatis blanditiis corrumpi* ⎬  by the allurements of plea-
                                   ⎭  sure.

*in voluptates se mergere*—to plunge into a life of pleasure.

*animum a voluptate sevocare*—to hold aloof from all
  amusement.

*voluptates* (*corporis*)—sensual pleasure.

*voluptatis* or *animi causa* (B. G. 5. 12)—for one's own
  diversion ; to satisfy a whim.

*deliciis diffluere*—to wanton in the pleasures of sense.

*animum relaxare, reficere, recreare* or simply *se reficere, se
  recreare, refici, recreari* (*ex aliqua re*)—to recruit oneself, seek relaxation.

*animum* or simply *se remittere* ⎱ to indulge oneself.
*animo* or simply *sibi indulgere* ⎰

## VI. THE MIND; ITS FUNCTIONS

### 1. GENIUS—TALENT—INTELLIGENCE

*magno animo esse*—to be magnanimous, broad-minded.

*animum attendere ad aliquid*—to turn one's attention to a thing.

*diligenter attendere (aliquid)*—to attend carefully.

*alias res* or *aliud agere*—to be inattentive.

*animo adesse*[1]—(1) to be attentive; (2) to keep one's presence of mind.

*vir magno ingenio, ingeniosus*⎱
*vir magno ingenio praeditus* ⎰a man of ability.

*ingenio valere*—to be talented, gifted.

*ingenio abundare*—to be very talented.

*natura et ingenium*—natural gifts.

*ingenium acuere*—to sharpen the wits.

*ingenii acumen*—penetration; sagacity.

*ingenii tarditas* (opp. *celeritas*)—dulness of intellect.

*ingenii infirmitas* or *imbecillitas*—weakmindedness.

*mentis compotem esse*—to be of sane mind.

*mente captum esse, mente alienata esse*—to be out of one's mind.

*sanae mentis esse*—to be of sound mind.

*mentis quasi luminibus officere (vid.* p. 208) or *animo caliginem offundere*—to obscure the mental vision.

*intellegentia* or *mente multum valere*[2]—to possess great ability.

[1] For the second meaning cf. Cicero, *ades animo et omitte timorem, Scipio.*

[2] *captus,* in the meaning ability, capacity, only occurs in the phrase *ut captus est servorum;* while *capacitas* merely means capacity, content, e.g. *vasorum.*

*ad intellegentiam communem* or *popularem accommodare
   aliquid*—to accommodate something to the standard of the popular intelligence.

## 2. IMAGINATION—THOUGHT

*animo, cogitatione aliquid fingere* (or
   simply *fingere*, but without *sibi*),   ⎫ to form an idea of
   *informare*     ⎬   a thing, imagine,
*animo concipere aliquid*     ⎭   conceive.

*animo, cogitatione aliquid praecipere* (Off. 1. 23. 81)—to
   form a conception of a thing beforehand.

*cogitatione sibi aliquid depingere*—to picture to oneself.

*ingenium, cogitatio*—imagination.

*ingenii vis* or *celeritas*—vivid, lively imagination.

*rerum imagines*     ⎫
*res cogitatione fictae* or *depictae* ⎬ creatures of the imagination.

*opinionum commenta, ineptiae, monstra, portenta*—extra-
   vagant fictions of fancy.

*animo, mente, cogitatione aliquid comprehendere, complecti*—
   to grasp a thing mentally.

*in eam cogitationem incidere*—to happen to think of . . .

*haec cogitatio subit animum* ⎫
*illud succurrit mihi*     ⎬ an idea strikes me.

*mihi in mentem venit alicuius rei*—something comes into
   my mind.

*aliquid animo meo obversatur* (cf. p. 27, s. v. *oculi*) — a
   vague notion presents itself to my mind.

*aliquem ad eam cogitationem adducere ut*—to induce a
   person to think that . . .

*alicuius animum ab aliqua re abducere*—to draw away
   some one's attention from a thing.

*cogitationem, animum in aliquid intendere* (Acad. 4. 46)—to direct one's attention . . .

*omnes cogitationes ad aliquid conferre*—to give all one's attention to a thing.

*mentem in aliqua re defigere*—to fix all one's thoughts on an object.

*in cogitatione defixum esse*—to be deep in thought.

*cogitationes in res humiles abicere* (De Amic. 9. 32) (opp. *alte spectare, ad altiora tendere, altum, magnificum, divinum suspicere*)—to study the commonplace.

## 3. CONCEPTIONS—IDEALS—PERFECTION

*notiones animo (menti) insitae, innatae*—innate ideas.

*intellegentiae adumbratae*[1] or *incohatae* (De Leg. 1. 22. 59) —vague, undeveloped ideas.

*notionem* or *rationem alicuius rei in animo informare* or *animo concipere*—to form a conception, notion of a thing.

*absolutus et perfectus*—absolutely perfect.

*omnibus numeris absolutus* (N. D. 2. 13)—perfect in every detail.

*ad summum perducere* 
*perficere et absolvere* } to bring to the highest perfection.

*ad perfectionem, (ad summum) pervenire*—to attain perfection.

*absolutio et perfectio* (not *summa perfectio*)—ideal perfection.

---

[1] *adumbrare* is a technical term of painting = to make a sketch, outline of an object ; then metaphorically, to merely hint at a thing. Its opposite is *exprimere*, technical term of sculpture, = figuratively, to represent exactly, clearly.    It never has the simple meaning "to express."

*cogitatione, non re*—ideally, not really.

*undique expleta et perfecta forma*
*species optima* or *eximia, speci-* }-an ideal.
   *men,* also simply *species, forma*

*comprehensam quandam animo speciem (alicuius rei) habere*
    —to have formed an ideal notion of a thing.

*singularem quandam perfectionis imaginem animo concipere*
    —to conceive an ideal.

*imaginem perfecti oratoris adumbrare*—to sketch the ideal
    of an orator.

*civitas optima, perfecta Platonis*
*illa civitas Platonis commenticia* }-Plato's ideal republic.
*illa civitas, quam Plato finxit*

## 4. OPINION—PREJUDICE—CONJECTURE

*in sententia manere, permanere, perseverare, perstare*—to
    abide by, persist in one's opinion.

*illud, hoc teneo*—I abide by this opinion.

*a sententia sua discedere*
*de sententia sua decedere* }-to give up one's opinion.
*(de) sententia desistere*

*de sententia deici, depelli, deterreri*—to be forced to change
    one's mind.

*de sententia aliquem deducere, movere*—to make a man
    change his opinion.

*aliquem ad suam sententiam perducere* or *in suam sententiam*
    *adducere*—to win a man over to one's own way of
    thinking.

*ad alicuius sententiam accedere, sententiam alicuius sequi*—
    to adopt some one's opinion.

*idem sentire* (opp. *dissentire ab aliquo*)—to hold the same views.

*sententiam suam aperire*[1]—to freely express one's opinions.

*sententiam fronte celare, tegere*—not to betray one's feelings by one's looks.

*dic quid sentias*[2]—give me your opinion.

*in hac sum sententia, ut . . . putem*—I think that . . .

*plura in eam sententiam disputare*—to discuss a subject more fully on the same lines.

*ut mea fert opinio*
*ut mihi quidem videtur* }-according to my opinion.
*mea (quidem) sententia*

*quot homines, tot sententiae*—many men, many minds.

*opiniones falsas animo imbibere* } to be imbibing false
*opinionibus falsis imbui* } opinions.

*opinionis error*—erroneous opinion.

*opinio praeiudicata*, also simply *opinio* (not *praeiudicium* = a preliminary decision)—prejudice.

*opinio confirmata, inveterata*—a rooted opinion.

*opinionum pravitate inficí*—to be filled with absurd prejudices.

*opinionum commenta* (N. D. 2. 2. 5)—chimeras.

*monstra* or *portenta*—marvellous ideas ; prodigies.

*coniectura assequi, consequi, aliquid coniectura colligere*—to conjecture.

*quantum ego coniectura assequor, augŭror*—as far as I can guess.

*coniecturam alicuius rei facere* or *capere ex aliqua re*—to infer by comparison, judge one thing by another.

---

[1] *se aperire* = to betray oneself ; cf. *se indicare* (Liv. 2. 12).

[2] Not *sententiam dicere,* which is used of senators giving their vote ; cf. *suffragium ferre.*

*de se (ex se de aliis) coniecturam facere*—to judge others by
oneself.

*aliquid in coniectura positum est*
*aliquid coniectura nititur, con-* } it is a matter of conjec-
*tinetur* (Div. 1. 14. 24) } ture, supposition.

*probabilia coniectura sequi*—to try to conjecture probabili-
ties.

*aliquid mihi nec opinanti, insperanti accidit*—a thing has
happened contrary to my expectation.


## 5. TRUTH—ERROR

*verum dicere, profiteri*—to speak the truth, admit the
truth.

*omnia ad veritatem*[1] *dicere*—to be truthful in all one's
statements.

*veritatis amans, diligens, studiosus*—truthful ; veracious.

*a vero aversum esse* (Catil. 3. 1. 29)—to be averse to
truth.

*a veritate deflectere, desciscere*—to swerve from the truth.

*veri videndi, investigandi cupiditas*—love of truth.

*veri inquisitio atque investigatio*—zealous pursuit of truth.

*a vero abduci*—to be led away from the truth.

*proxime ad verum accedere*—to be very near the truth.

*a vero non abhorrere*
*veri simile esse* } to be probable.

*haec speciosiora quam veriora sunt*—this is more plausible
than true.

*vera et falsa (a falsis) diiudicare*—to distinguish true and
false.

---

[1] *verum* = the truth, concrete ; *veritas* = truth in the abstract.

*vera cum falsis confundere*—to confuse true with false.

*veritas*—veracity.

*re (vera), reapse* (opp. *specie*)—in truth ; really

*in errore versari*—to be mistaken.

*magno errore teneri*
*in magno errore versari* } to be in gross error, seriously
*vehementer errare* misled.

*erroribus implicari* (Tusc. 4. 27. 58)—to fall into error.

*per errorem labi,* or simply *labi*—to take a false step.

*aliquem in errorem inducere, rapere*—to lead a person into
error.

*errorem animo imbibere*—to get a mistaken notion into
the mind.

*errorem cum lacte nutricis sugere* (Tusc. 3. 1. 2)—to imbibe
error from one's mother's breasts.

*error longe lateque diffusus*—a wide-spread error.

*errorem tollere*
*errorem amputare et* } to banish an error, do away with a
*circumcīdere* false impression.

*errorem stirpitus extrahere* — to totally eradicate false
principles.

*errorem deponere, corrigere* — to amend, correct one's
mistake.

*alicui errorem demere, eripere, extorquere*—to undeceive a
person.

*nisi fallor*
*nisi (animus) me fallit* } if I am not mistaken.

*nisi omnia me fallunt*—unless I'm greatly mistaken.

## 6. CHOICE—DOUBT—SCRUPLE

*optionem alicui dare* (Acad. 2. 7. 19)—to give a person his choice.

*optionem alicui dare, utrum . . . an*—to offer a person the alternative of . . . or . . .

*in dubium vocare*⎫
*in dubio ponere*⎭ to throw doubt upon a thing.

*in dubium venire*—to become doubtful.

*quod aliquam (magnam) dubitationem habet* (Leg. Agr. 1. 4. 11)—a thing which is rather (very) dubious.

*dubitatio mihi affertur, inicitur*—a doubt arises in my mind.

*dubitationem alicui tollere* — to relieve a person of his doubts.

*aliquid in medio, in dubio relin-*
  *quere* (Cael. 20. 48)
*aliquid dubium, incertum relin-*
  *quere* ⎭ to leave a thing undecided.

*sine dubio* (not *sine ullo dubio*)—without doubt, beyond all doubt.

*sine ulla dubitatione*—without any hesitation ; without the least scruple.

*scrupulum ex animo alicuius evellere* (Rosc. Am. 2. 6)—to relieve a man of his scruple.

*unus mihi restat scrupulus* (Ter. Andr. 5. 4. 37) (cf. too *religio*, p. 179)—one thing still makes me hesitate.

## 7. KNOWLEDGE—CERTAINTY—PERSUASION

*certo (certe) scio*[1] (Arch. 12. 32)—I know for a fact.

*probe scio, non ignoro*
*non sum ignarus, nescius* } I know very well
  (not *non sum inscius*)

*me non fugit, praeterit*—I am not unaware.

*quantum scio*
*quod sciam* } as far as I know.

*hoc* (not *tantum*) *certum est*—this much is certain.

*aliquid compertum habere*—to know a thing for certain.

*illud pro certo affirmare licet*—this much I can vouch for.

*mihi exploratum est, exploratum (certum) habeo*—I am quite certain on the point.

*inter omnes constat*—it is a recognised fact.

*mihi persuasum est*[2]
*mihi persuasi* } I am persuaded, convinced.

*sic habeto*
*persuade tibi*
*velim tibi ita persuadeas*
*sic volo te tibi persuadere* } convince yourself of this; rest assured on this point.

*addūcor, ut credam*—I am gradually convinced that . . .

*non possum adduci, ut (credam)*—I cannot make myself believe that . . .

*ex animi mei sententia (vid.* p. 179)—according to my strong conviction.

*suo iudicio uti*—to act in accordance with one's convictions.

---

[1] With *certe scio*, which is the form Cicero usually employs, the certitude lies in our knowledge, *certum est me scire;* with *certo scire* the certitude lies in the object of our knowledge. *certo* rarely occurs except with *scio*.

[2] Caesar occasionally uses *persuasum sibi habere*.

## 8. PLAN—ADVICE—DELIBERATION

*consilium capere, inire (de aliqua re*, with Gen. gerund., with Inf., more rarely *ut)*—to form a plan, make a resolution.

*consilio desistere*—to give up a project, an intention.

*consilium abicere* or *deponere*—to let a plan fall through.

*a consilio deterreri aliqua re*—to be deterred from one's intention by something.

*mediocribus consiliis uti*—to adopt half-measures.

*consilium, sententiam mutare*—to alter one's views, intentions.

*suo consilio uti*[1]—to go one's own way, proceed independently.

*magna moliri*—to be busy with ambitious projects.

*consilia cum aliquo communicare*[2]—(1) to communicate one's plans to some one; (2) to make common cause with a person. Similarly *c. causam, rationem.*

*consilia inter se communicare*—to take common counsel.

*aliquem in* or *ad consilium adhibere*—to consult a person, take his advice.

---

[1] *uti* is similarly used in several phrases, especially with the meaning of having, showing, enjoying, practising, proving, etc., e.g. *uti ventis secundis, adversis ; praesenti animo uti*, to show presence of mind ; *perpetua felicitate*, to enjoy . . . ; *prudentia, severitate, crudelitate*, to show . . . ; *bona valetudine, prospero fortunae flatu*, to enjoy . . . ; cf. v. 6.

[2] *communicare (aliquid cum aliquo)* means properly to share a thing with some one. From this are developed the two senses—1. to give some one something, e.g. *consilia, laudem, gloriam alicuius rei ;* 2. to receive a share of a thing, e.g. *pericula, paupertatem.* "To communicate," *i.e.* to announce, inform, is represented by *dicere, tradere, narrare, exponere, certiorem facere*, etc.

*consilium habere* (*de aliqua re*)—to deliberate together (of a number of people).

*consultare* or *deliberare* (*de aliqua re*)—to deliberate, consider (of individuals).

*consiliis arcanis interesse* (Liv. 35. 18)—to be present at secret consultations.

*consilium dare alicui*  
*auctorem esse alicui, ut* } to give a person advice.

*aliquem consilio* (*et re*) *iuvare*—to give a person the advantage of one's advice (and actual support).

*consilii mei copiam facio tibi*—I put myself at your disposal as regards advice.

*consilium petere ab aliquo*—to apply to a person for advice.

*consilii inopem esse*—to be perplexed.

*omnia consilia frigent* (Verr. 2. 25)—advice is useless in this case; the situation is very embarrassing.

*nullo consilio, nulla ratione, temere*—without reflection; inconsiderately; rashly.

*secum* (*cum animo*) *reputare aliquid*  
*considerare in, cum animo, secum aliquid* } to think over, consider a  
*agitare* (*in*) *mente* or (*in*) *animo aliquid* } thing.

*aliquid cadit in deliberationem* (Off. 1. 3. 9)—a subject becomes matter for reflection.

*re diligenter considerata, perpensa*  
*omnibus rebus circumspectis* } after mature deliberation.  
*inita subductaque ratione*

## 9. RESOLVE—DESIGN—INTENTION

*in animo habeo* or *mihi est in animo* c. Inf.—I am resolved; it is my intention.

*certum* (*mihi*) *est*—I am determined.

*certum deliberatumque est* ⎱
*stat mihi sententia* (Liv. 21. 30) ⎰ I am firmly resolved.

*incertus sum, quid consilii capiam*—I am undecided . . .

*mihi non constat* (with indirect question)—I have not made up my mind.

*propositum est mihi* c. Inf.—I intend, propose to . . .

*propositum, consilium tenere* (opp. *a proposito deterreri*)— to abide by one's resolution.

*propositum* [1] *assequi, peragere*—to carry out one's plan.

*magna sibi proponere* or *magna spectare*—to have a high object in view; to be ambitious.

*in incepto* or *conatu perstare* ⎫
*in proposito susceptoque con-* ⎬ to persevere in one's resolve
*silio permanere* ⎭

*incepto* or *conatu desistere*—to give up one's project.

*parare aliquid*—to take measures for . . .

*animum inducere* c. Inf. (*in animum inducere* rare)— to persuade oneself to . . .

*a me impetrare non possum, ut*—I cannot bring myself to . . .

*descendere ad aliquid, ad omnia* (*vid.* note, p. 54)—to consent to . . ., lend oneself to . . .

*descendere ad extrema consilia* (Fam. 10. 33. 4)—to have recourse to extreme measures.


## 10. OBJECT—AIM—HESITATION—DELAY

*consilium est* c. Inf. or *ut* ⎱
*id sequor, ut* ⎰ my intention is . . .

---

[1] In classical prose *propositum* is still semi-adjectival and has not yet acquired all the functions of a substantive; consequently it cannot be joined to a genitive, an adjective, or a pronoun. Cf. the treatment of *factum, dictum*, etc., in Augustan Latin.

*spectare aliquid* or *ad aliquid*—to have an object in view.

*res eo spectat, ut*—the matter tends towards . . ., has
     this object.[1]

*res spectat ad vim (arma)*—there seems a prospect of
     armed violence ; things look like violence.

*id quod voluit consecutus est*⎫
*ad id quod voluit pervenit*    ⎬he attained his object.

*quid tibi vis ?*—what do you mean to do ?

*quid hoc sibi vult ?*⎫
*quid hoc rei est ?*  ⎬what is the meaning of this ?

*eo consilio, ea mente, ut*—with the intention of . . .

*de industria, dedita opera* (opp. *imprudens*)—designedly ;
     intentionally.

*ad id ipsum* [2]—with this very object.

*infecta re* (Liv. 9. 32)—to no purpose ; ineffectually.

*moram alicui rei afferre, inferre, facere*—to retard, delay
     a thing.

*in mora alicui esse*—to detain a person.

*nullam moram interponere, quin* (Phil. 10. 1. 1)—to make
     all possible haste to . . .

*sine mora* or *nulla mora interposita*—without delay.

*diem ex die ducere, differre*—to put off from one day to
     another.


## 11. REMEMBRANCE—FORGETFULNESS

*memoriâ tenere aliquid*       ⎫to remember a thing per-
*memoriam alicuius rei tenere*⎬   fectly.

---

[1] Note *Athenae a Persis petuntur*, the object of the Persian
invasion is Athens (Nep. Them. 2. 6).

[2] The aim, tendency of a writing or a poem is *consilium, quo liber
scriptus est, quo carmen compositum est*, or *quod quis in libro scribendo secutus est*, not *consilium libri*.

*recenti memoria tenere aliquid*—to have a vivid recollection
  of a thing.

*memoriâ (multum) valere* (opp.
  *memoriâ vacillare*)
*memorem esse* (opp. *obliviosum
  esse*)
⎱to have a good memory.

*memoria tanta fuit, ut*—he had such an extraordinary
  memory that . . .

*memoriâ labi*—to make a slip of the memory.

*memoriae mandare aliquid*[1]—to impress on the memory.

*ex memoria* (opp. *de scripto*)—from memory ; by heart.

*memoriter*—(1) with good memory ; (2) from personal
  recollection.

*memoria custodire*—to keep in mind.

*memoriam alicuius rei renovare, revocare (redintegrare)*—to
  recall a thing to one's recollection.

*memoriam alicuius rei repetere*⎱ to recall to mind a thing or
*in memoriam alicuius redire*  ⎰      person.

*in memoriam alicuius redigere, reducere aliquid* (not *revocare*)
  —to recall a thing to a person's mind.

*memoria et recordatio*—vivid recollection.

*grata memoria aliquem prosequi*[2]—to show a thankful
  appreciation of a person's kindness.

*nomen alicuius grato animo prosequi*—to think of a person
  with a grateful sense of his goodness.

*memoriam alicuius rei repraesentare* (opp. *memoriam alicuius
  rei deponere, abicere*)—to picture to oneself again.

---

[1] Distinguish this expression from *ediscere* which = to learn by
heart ; also from *memoriae prodere, tradere* = to hand down as
tradition (*vid.* p. 110).

[2] *Prosequi* used figuratively, with an ablative, occurs in several
phrases—e.g. *prosequi aliquem honore ; verbis honorificis ; beneficiis,
officiis, studiis suis ; ominibus, votis, lacrimis.*

*memoriam alicuius rei conservare, retinere*—to retain the recollection of a thing.

*memoriam alicuius pie inviolateque servare*—to show an affectionate regard for a person's memory.

*gratam (gratissimam) alicuius memoriam retinere*—to retain a (most) pleasant impression of a person.

*numquam ex animo meo memoria illius rei discedet*—the memory of this will never fade from my mind.

*aliquid in memoria nostra penitus insidet* (de Or. 2. 28. 122)—a thing has been vividly impressed on my memory.

*memoriam eius nulla umquam delebit (obscurabit) oblivio* (Fam. 2. 1)
*semper memoria eius in (omnium) mentibus haerebit*
} nothing will ever make me forgetful of him.

*nomen suum posteritati aliqua re commendare, propagare, prodere*—to win renown amongst posterity by some act.

*memoriam nominis sui immortalitati tradere, mandare, commendare*—to immortalise one's name.

*post hominum memoriam*
*post homines natos*
} within the memory of man.

*memoriae causa, ad* (not *in*) *memoriam* [1] (Brut. 16. 62)—in memory of . . .

*oblivio alicuius rei me capit*—I forget something.

*aliquem in oblivionem alicuius rei adducere* (pass. *in oblivionem venire*)—to make a person forget a thing.

*aliquid excidit e memoria, effluit, excidit ex animo*—a thing escapes, vanishes from the memory.

---

[1] One can also say *monumenti causa*—e.g. *aliquid alicui monumenti causa relinquere.* Cf. such turnings as *alicuius memoriam aliqua re prosequi, celebrare, renovare.*

*memoria alicuius rei excidit, abiit, abolevit*—the recollection of a thing has been entirely lost.

*obliterari*[1] (Liv. 26. 41)

*memoria alicuius rei obscuratur,*
   *obliteratur, evanescit*

*oblivioni esse, dari*

*in oblivionem adduci*

*oblivione obrui, deleri, exstingui*

*in oblivione iacēre* (of persons)

} to be forgotten, pass into oblivion.

*aliquid ab oblivione vindicare*—to rescue from oblivion.

*mementote* with Acc. c. Inf.—do not forget.


## 12. THEORY—PRACTICE—EXPERIENCE

*ratione, doctrina* (opp. *usu*) *aliquid cognitum habere*—to have a theoretical knowledge of a thing.

*ad artem, ad rationem revocare aliquid* (De Or. 2. 11. 44) —to reduce a thing to its theoretical principles; to apply theory to a thing.

*doctrinam ad usum adiungere*—to combine theory with practice.

*in rebus atque in usu versatum esse*—to have had practical experience.

*usu*[2] *praeditum esse*—to possess experience.

*magnum usum in aliqua re habere*—to have had great experience in a thing.

*multarum rerum usus*—varied, manifold experience.


[1] This and the following expressions are useful to express the passive of *oblivisci.*

[2] Not *experientia,* which in classical prose means attempt, proof.

*usu rerum (vitae, vitae commu-*
*nis) edocti scimus*
*experti scimus, didicimus*  } we know from experience.
*usu cognitum habemus*

*res ipsa, usus rerum (cotidie) docet*—everyday experience tells us this.

*(rerum) imperitum esse*—to have had no experience of the world.

*multa acerba expertus est*[1]—he has had many painful experiences.

*usus me docuit*—experience has taught me.

# VII. THE ARTS AND SCIENCES

## 1. SCIENTIFIC KNOWLEDGE IN GENERAL— LITERATURE

*optima studia, bonae, optimae, liberales, ingenuae artes,*
*disciplinae*—the sciences; the fine arts.

*litterarum*[2] *studium* or *tractatio* (not *occupatio*)—the study of belles-lettres; literary pursuits.

*homines litterarum studiosi*) learned, scientific, literary
*homines docti*　　　　　 } 　 men.

---

[1] *experiri* is only used of personal experience.

[2] *littera* in sing. = letter of the alphabet, e.g. *litteram nullam ad me misit.* In plur. = 1. letters of the alphabet, characters (cf. viii. 9); 2. a letter (*epistola*); 3. writings, books, e.g. *graecae de philosophia litterae;* 4. literature, *graecas litteras discere;* 5. literary pursuits; 6. science; 7. culture, erudition, learning, *erant in eo plurimae litterae, neque eae vulgares, sed interiores quaedam et reconditae.*

*artium studia* or *artes vigent* (not *florent*)—learning, scientific knowledge is flourishing.

*litterae iacent, neglectae iacent*[1]—scholarship, culture, literature is at a low ebb.

*litteras colere* — to be engaged in the pursuit of letters.

*litteras amplecti*
*litteras adamasse* ( only in } to be an enthusiastic devotee of letters.
   perf. and plup.)

*in studio litterarum versari*—to be engaged in literary pursuits.

*in aliquo litterarum genere versari*—to be engaged in some one branch of study.

*summo studio in litteris versari*—to be an ardent student of . . .

*se totum litteris tradere, dedere*—to devote oneself entirely to literature.

*se totum in litteras* or *se litteris abdere*—to be quite engrossed in literary studies.

*in litteris elaborare* (De Sen. 8. 26)—to apply oneself very closely to literary, scientific work.

*in litteris acquiescere* or *conquiescere*—to find recreation in study.

*aetatem in litteris ducere, agere*—to devote one's life to science, study.

*omne (otiosum) tempus in litteris consumere*—to devote all one's leisure moments to study.

*omne studium in litteris collocare, ad litteras conferre*—to employ all one's energies on literary work.

---

[1] *iacēre* metaphorically is used not only of things neglected and abandoned, but of persons (cf. *frigere*) who have lost all their political influence.

*optimarum artium studio incensum esse*—to be interested in, have a taste for culture.

*litterarum studio trahi*
*trahi, ferri ad litteras* } to feel an attraction for study.

*litterarum studia remittere*—to relax one's studies.

*intermissa studia revocare*—to resume one's studies.

*primis (ut dicitur)*[1] or *primoribus labris gustare* or *attingere litteras*—to have a superficial knowledge, a smattering of literature, of the sciences.

*litterae*—literature.

*litterae ac monumenta*, or simply *monumenta*—written records; documents.

*litterae latinae*[2]—Roman literature.

*clarissima litterarum lumina*—shining lights in the literary world.

*graecis litteris studere*—to study Greek literature.

*multum (mediocriter) in graecis litteris versari*—to be well (slightly) acquainted with Greek literature.


## 2. LEARNING—ERUDITION

*vir* or *homo doctus, litteratus*—a man of learning; a scholar; a savant.

*vir doctissimus*—a great scholar.

*vir perfecte planeque eruditus*—a man of profound erudition.

*vir omni doctrina eruditus*—a man perfect in all branches of learning.

---

[1] Cf. Pro Caelio 12, 28 *extremis ut dicitur digitis attingere.*

[2] *latinus* is only used of language and literature, *Romanus* of nationality.

*multi viri docti,* or *multi et ii docti* (not *multi docti*)—many
learned men ; many scholars.

*omnes docti, quivis doctus, doctissimus quisque*—all learned
men.

*nemo doctus*—no man of learning.

*nemo mediocriter doctus*—no one with any pretence to
education.

*latinis litteris* or *latine doctus*—acquainted with the Latin
language.

*bene*[1] *latine doctus* or *sciens*—a good Latin scholar.

*doctrina abundare* (De Or. 3. 16. 59)—to be a man of
great learning.

*a doctrina mediocriter instructum esse*—to have received
only a moderate education (lit. on the side of
learning).

*doctrina exquisita, subtilis, elegans*[2]—sound knowledge ;
scholarship.

*doctrina recondita*—profound erudition.

*studia, quae in reconditis artibus versantur* (De Or. 1. 2. 8)
—abstruse studies.

*magnam doctrinae speciem prae se ferre*—to pass as a man
of great learning.

*vita umbratilis* (*vid.* p. 98)—the contemplative life of a
student.

---

[1] For the use of adverbs to modify adjectives and other adverbs
*vid.* Nägelsbach Lat. Stil. p. 278 ; cf. *bene multi, bene mane, bene
penitus* (Verr. 2. 70. 169), *impie ingratus* (Tusc. 5. 2. 6) etc.
Such combinations are especially frequent in Tacitus, Velleius,
Seneca, and Quintilian. For *latine* by itself cf. Cic. Opt. Gen. 4
*latine, id est pure et emendate, loqui.* If the style is to be criticised,
adverbs can be added—e.g. *bene, perbene, pessime, eleganter,* etc., cf.
vii. 7.

[2] Not *solida,* which means properly entire, massive—e.g. *marmor
solidum, crateres auro solidi,* then metaph. e.g.—*solida laus, utilitas.*

*litterarum scientiam* (only in sing.) *habere*—to possess
   literary knowledge.

*scientiam alicuius rei consequi* ⎱ to acquire knowledge of a
*scientia comprehendere aliquid* ⎰  subject.

*penitus percipere et comprehendere aliquid* (De Or. 1. 23.
   108)—to have a thorough grasp of a subject.

*scientia augere aliquem*—to enrich a person's knowledge.

*multa cognita, percepta habere,*⎫
   *multa didicisse* ⎪
*multarum rerum cognitione im-*⎬ to be well-informed, eru-
   *butum esse* (opp. *litterarum* ⎪  dite.
   or *eruditionis expertem esse*⎪
   or [*rerum*] *rudem esse*) ⎭


## 3. CULTURE—CIVILISATION

*animum, ingenium excolere* (not *colere*)—to cultivate the
   mind.

*animi, ingenii cultus* (not *cultura*)—mental culture.

*optimis studiis* or *artibus, opti-*⎫
   *marum artium studiis erudi-*⎬ to have received a liberal
   *tum esse* ⎪  education.
*litteras scire* ⎭

*litterae interiores et reconditae, artes reconditae*—profound
   scientific education.

*sunt in illo, ut in homine Romano, multae litterae* (De Sen.
   4. 12)—for a Roman he is decidedly well educated.

*litteris leviter imbutum* or *tinctum esse*—to have received
   a superficial education.

*omni vita atque victu. excultum atque expolitum esse* (Brut.
   25. 95)—to have attained to a high degree of
   culture.

*omnis cultus et humanitatis ex-*
    *pertem esse*[1]
                       to be quite uncivilised.
*ab omni cultu et humanitate*
    *longe abesse* (B. G. 1. 1. 3)

*homines, gentem a fera agrestique vita ad humanum cultum*
    *civilemque deducere* (De Or. 1. 8. 33)—to civilise
    men, a nation.

## 4. EDUCATION—INSTRUCTION—SCHOOL— PROFESSION

*liberaliter, ingenue, bene educari*—to receive a liberal
    education.

*severa disciplina contineri*—to be brought up under strict
    discipline.

*aliquem ad humanitatem informare* or *instituere*—to teach
    a person refinement.

*mores alicuius corrigere*—to improve a person.

*in viam reducere aliquem*—to bring a person back to the
    right way.

*in viam redire*—to return to the right way.

*litteras discere ab aliquo*—to be educated by some one.

*institui* or *erudiri ab aliquo*
                       to receive instruction from
*disciplina alicuius uti, magistro*
    *aliquo uti*                         some one.

*e disciplina alicuius profectum esse*—to be brought up in
    some one's school.

*puerum alicui erudiendum* or *in disciplinam tradere*—to en-
    trust a child to the tuition of . . .

*operam dare* or simply *se dare alicui, se tradere in discip-*

---

[1] Not *incultum esse,* which refers only to external appearance.

*linam alicuius, se conferre, se applicare ad aliquem*—
to become a pupil, disciple of some one.

*multum esse cum aliquo* (Fam. 16. 21)—to enjoy close
intercourse with . . . (of master and pupil).

*ludus (discendi* or *litterarum)*—an elementary school.

*schola*—a school for higher education.

*scholam frequentare*—to go to a school.

*disciplina (institutio) puerilis* (not *liberorum)*—the teaching
of children.

*pueros elementa (prima) docere*—to teach children the
rudiments.

*primis litterarum elementis imbui*—to receive the first elements of a liberal education.

*doctrinae, quibus aetas puerilis*
  *impertiri solet* (Nep. Att.
  1. 2)
*artes, quibus aetas puerilis ad*
  *humanitatem informari solet*
} the usual subjects taught
to boys.

*erudire aliquem artibus, litteris* (but *erudire aliquem in
iure civili, in re militari)*—to teach some one
letters.

*natum, factum esse ad aliquid (faciendum)*—to be born for
a thing, endowed by nature for it.

*adversante et repugnante natura* or *invitâ Minervâ (ut aiunt)
aliquid facere* (Off. 1. 31. 110)—to do a thing which
is not one's vocation, which goes against the
grain

*crassa* or *pingui Minerva* (proverb.)—with no intelligence
or skill.

*calcaria alicui adhibere, admovere ; stimulos alicui admovere*
—to spur, urge a person on.

*frenos adhibere alicui*—to restrain some one.

*bona indole* (always in sing.)⎫
  *praeditum esse*       ⎬ to be gifted, talented (not
*ingenio valere*          ⎭   *praeditum esse* by itself).

*summo ingenio praeditum esse*—to possess rich mental endowments.

*in aliqua re progressus facere, proficere, progredi*—to make progress in a subject.

*aliquid efficere, consequi in aliqua re* (De Or. 1. 33. 152)—to obtain a result in something.

*adulescens alios bene de se sperare iubet, bonam spem ostendit* or *alii de adulescente bene sperare possunt*—he is a young man of great promise.

*adulescens bonae (egregiae) spei*—a promising youth.

*magna est exspectatio ingenii tui*—we expect a great deal from a man of your calibre.

*desudare in scholae umbra* or *umbraculis* [1]—to exert oneself in the schools.

*genus vitae (vivendi)* or *aetatis degendae deligere* [2]—to choose a career, profession.

*viam vitae ingredi* (Flacc. 42. 105)—to enter upon a career.

*philosophiam, medicinam profiteri*⎫ to be a philosopher,
*se philosophum, medicum (esse)* ⎬ physician by profes-
  *profiteri*                ⎭ sion.

*qui ista profitentur*—men of that profession.

---

[1] Cf. *umbra, umbracula (-orum)*, and *umbratilis* (*vid.* vii. 2, *vita umbratilis*), used of the retired life of a savant as opposed to *sol, lux ori* or *forensis.* Cf. De Legg. 3. 6. 14 *Phalereus ille Demetrius mirabiliter doctrinam ex umbraculis eruditorum otioque non modo in solem atque in pulverem sed in ipsum discrimen aciemque produxit.*

[2] The *locus classicus* on the choice of a profession is De Officiis 1. 32. 115-122.

## 5. EXAMPLE—PATTERN—PRECEDENT

*exemplum clarum, praeclarum*⎫
*exemplum luculentum* ⎬ a good,[1] brilliant example ;
*exemplum illustre* ⎭ a striking example.

*exemplum magnum, grande*—a weighty example, precedent.

*exemplum afferre*⎫
*exemplo uti* ⎬to quote an example.

*aliquem (aliquid) exempli causa* [2] *ponere, proferre, nominare, commemorare*—to cite a person or thing as an example.

*aliquid exemplis probare, comprobare, confirmare*—to quote precedents for a thing.

*aliquid exemplis ostendere*—to demonstrate by instances.

*exempla petere, repetere a rerum gestarum memoria* or *historiarum (annalium, rerum gestarum) monumentis*—to borrow instances from history.

*exempla a rerum Romanarum (Graecarum) memoria petita*—examples taken from Roman (Greek) history.

*multa exempla in unum (locum) colligere*—to collect, accumulate instances.

*ex infinita exemplorum copia unum (pauca) sumere, decerpere (eligere)*—to choose one from a large number of instances.

---

[1] Not *bonum exemplum*, which means an example morally good for us to follow.

[2] " For example " must not be translated by *exempli causa*, which is only used in complete sentences with such verbs as *ponere, afferre, proferre, nominare*. *verbi causa (gratia)* = " for instance," " we will say," usually refers to a single expression, e.g. *quid dicis igitur ? miserum fuisse verbi causa M. Crassum ?* (Tusc. 1. 4. 12). Often examples are introduced by such words as *ut, velut, in his*, etc., e.g. *bestiae quae gignuntur in terra, veluti crocodili* (N. D. 2. 48. 124).

*a Socrate exemplum virtutis petere, repetere*—to quote Socrates as a model of virtue.

*similitudines afferre*—to cite parallel cases.

*auctore aliquo uti ad aliquid*
*auctorem aliquem habere ali-*
*cuius rei*
} to have as authority for a thing.

*auctoritatem alicuius sequi*—to be guided by another's example.

*auctoritas et exemplum* (Balb. 13. 31)—standard and pattern.

*sibi exemplum alicuius proponere ad imitandum* or simply *sibi aliquem ad imitandum proponere*—to set up some one as one's ideal, model.

*sibi exemplum sumere ex aliquo* or *exemplum capere de aliquo* — to take a lesson from some one's example.

*ad exemplum alicuius se conformare*—to shape one's conduct after another's model.

*exemplum edere, prodere*
*exemplo esse*
} to set an example.

*exemplum in aliquo* or *in aliquem statuere*
*exemplum (severitatis) edere in aliquo* (Q. Fr. 1. 2. 2. 5)
} to inflict an exemplary punishment on some one.

*bene (male) praecipere alicui*—to inculcate good (bad) principles.

*praecepta dare, tradere de aliqua re*—to give advice, directions, about a matter.

*ad praecipiendi rationem delābi* (Q. Fr. 1. 1. 6. 18)—to adopt a didactic tone.

*aliquid in animo haeret, penitus insedit* or *infixum est*—a thing is deeply impressed on the mind.

*aliquid animo mentique penitus mandare* (Catil. 1. 11. 27)—
to impress a thing on one's memory, mind.

*demittere aliquid in pectus* or *in pectus animumque suum*—
to take a thing to heart.

*hoc verbum alte descendit in pectus alicuius*—what he said
made a deep impression on . . .


## 6. PHILOSOPHY

*se conferre ad philosophiam, ad philosophiae* or *sapientiae*
*studium* (Fam. 4. 3. 4)—to devote oneself to philosophy.

*animum appellere* or *se applicare ad philosophiam*—to apply
oneself to the study of philosophy.

*philosophiae (sapientiae) studio teneri* (Acad. 1. 2. 4)—to be
enamoured of philosophy.

*in portum philosophiae confugere*—to take refuge in
philosophy.

*in sinum philosophiae compelli*—to be driven into the arms
of philosophy.

*philosophia (neglecta) iacet (vid.* p. 92, note)—philosophy
is neglected, at low ebb.

*philosophiam latinis litteris illustrare* (Acad. 1. 1. 3)—to
write expositions of philosophy in Latin.

*Ciceronis de philosophia libri*—Cicero's philosophical writings.

*decreta, inventa philosophorum*—the tenets, dogmas of
philosophers.

*quae in philosophia tractantur*—philosophical subjects.

*praecepta philosophorum (penitus) percepta habere*—to be well
acquainted with the views of philosophers.

*illae sententiae evanuerunt*—those views are out of date.

*illae sententiae iam pridem explosae et eiectae sunt* (Fin. 5. 8. 23)—those ideas have long ago been given up.

*schola, disciplina, familia ; secta*—a sect, school of thought.

*sectam alicuius sequi* (Brut. 31. 120)

*disciplinam alicuius profiteri* } to be a follower, disciple of some one.

*qui sunt a Platone* or *a Platonis disciplina ; qui profecti sunt a Platone ; Platonici*—disciples of Plato, Platonists.

*Solo, unus de septem* (*illis*)—Solon, one of the seven sages.

*Pythagorae doctrina longe lateque fluxit* (Tusc. 4. 1. 2)— Pythagoras' principles were widely propagated.

*scholas habere, explicare* (Fin. 2. 1. 1)—to give lectures.

*scholis interesse*—to attend lectures.

*tradere (aliquid de aliqua re)*—to teach.

*audire Platonem, auditorem esse Platonis*—to attend Plato's lectures.


## 7. THE PARTS OF PHILOSOPHY

*physica*[1] (*-orum*) (Or. 34. 119); *philosophia naturalis*— physics ; natural philosophy.

*dialectica* (*-ae* or *-orum*) (pure Latin *disserendi ratio et scientia*)—logic, dialectic.

*disserendi praecepta tradere*—to teach logic.

*disserendi elegantia*—logical minuteness, precision.

*disserendi subtilitas* (De Or. 1. 1. 68)—dialectical nicety.

*disserendi spinae* (Fin. 4. 28. 79)—subtleties of logic ; dilemmas.

*disserendi peritus et artifex*

*homo in dialecticis versatissimus* } an accomplished dialectician.

---

[1] Cf. Acad. 1. 5. 19 *philosophandi ratio triplex ; una de vita et moribus, altera de natura et rebus occultis, tertia de disserendo.*

*disserendi artem nullam habere*—to know nothing of logic.

*dialecticis ne imbutum*[1] *quidem esse*—to be ignorant of even the elements of logic.

*ratione, eleganter* (opp. *nulla ratione, ineleganter, confuse*) *disponere aliquid*—to arrange on strictly logical principles.

*philosophia, quae est de vita et moribus* (Acad. 1. 5. '19)

*philosophia, in qua de bonis rebus et malis, deque hominum vita et moribus disputatur*

⎫ moral science ; ethics.

*philosophia, quae in rerum contemplatione versatur,* or *quae artis praeceptis continetur* — theoretical, speculative philosophy.

*philosophia,*[2] *quae in actione versatur*—practical philosophy.

*omnes philosophiae loci*—the whole domain of philosophy.

## 8. SYSTEM—METHOD—PRINCIPLES

*ratio ; disciplina, ratio et disciplina ; ars*—system.

*ad artem redigere aliquid*

*ad rationem, ad artem et praecepta revocare aliquid* (De Or. 1. 41)

⎫ to systematise.

*arte conclusum esse*—to have been reduced to a system.

*ratio et doctrina*—systematic, methodical knowledge.

*artificio et via tradere aliquid*—to give a scientific explanation of a thing.

---

[1] *imbuere* is properly to give the first touch to, tinge, bathe, e.g. *gladii sanguine imbuti.* Metaph. it =(1) to fill with, e.g. *religione, pietate, superstitione, crudelitate ;* (2) to teach, initiate, e.g. *animum honestis artibus,* and is used especially of a superficial knowledge.

[2] Cf. Sen. Ep. 25. 10 *philosophia activa.*

*artificiose redigere aliquid*

*ad rationis praecepta accommo-* } to treat with scientific
      *dare aliquid*                          exactness; to classify.

*totam rationem evertere* (pass. *iacet tota ratio*)—to upset the
      whole system.

*ratione et via, via et ratione progredi, disputare* (Or. 33. 116)
      to proceed, carry on a discussion logically.

*novam rationem ingredi*—to enter on a new method.

*a certa ratione proficisci* — to be based on a sound
      principle.

*a falsis principiis proficisci*—to start from false premises.

*ad philosophorum* or *philosophandi rationes revocare aliquid*
      —to deal with a subject on scientific prin-
      ciples.

*perpetuitas et constantia* (Tusc. 5. 10. 31)—logical con-
      sistency.


## 9. SPECIES—DEFINITION—CLASSIFICATION— CONNECTION

*partes* [1] *generibus subiectae sunt*—the species is subordinate
      to the genus.

*genus universum in species certas partiri et dividere* (Or. 33.
      117)—to analyse a general division into its specific
      parts.

*genere, non numero* or *magnitudine differre*—to differ
      qualitatively not quantitatively.

---

[1] Cf. Cic. De Or. 1. 42 for the definition.  gen us *autem id est,
quod sui similes communione quadam, specie autem differentes, duas
aut plures complectitur partes.*  partes *autem sunt, quae generibus
eis ex quibus manant subiciuntur; omniaque quae sunt vel generum vel
partium nomina, definitionibus, quam vim habeant, est exprimendum.*
est enim defi nitio *rerum earum, quae sunt eius rei propriae, quam
definire volumus, brevis et circumscripta quaedam explicatio.*

*spinae partiendi et definiendi* (Tusc. 5. 8. 22)—minute, captious subdivisions and definitions.

*rem (res) definire*—to define a thing.

*a definitione proficisci*—to start from a definition.

*involutae rei notitiam definiendo aperire* (Or. 33. 116)—to make an obscure notion clear by means of definition.

*sub metum subiectum esse*—to be comprised under the term "fear."

*constituere, quid et quale sit, de quo disputetur*—to determine the nature and constitution of the subject under discussion.

*in ordinem redigere aliquid*—to systematise, classify a thing.

*conexum et aptum esse inter se*—to be closely connected with each other.

*cohaerere, coniunctum esse cum aliqua re*—to be closely connected with a thing.

*arte (artissime) coniunctum esse* ⎫ to be very intimately re-
*apte (aptissime) cohaerere* ⎭ lated.

*continuatio seriesque rerum, ut alia ex alia nexa et omnes inter se aptae colligataeque sint* (N. D. 1. 4. 9)—systematic succession, concatenation.

*diffusum, dissipatum esse*—to have no coherence, connection.

*confusum, perturbatum esse*—to be confused.

*rem dissolutam conglutinare, coagmentare*—to reunite disconnected elements.

## 10. PROOF—REFUTATION

*argumentum* [1] *firmum, magnum*—a strong, striking proof.

*argumentum afferre*—to bring forward a proof.

*argumentum immortalitatis afferre* (not *pro*)—to quote an argument in favour of immortality.

*argumentum afferre, quo animos immortales esse demonstratur* —to bring forward a proof of the immortality of the soul.

*argumento huic rei est, quod*—a proof of this is that . . .

*aliquid planum facere* (Ad Herenn. 2. 5)—to demonstrate, make a thing clear.

*aliquid alicui probare* (or c. Acc. c. Inf.)—to prove one's point to a person's satisfaction.

*argumentis confirmare, comprobare, evincere aliquid* (or c. Acc. c. Inf.)—to prove a thing indisputably.

*argumentum ducere, sumere ex aliqua re* or *petere ab aliqua re* —to derive an argument from a thing.

*argumentum premere* (not *urgere*)—to persist in an argument, press a point.

*loci* (τόποι) *argumentorum* (De Or. 2. 162)—the points on which proofs are based ; the grounds of proof.

*argumenta refellere, confutare*—to refute arguments.

*rationem* [1] *afferre* (Verr. 3. 85. 195)—to bring forward an argument (based on common-sense).


## 11. CONCLUSION—HYPOTHESIS—INFERENCE

*concludere, colligere, efficere, cogere ex aliqua re*—to draw a conclusion from a thing.

---

[1] *argumentum*=a proof resting on facts ; *ratio*=an argument drawn from the general reasonableness of the proposition.

*acute, subtiliter concludere*—to draw a subtle inference.

*ratio* or *rationis conclusio efficit*—the conclusion proves that . . .

*ratiocinatio, ratio*—the syllogism ; reasoning.

*prima*[1] *(superiora) ; consequentia* (Fin. 4. 19. 54)—premises ; consequences.

*conclusiuncula fallax* or *captio*—a fallacious argument ; sophism.

*positum est a nobis primum* (c. Acc. c. Inf.)—we start by presupposing that . . .

*hoc posito*—on this supposition, hypothesis.

*hoc probato consequens est*—it follows from what we have shown.

*sequitur* (not *ex quo seq.*) *ut* ⎫
*ex quo, unde, hinc efficitur ut* ⎭ it follows from this that . . .


## 12. DEBATE—CONTROVERSY

*disputatio, quaestio*—systematic, scientific discussion.

*disputare*[2] *(de aliqua re, ad aliquid)*—to discuss, investigate a subject scientifically.

*subtiliter disputare*—to thoroughly discuss.

*in utramque partem, in contrarias partes disputare* (De Or. 1. 34)—to discuss both sides of a question.

*in nullam partem disputare*—to say nothing either for or against an argument.

---

[1] In a syllogism the technical term for the major premise is *propositio* or *propositio major ;* for the minor, *propositio minor ;* for the conclusion, *conclusio.*

[2] *disputare*=to discuss, considering the arguments *pro* and *con*, used of a number of people with different opinions. *disserere de aliqua re*=to discourse on a matter for the benefit of those present ; but in both cases the substantive is *disputatio.*

*non repugno*—I have nothing to say against it.

*pertinacem* (opp. *clementem*) *esse in disputando*—to be dogmatic ; positive.

*opponere alicui aliquid*—to object, to adduce in contradiction.

*dare, concedere aliquid*—to grant, admit a thing.

*sumere* (opp. *reicere*) *aliquid*—to assume a thing.

*tenere aliquid ; stare in aliqua re*—to insist on a point.

*obtinere aliquid*—to maintain one's assertion, prove oneself right.

*in controversia* (*contentione*) *esse, versari*⎫ to be at variance
*in controversiam cadere*                         ⎭   with.

*in controversiam vocare, adducere aliquid*—to make a thing the subject of controversy.

*in controversiam vocari, adduci, venire* (De Or. 2. 72. 291) —to be contested, become the subject of debate.

*in controversia relinquere aliquid*—to leave a point undecided.

*controversiam* (*contentionem*) *habere cum aliquo*—to maintain a controversy with some one.

*in contentione ponitur, utrum . . . an*—it is a debated point whether . . . or . . .

*id, de quo agitur* or *id quod cadit in controversiam*—the point at issue.

*controversiam sedare, dirimere, componere, tollere*—to put an end to, settle a dispute.

*controversiam diiudicare*—to decide a debated question.

*transigere aliquid cum aliquo*—to come to an understanding with a person.

*res mihi tecum est*—I have a point to discuss with you.

*sine* (*ulla*) *controversia*—indisputably ; incontestably.

*hoc est a* (*pro*) *me*—this goes to prove what I say.

*res ipsa docet*—the very facts of the case show this.

*res ipsa* (*pro me apud te*) *loquitur*—the matter speaks for itself.

*res confecta est*—the question is settled, finished.


## 13. AGREEMENT—CONTRADICTION

*consentire, ĭdem sentire cum aliquo*—to agree with a person.

*dissentire, dissidere ab* or *cum aliquo*—to disagree with a person.

*omnes* (*uno ore*) *in hac re consentiunt*—all agree on this point.

*una et consentiens vox est*—all are unanimous.

*una voce ; uno ore*
*uno, communi, summo* or *omnium* ⎱unanimously.
   *consensu* (Tusc. 1. 15. 35) ⎰

*re concinere, verbis discrepare*—to agree in fact but not in word.

*hoc convēnit inter nos*—we have agreed on this point.

*hoc mihi tecum convēnit* (Att. 6. 1. 14)—I agree with you there.

*quī convĕnit ?*—how is this consistent? how are we to reconcile this . . .?

*summa est virorum doctissimorum consensio* (opp. *dissensio*) —the learned are most unanimous in . . .

*constantia* (opp. *inconstantia*) (Tusc. 5. 11. 32)—consistency.

*inter se pugnare* or *repugnare*—to be mutually contradictory.

*secum pugnare* (without *sibi*); *sibi* ⎤
   *repugnare* (of things)         ⎟ to contradict oneself,
*a se dissidere* or *sibi non constare* ⎟   be inconsistent.
   (of persons) ⎦

*pugnantia loqui* (Tusc. 1. 7. 13)—to make contradictory,
   inconsistent statements.

*dicere contra aliquem* or *aliquid* (not *contradicere alicui*)—
   to contradict some one.

## 14. PARTICULAR SCIENCES

(History, Mythology, Chronology, Geography,
Mathematics, Natural Science, Astronomy.)

*res Romanae*[1]       ⎤ Roman history (*i.e.* the events in
*res gestae Romanorum* ⎦   it).

*historia*—history (as a science).

*historia Romana*[2] or *rerum Romanarum historia*—Roman
   history (*i.e.* the exposition, representation of it by
   writers).

*memoria rerum Romanarum*—Roman history (as tradition).

*historiam (-as) scribere*—to write a history.

*res populi Romani perscribere*—to write a history of
   Rome.

---

[1] But *res Romana* = the Roman power, Rome.

[2] *historia* has several different senses.   (1) The narration,
exposition of the facts (*res gestae, res*), cf. *rerum exemplum,* historic
precedent; *res facta,* historic fact.   (2) Historical composition, e.g.
*historiam scribere, historia graeca* = either a history written in Greek
or a history of Greece (*rerum graecarum historia*); *historia latina,*
history written in Latin; *historia romana* or *rerum romanarum
historia* = a history of Rome.   (3) A place famous in history, e.g.
*quacunque ingredimur, in aliqua historia pedem ponimus.*  In the
plural *historiae* means specially histories, anecdotes (*narratiunculae*),
memoirs, e.g. *Taciti historiae.*

*rerum scriptor* [1]
*rerum auctor* (as authority) } an historian.

*evolvere historias, litterarum (veterum annalium) monumenta*—to study historical records, read history.

*memoriae traditum est, memoriae (memoria) proditum est* (without *nobis*)—tradition, history tells us.

*tradunt, dicunt, ferunt*—they say; it is commonly said.

*accepimus* [2]—we know; we have been told.

*historiae prodiderunt* (without *nobis*)—history has handed down to us.

*apud rerum scriptores scriptum videmus, scriptum est*—we read in history.

*duplex est memoria de aliqua re*—a twofold tradition prevails on this subject.

*rerum veterum memoria*
*memoria vetus* (Or. 34. 120)
*veterum annales* } ancient history.
*veterum annalium monumenta*
*antiquitatis memoria*

*recentioris aetatis memoria*—modern history.

*memoria huius aetatis (horum* } the history of our own
    *temporum)* } times; contemporary
*nostra memoria* (Cael. 18. 43) } history.

*omnis memoria, omnis memoria aetatum, temporum, civitatum* or *omnium rerum, gentium, temporum, saeculorum memoria*—universal history.

---

[1] *historicus* means an erudite student of history, one engaged on historical research. As an adjective its use in Cicero is limited, being only used when opposed to *oratorius*, e.g. *genus historicum*, historic style (Brut. 83. 286).

[2] *scimus, cognovimus* (=we know by experience) are not used of historical knowledge.

*memoriam annalium* or *temporum replicare*—to consult history.

*aetas heroica*[1] (Tusc. 5. 3. 7) | the mythical period;
*tempora heroica* (N. D. 3. 21. 54) | the heroic age.

*fabulae, historia fabularis*—mythology.

*repetere ab ultima* (*extrema, prisca*) *antiquitate* (*vetustate*), *ab heroicis temporibus*—to go back to the remote ages.

*ut a fabulis ad facta veniamus*—to pass from myth to history.

*historicorum fide contestata memoria*—historic times.

*historiae, rerum fides*—historic truth.

*narrare aliquid ad fidem historiae*—to give a veracious and historic account of a thing.

*res historiae fide comprobata*—an acknowledged historical fact.

*incorrupta rerum fides*—genuine historical truth.

*ad historiam* (*scribendam*) *se conferre* or *se applicare*—to devote oneself to writing history.

*homo in historia diligens*—a conscientious historian.

*memoriam rerum gestarum* (*rerum Romanarum*) *tenere*—to be well versed in Roman history.

*domestica* (*externa*) *nosse*—to be acquainted with the history of one's own land.

*temporum ratio, descriptio, ordo*—chronology.

*temporum ordinem servare* | to observe the chronological
*servare et notare tempora* | order of events.

*res temporum ordine servato narrare*—to narrate events in the order of their occurrence.

[1] *heroicus* only of time. *herous*=epic, e.g. *versus herous* (De Or. 3. 49. 191)=a dactylic hexameter; *pes herous* a dactyl; "epic" of other things is usually *epicus*, e.g. *carmen epicum; poetae epici*, or *epici* alone. For "heroic" of an action, cf. *praeclarum atque divinum factum; factum illustre et gloriosum*, etc.

*temporibus errare* (Phil. 2. 9. 23)—to make a chrono-
logical mistake.

*ad temporum rationem aliquid revocare*—to calculate the
date of an event.

*diligentem esse in exquirendis temporibus*—to be exact in
calculating dates.

*terrarum* or *regionum descriptio* (*geographia*)—geography.

*Africae situm paucis exponere*—to give a brief exposition
of the geography of Africa.

*regionum terrestrium aut maritimarum scientia*—geo-
graphical knowledge.

*mathematica* (*-ae*) or *geometria* (*-ae*), *geometrica* (*-orum*)
(Tusc. 1. 24. 57)—mathematics.

*mathematicorum ratione concludere aliquid*—to draw a
mathematical conclusion.

*formas* (not *figuras*) *geometricas describere* — to draw
geometrical figures.

*se conferre ad naturae investigationem*—to devote oneself to
the study of a natural science.

*astrologia* (pure Latin *sidera, caelestia*)—astronomy.

*spectator siderum, rerum caelestium* or *astrologus*[1]—an
astronomer.

*arithmetica*[2] (*-orum*) ⎱
*numeri* (*-orum*)        ⎰ arithmetic.

---

[1] It is only in later Latin after *astrologus* had acquired the meaning of astrologer, magician, that *astronomus* came to be used
(=astronomer).

[2] In Cicero always neut. plur., e.g. *in arithmeticis satis versatus;*
later writers use the fem. sing. The pure Latin word is *numeri,* cf.
De Fin. 1. 21. 72 *an ille se, ut Plato, in musicis, geometria,
numeris, astris contereret?* So De Fin. 5. 29. 87 *cur Plato
Aegyptum peragravit, ut a sacerdotibus barbaris numeros et caelestia
acciperet?* Cf. Nägelsb. Lat. Stil. p. 46.

*bis bina quot sint non didicisse*—to be absolutely ignorant of arithmetic.

## 15. ART IN GENERAL

*artis opus ; opus arte factum* or *perfectum*—a work of art.

*opus summo artifico factum* ⎱ a master-piece of classical
*opus omnibus numeris absolutum* ⎰     work.

*artem exercere*—to follow an artistic profession, practise an art.

*artem tradere, docere*—to teach an art.

*artem profiteri*—to profess an art.

*artium (liberalium) studium,* or simply *studium*—a taste for the fine arts.

*artis praecepta,* or also simply *ars*—the rules of art; aesthetics.

*(artis, artium) intellegens, peritus*[1] (opp. *idiota,* a layman) a connoisseur ; a specialist.

*existimator (doctus, intellegens, acerrimus)*—a (competent, intelligent, subtle) critic.

*in existimantium arbitrium venire* (Brut. 24. 92)—to come before the tribunal of the critics.

*iudicium facere*—to criticise.

*sensum, iudicium habere*—to be a man of taste.

*elegantia in illo est*—he possesses sound judgment in matters of taste.

*iudicium subtile, elegans, exquisitum, intellegens*—good taste ; delicate perception.

*iudicium acuere*—to cultivate one's powers of criticism.

---

[1] *idiota*=properly uninitiated, not the same as *rudis, indoctus, imperitus.*

*abhorrere ab artibus* (opp. *delectari artibus*)—to have no taste for the fine arts.

*veritatem*[1] *imitari* (Div. i. 13. 23)—(1) to make a lifelike, natural representation of a thing (used of the artist); (2) to be lifelike (of a work of art).

*in omni re vincit imitationem veritas*—in everything nature defies imitation.

*aliquid ad verum exprimere*—to make a copy true to nature.

*morum ac vitae imitatio*—a lifelike picture of everyday life.

*aliquid e vita ductum est*—a thing is taken from life.


## 16. POETRY—MUSIC—PAINTING—SCULPTURE

*poëma condere, facere, componere* ⎱ to write poetry.
*versus facere, scribere* ⎰

*carmina, versus fundere* (De Or. 3. 50)—to write poetry with facility.

*carmen epicum*—epic poetry.

*poëta epicus*—an epic, heroic poet.

*poësis scaenica*—dramatic poetry.

*poëta scaenicus*—a dramatic poet.

*scriptor tragoediarum, comoediarum,* also (*poëta*) *tragicus, comicus*[2]—a writer of tragedy, comedy.

*scriptor fabularum*[3]—a writer of fables.

---

[1] *veritas* means not merely truth (opp. *mendacium*), but also reality (opp. *opinio, imitatio*). Thus we often find the combination *res et veritas ipsa* (Tusc. 5. 5. 13), *natura rerum et ipsa veritas.*

[2] *tragicus, comicus* as adjectives = occurring in tragedy, comedy—e.g. *Orestes tragicus; senes comici.* Comic in the ordinary sense = *ridiculus,* cf. *homo ridiculus.*

[3] Not *fabulator,* which = a gossip, teller of anecdotes.

*divino quodam instinctu concitari, ferri* (Div. 1. 31. 66)—to feel inspired.

*divino quodam spiritu inflatus* or *tactus*—inspired.

*carmen, versum agere*—to recite a poem, line with appropriate action.

*carmen recitare*—to read a piece of verse with expression.

*carmen pronuntiare*—to recite a piece of verse (without gestures).

*carmen inconditum*—a rough poem ; an extempore effusion.

*se conferre ad poësis studium*—to devote oneself to poetry.

*poëtica laude florere*—to be distinguished as a poet.

*poësis genus ad Romanos transferre*—to transplant to Rome one of the branches of poesy.

*alicuius laudes versibus persequi*
*alicuius laudes (virtutes) canere* } to sing the praises of some one (not *canere aliquem*).

*alicuius res gestas versibus ornare, celebrare*—to celebrate some one's exploits in song.

*ut ait Homerus*—as Homer sings (not *canit*).

*numerus poëtice vinctus*—poetical rhythm.

*artem musicam*[1] *discere, tractare*—to learn, study music.

*nervorum et tibiarum cantus*—instrumental music.

*vocum et fidium (nervorum) cantus*—vocal and instrumental music.

*docere aliquem fidibus*—to teach some one to play a stringed instrument.

*fidibus discere* (De Sen. 8. 26)—to learn to play a stringed instrument.

*fidibus canere*—to play on the lyre.

*pellere nervos in fidibus*—to strike the strings of the lyre.

---

[1] *musica (-orum)* is also used for music, cf. *in musicis se conterere.*

*tibias inflare*
*tibiis* or *tibiā canere* } to play the flute.

*ad tibiam* or *ad tibicinem canere*—to sing to a flute
    accompaniment.

*(homo) symphoniacus*—a singer, member of a choir.

*symphōnīa canit* (Verr. 3. 44. 105)—the orchestra is
    playing.

*acroāma*[1]—a professional performer.

*modi* (De Or. 1. 42. 187)—the melody.

*modos facere*—to compose, put to music.

*numerus, numeri*—the tune; rhythm.

*numerose cadere*—to have a rhythmical cadence.

*ars pingendi, pictura* (De Or. 2. 16. 69)—the art of
    painting.

*ars fingendi*—the art of sculpture.

*signa et tabulae* (*pictae*)—statues and pictures.

*simulacrum e marmore facere*—to make a marble statue.

*statuas*[2] *inscribere* (Verr. 2. 69. 167)—to put an inscrip-
    tion on statues.

## 17. THE DRAMA

*ars ludicra* (De Or. 2. 20. 84)—the dramatic art.

*fabula, ludus scaenicus*—the piece; the play.

*argumentum*—the plot of the piece.

*actio*—the treatment of the piece.

*actus*—an act.

[1] *acroama* = originally anything performed to give pleasure, then
a performer. The Greeks applied the term to music; the Romans
used it of any professional performer who entertained guests while at
table.

[2] *statua* is not used of statues of the gods, but *signum, simulacrum*.

*fabulam docere* (διδάσκειν) (of the writer) (opp. *fabulam discere*—to study a piece, of the actor)—to get a piece played, rehearse it.

*fabulam agere*—to act a play (said of the actors).

*fabulam edere*—to bring out a play, put it on the stage (used of the man who finds the money).

*fabulam dare*—to produce a play (of the writer).

*in scaenam producere aliquem*—to introduce a character on the stage.

*in scaenam prodire*—to come upon the stage.

*in scaenam redire*—to reappear on the scene.

*de scaena decedere*—to retire from the stage.

*in scaenam aliquid inducere*—to bring a thing upon the stage.

*familia, grex, caterva histrionum* — a theatrical company.

*dominus gregis*—the manager.

*theatrum* [1]—the playhouse.

*theatra reclamant*—the spectators protest.

*populum facilem, aequum habere*—to have an appreciative audience.

*plaudere* (not *applaudere*)  
*plausum dare (alicui)* } to applaud, clap a person.

*clamores (coronae) facere, excitare*—to elicit loud applause.

*saepius revocatur* (Liv. 7. 2. 9)—he is encored several times.

*fabulam exigere* (Ter. Andr. Prol.)—to hiss a play.

*fabula cadit*—a piece is a failure, falls flat.

---

[1] *theatrum* = (1) the playhouse, theatre; (2) the audience, house. It is used metaphorically for the sphere of activity, theatre, scene, e.g. *theatrum magnum habet ista provincia* (Cic.); *nullum theatrum virtuti conscientia majus* (ibid.)

*histrionem exsibilare, explodere, eicere, exigere*—to hiss an actor off the stage.

*histrioni acclamare* [1]—to interrupt an actor by hooting him.

*partes agere alicuius* [2]—to play the part of some one.

*agere servum, lenonem* — to act the rôle of a slave, pander.

*actor primarum (secundarum, tertiarum) partium* — the actor who plays the leading part.

*tragoedia* or *fabula Antigona* (not *Antigona trag.* or *fab.*) —the Antigone.

*in Sophoclis* (not *Sophoclea*) *Aiace* or *apud Sophoclem in Aiace*—in Sophocles' Ajax.

*caterva, chorus*—the Chorus in Tragedy.

*carmen chori, canticum*—a choric ode in a tragedy.

*loci melici*—the lyric portions of a tragedy.

*diverbium*—stage dialogue.

*canticum*—a choric ode.

*ludi circenses, scaenici* — performances in the circus ; theatrical performances.

*ludos apparare*—to institute games.

*ludos facere, edere (Iovi)* — to give public games in honour of Jupiter.

---

[1] Livy is the first writer who uses *acclamare* in a good sense.

[2] Also used metaphorically of the part played in life, e.g. *partes suscipere, sustinere, dare, tribuere, defendere, tueri*. Similarly *persona* (properly mask) is used in several phrases, e.g. *personam alicuius agere, ferre, tenere ; personam suscipere* or *induere ; personam tueri* (Phil. 8. 10) ; *personam alicui imponere* (Sull. 3. 8). *persona* thus got the meaning of personality, individuality, character, and lastly in a concrete sense a personage of distinction. N.B.—It never represents our " person," cf. many persons were present, *multi (homines) aderant.*

*ludos instaurare*—to revive public games.

*munus gladiatorium edere, dare*⎫
   (or simply *munus edere, dare*)⎬ to give a gladiatorial
*gladiatores dare*⎭ show.

*familia*[1] *gladiatoria* (Sest. 64. 134)—a band, troupe of gladiators under the management of a lanista.

*ludus gladiatorius*—a school for gladiators.

*gladiatoribus* (Att. 2. 19. 3)—at the gladiatorial games.

*celebritas ludorum*—crowded games.

*magnificentia ludorum*⎫
*ludi apparatissimi*⎬ sumptuous public games.

*ludi Olympia* (not *ludi Olympici*), *Pythia*—the Olympian, Pythian games.

*Olympia vincere* ('Ολύμπια νικᾶν)—to win a prize at the Olympian games.

*ludi gymnici*⎫
*certamina gymnica*⎬ gymnastic contests.

*stadium currere* (Off. 3. 10. 42)—to run a foot-race.


# VIII. SPEECH AND WRITING

## 1. SPEECH IN GENERAL

*ars dicendi*—the art of speaking; oratory.

*ad dicendum se conferre*—to devote oneself to oratory.

*dicendi*[2] *praecepta tradere*—to teach rhetoric.

---

[1] Hence *familiam ducere*, metaphorically to be at the head of a movement, to play the leading part, e.g. *in iure civili* (Cic.) For other phrases drawn from the wrestling-school *vid.* ix. 6.

[2] Note the way in which the Latin language prefers a concrete expression in the plural to represent our abstract "rhetoric," cf. *musica* (*-orum*), *astra, numeri, soni* = music, astronomy, arithmetic, acoustics (*vid.* vii. 14).

*rhetor, dicendi magister*—a teacher of rhetoric.

*facultas dicendi*—oratorical talent.

*natum, factum esse ad dicendum*—to be a born orator.

*facilem et expeditum esse ad dicendum* (Brut. 48. 180)—to be
    a ready, fluent speaker.

*rudem, tironem ac rudem* (opp. *exercitatum*) *esse in dicendo*
    —to be an inexperienced speaker.

*disertum esse* (De Or. 1. 21. 94)—to be fluent.

*eloquentem esse* (De Or. 1. 21. 94)—to be a capable, fin-
    ished speaker.

*eloquentia valere* ⎱
*dicendi arte florere* ⎰ to be very eloquent.

*eloquentiae laude florere*—to be a distinguished orator.

*vis dicendi*—oratorical power.

*multum dicendo valere, posse*—to have great weight as a
    speaker.

*eloquentiae principatum tenere* ⎫
*primum* or *principem inter ora-* ⎪ to be considered the fore-
   *tores locum obtinere* ⎬     most orator.
*oratorum principem esse* ⎭

*orationem conficere*—to compose a speech.

*orationem commentari* (Fam. 16. 26)—to prepare, get up a
    speech.

*oratio meditata* (Plin. 26. 3. 7)—a prepared speech.

*subito, ex.tempore* (opp. *ex praeparato*) *dicere*—to speak ex-
    tempore.

*oratio subita*—an extempore speech.

*oratio perpetua*—a continuous discourse.

*oratio accurata* [1] *et polita*—a carefully prepared speech.

*oratio composita*—an elaborate speech.

---

[1] *accuratus* is only used of things, never of persons.

*contentio* (opp. *sermo*) (Off. 2. 48)—animated address ; emotional language.

*copiose dicere*—to speak very fluently.

*ornate dicere*—to speak well, elegantly.

*libere dicere* (Verr. 2. 72. 176)—to speak frankly, independently.

*plane, aperte dicere*—to speak openly, straightforwardly.

*perspicue, diserte dicere*—to speak in clear, expressive language.

*missis ambagibus dicere*—to speak without circumlocution.

*accommodate ad persuadendum dicere*—to be a persuasive speaker.

*aggredi ad dicendum* [1]—to come forward to make a speech ; to address the house.

*verba facere apud* [2] *populum, in contione*—to address a meeting of the people.

*in contionem* (*in rostra*) *escendere* [3] (only of Romans)—to mount the rostra.

*orationem habere* (Tusc. 5. 33. 94)—to make a speech.

*initium dicendi facere*—to begin to speak.

*finem dicendi facere*—to cease speaking.

*perorare*—(1) to make one's peroration ; (2) to deliver the closing speech (in a case where several speeches have been made).

---

[1] *surgere ad dicendum* is only used of some one who has been till now seated (De Or. 2. 78. 316).

[2] *apud* is used of appearing before an official assembly, e.g. *apud populum, apud senatum, apud iudices.* *coram* is used of an informal casual meeting.

[3] *escendere* is more common than *ascendere*, cf. *in contionem escendere* (Cic. Att. 4. 2. 3 ; Liv. 2. 7. 7, etc. etc.) Similarly *in rostra escendere* (Cic. Liv.), *in tribunal escendere* (Liv.) Later *suggestum, rostra escendere* (Tac. Ann. 15. 59 ; ibid. 13. 5).

*animos audientium permovere, inflammare*—to make an impression on one's audience.

*animos tenere*—to rivet the attention of . . .

*audientiam sibi (orationi) facere*—to obtain a hearing.

*solutum et expeditum esse ad dicendum*—to be never at a loss for something to say.

*lingua promptum esse*—to have a ready tongue.

*celeritas in respondendo*—readiness in debate, in repartee.

*bonis lateribus*[1] *esse*—to have good lungs.

*linguae solutio*—volubility.


## 2. STYLE—EXPRESSION

*genus dicendi (scribendi) ; oratio*[2]—style.

*genus dicendi grave* or *grande, medium, tenue*[3] (cf. Or. 5. 20 ; 6. 21)—elevated, moderate, plain style.

*fusum orationis genus*—a running style.

*inconditum dicendi genus* (Brut. 69. 242)—a rough, unpolished style.

---

[1] *latus* is never used in the singular in good Latin with the meaning "lungs," "breath," "vigour," cf. Cic. *iam me dies, vox, latera deficient si . . .* In a somewhat similar way *lacerti* is used of oratorical vigour, e.g. *ipse hastas . . . oratoris lacertis viribusque torquebit* (De Or. 1. 57. 242).

[2] Not *stilus*, which means the writing instrument the stylus, hence the expression *stilum vertere* (Verr. 2. 3. 41), to erase what has been written. Metaphorically it denotes—(1) the action of writing, e.g. *stilus optimus est et praestantissimus dicendi effector et magister ;* (2) the manner of writing, mode of composition, e.g. *unus enim sonus est totius orationis et idem stilus.*

[3] Speeches belong according to their subject-matter to *genus deliberativum* (συμβουλευτικόν), *genus iudiciale* (δικανικόν), or *genus demonstrativum* (ἐπιδεικτικόν), cf. Cic. de Inv. 1. 5. 7 ; Arist. Rhet. bk. iii.

*inflatum orationis genus*⎫
*oratio altius exaggerata* ⎭a bombastic style.

*elatio atque altitudo orationis*—the exalted strain of the speech.

*exsurgere altius* or *incitatius ferri*—to take a higher tone (especially of poets and orators).

*magnifice loqui, dicere*—(1) to speak vehemently, passionately; (2) to speak pompously, boastfully.

*magniloquentia, granditas verborum*—pathos; passion.

*tragoediae*—tragic pathos.

*expedita et facile currens oratio*⎫
*oratio aequabiliter fluens* ⎭an easy, fluent style.

*flumen*[1] *orationis* (De Or. 2. 15. 62)—flow of oratory.

*siccitas, sanitas orationis* ⎫
*verborum tenuitas, oratio subtilis*⎭the plain style.

*oratio exilis, ieiuna, arida, exsanguis*—the dry, lifeless style.

*ornatus orationis, verborum*—well-chosen language, grace of style.

*elegantia orationis*—tasteful description.

*oratio pura, pura et emendata*—pure, correct language.

*integritas, sinceritas orationis* (not *puritas*) — purity of style.

*oratio inquinata*[2] (De Opt. Gen. Or. 3. 7)—incorrect language.

*orationes Catonis antiquitatem redolent* (Brut. 21. 82)— Cato's speeches sound archaic.

*ex illius orationibus ipsae Athenae redolent*—there is a flavour of Atticism about his discourse.

*oratio soluta* (not *prosa*) or simply *oratio*—prose.

---

[1] On the other hand, *oratio fluit* (De Or. 3. 49. 190)= the language has no rhythm.

[2] Not *impura*, which means unchaste, obscene.

*oratio numerose cadit*—his style has a well-balanced cadence.

*numeris orationem astringere, vincire*—to make a speech rhythmical.

*lumina, flores dicendi* (De Or. 3. 25. 96)—flowers of rhetoric ; embellishments of style.

*sententias (verbis) explicare, aperire*—to explain one's sentiments.

*sententiae reconditae et exquisitae* (Brut. 97. 274)—profound sentiments.

*ubertas* (not *divitiae*) *et copia orationis*—a full and copious style of speech.

*crebritas* or *copia* (opp. *inopia*) *sententiarum* or simply *copia* —richness of ideas.

*sententiis abundans*[1] or *creber* (opp. *sententiis inanis*)—rich in ideas.

*adumbrare aliquid* (Or. 14. 43)—to roughly sketch a thing.

*exprimere aliquid verbis* or *oratione* (*vid.* p. 77, note)—to express clearly, make a lifelike representation of a thing.

*exponere aliquid* or *de aliqua re*—to give an account of a thing (either orally or in writing).

| | |
|---|---|
| *sententiae inter se nexae*<br>*perpetuitas verborum*<br>*contextus orationis* (not *nexus,*<br>  *conexus sententiarum*) | the connection. |
| *ratio sententiarum*<br>*ratio, qua sententiae inter se*<br>  *excipiunt* | the connection of thought. |

---

[1] Not *dives* which Cicero uses only absolutely and almost always of persons, cf. however *animus hominis dives* (Parad. 6. 44), *divitior mihi et affluentior videtur esse vera amicitia,* (De Am. 16. 58).

*vitam alicuius exponere*—to give an account of a man's life.

*vitam alicuius depingere*—to make a sketch of a man's life.

*de ingenio moribusque alicuius exponere*—to make a character-sketch of a person.

*summo colore aliquid illustrare*—to depict a thing in lively colours.

*ante oculos ponere aliquid*—to bring a thing vividly before the eyes.

*oculis* or *sub oculos, sub aspectum subicere aliquid*—to represent a thing vividly.

*rerum sub aspectum paene subiectio* (De Or. 3. 53. 202)—graphic depiction.

*perlustrare, lustrare oculis aliquid*—to scrutinise, examine closely.

*sic exponere aliquid, quasi agatur res (non quasi narretur)*—to represent a thing dramatically.

*aliquem disputantem facere, inducere, fingere (est aliquis apud aliquem disputans)*—to introduce a person (into a dialogue) discoursing on . . .

*in uno conspectu ponere aliquid*
*sub unum aspectum subicere aliquid* } to give a general idea of a thing.

*in brevi conspectu ponere aliquid*—to make a short survey of a thing.

*uno conspectu videre aliquid*—to have a general idea of a thing.

*breviter tangere, attingere aliquid*—to touch briefly on a thing.

*strictim, leviter tangere, attingere, perstringere aliquid*
*quasi praeteriens, in transitu attingere aliquid* } to make a cursory mention of a thing ; to mention by the way (not *obiter* or *in transcursu*).

*res summas attingere*
*summatim aliquid exponere*
} to dwell only on the main points.

*multa verba facere*
*multum, nimium esse (in ali-*
*qua re)* (De Or. 2. 4. 17)
} to go deeply into a matter, discuss it fully.

*pluribus verbis, copiosius explicare, persequi*[1] *aliquid*—to give a full, detailed account of a thing.

*fusius, uberius, copiosius disputare, dicere de aliqua re*—to speak at great length on a subject, discuss very fully.

*breviter, paucis explicare aliquid*
*rem paucis absolvere* (Sall. Iug. 17. 2)
} to explain a matter briefly, in a few words (not *paucis verbis*).

*rebus ipsis par est oratio*
*rebus verba respondent*
} the circumstances are described in language worthy of them.

*copiam quam potui persecutus sum*—I have exhausted all my material.

*verbis non omnia exsequi posse*—to be unable to say all one wants.

*in medium proferre aliquid*—to bring a subject forward into discussion.

*in medio ponere (proponere)*—to publish, make public.

*silentio praeterire* (not *praetermittere*) *aliquid*—to pass over in silence.

*significare aliquem* or *aliquid*
*significatione appellare aliquem*
*describere aliquem* (Cael. 20. 50)
} to allude to a person or thing (not *alludere*).

*leviter significare aliquid*—to hint vaguely at a thing.

---

[1] *persequi* is often used in the meaning to expound, treat of either orally or in writing, e.g. *alicuius vitam, alicuius laudes versibus, res Hannibalis.*

*ordine narrare, quomodo res gesta sit*—to detail the whole history of an affair.

*dicendo ornare aliquid*—to embellish a narrative.

*rhetorice, tragice ornare aliquid* (Brut. 11. 43)—to add rhetorical, dramatic embellishments to a subject.

*digressus, digressio, egressio*
*quod ornandi causa additum est* }—a digression, episode.

*includere in orationem aliquid*
*inserere orationi aliquid*
*interponere aliquid* (De Am. 1. 3) }—to interpolate, insert something.

*dicendo augere, amplificare aliquid* (opp. *dicendo extenuare aliquid*)—to lend lustre to a subject by one's description.

*in maius ferre, in maius extollere aliquid*—to exaggerate a thing.

*in maius accipere aliquid*—to overestimate a thing.

*digredi (a proposito)* (De Or. 2. 77. 311)—to digress, deviate.

*studio alicuius rei provectus sum*—my zeal for a thing has led me too far.

*longe, alte (longius, altius) repetere* (either absolute or *ab aliqua re*)—to go a long way back (in a narrative).

*oratio longius repetita* (De Or. 3. 24. 91)—a rather recondite speech.

*accedere ad cotidiani sermonis genus*—to adopt the language of everyday life.

*ad vulgarem sensum* or *ad communem opinionem orationem accommodare* (Off. 2. 10. 35)—to express oneself in popular language.

## 3. DELIVERY—VOICE

*actio* (Brut. 38)—delivery.

*pronuntiatio*[1] c. Gen.—artistic delivery; declamation.

*actio paulum claudicat*[2]—the delivery is rather halting, poor.

*haerere, haesitare* (Catil. 2. 6. 13)—to stop short, hesitate.

*perturbari, permoveri*—to be nervous, embarrassed.

*de scripto orationem*[3] *habere, dicere* (opp. *sine scripto, ex memoria*)—to read a speech.

*interpellare aliquem (dicentem)*—to interrupt.

*vox magna, clara* (Sulla 10. 30)—a strong, loud voice.

*vox gravis, acuta, parva, mediocris*—a deep, high, thin, moderate voice.

*vox canōra* (Brut. 63. 234)—a melodious, ringing voice.

*vox lenis, suppressa, summissa*—a gentle, subdued voice.

*vocem mittere (sonitum reddere* of things)—to speak, utter a sound.

*vocem summittere*—to lower one's voice.

*contentio, remissio vocis*—raising, lowering the voice.

*vocem intercludere* (Just. 11. 8. 4)—to prevent some one from speaking.

*nulla vox est ab eo audita*—no sound passed his lips.

*magna voce clamare*—to shout at the top of one's voice.

*clamorem tollere* (Liv. 3. 28)—to raise a shout, a cry.

*gestum* (always in the sing.) *agere*—to gesticulate.

---

[1] Not *declamatio* which = an oratorical exercise. Distinguish *pronuntiare* (De Or. 1. 59. 251), to declaim a thing according to the rules of rhetoric; and *declamare* = to go through rhetorical exercises as a practice in speaking.

[2] *claudicare* often metaph. of things which are unequal, weak, e.g. *amicitia claudicat* (Fin. 1. 69).

[3] But to read a speech *orationem legere* (Brut. 51. 191); to read with expression, *recitare* (Phil. 10. 2. 5).

## 4. SUBJECT-MATTER—ARGUMENT

*non habeo argumentum scribendi*
*deest mihi argumentum ad scri-* } I have nothing to write
   *bendum* (Att. 9. 7. 7)     about.
*non habeo, non est quod scribam*

*res* (opp. *verba*) *mihi suppetit*—I have abundance to say.

*materia mihi crescit*—my subject grows as I write.

*res componere ac digerere*—to arrange and divide the
   subject-matter.

*dispositio rerum* (De Inv. 1. 7. 9)—the arrangement of the
   subject-matter.

*materia rerum et copia uberrima* }
*infinita et immensa materia*   } abundance of material.

*materiem ad ornatum praebere*—to afford matter for
   elaboration, embellishment.

*id quod* (*mihi*) *propositum est*
*res proposita*            } a theme, subject proposed
*id quod quaerimus* (*quaeritur*) }  for discussion.
*institutum* or *id quod institui*

*a proposito aberrare, declinare, deflectere, digredi, egredi*—to
   digress from the point at issue.

*ad propositum reverti, redire* }
*ad rem redire*         } to come back to the point.

*sed redeat, unde aberravit oratio*
*sed ad id, unde digressi sumus,*  but to return from the
   *revertamur*           } digression we have
*verum ut ad id, unde digressa est*  been making.
   *oratio, revertamur*

*mihi propositum est* c. Inf. (or *mihi proposui, ut*)—the task
   I have put before myself is . . .

*ponere*—to propose, set a theme.

*verba composita* [1]—well-arranged words.

*verborum immutatio*—a trope ; metonymy.

*continua translatio* (Or. 27. 94)—an allegory ; continuous
    metaphor.

*simili uti*—to employ a comparison, simile.

*dissimulatio* (Off. 1. 30. 108)—irony.

*vetus (verbum) est* (c. Acc. c. Inf.)—it was said long ago
    that . . .

*ut est in proverbio*
*ut* or *quod* or *quomodo aiunt,* }—as the proverb says.
  *ut* or *quemadmodum dicitur*

*in proverbii consuetudinem* or simply *in proverbium venire*—
    to pass into a proverb.

*proverbii locum obtinere* (Tusc. 4. 16. 36)—to be used as
    a proverb.

*hoc est Graecis hominibus in proverbio*—this is a proverb
    among the Greeks.

*bene illo Graecorum proverbio praecipitur*—that Greek
    proverb contains an excellent lesson.

*vetamur vetere proverbio*—an old proverb tells us not
    to . . .

*proverbium vetustate* or *sermone tritum* (*vid.* p. 11, note)—
    an old proverb which every one knows.

*syllabam, litteram producere* (opp. *corripere*) (Quintil. 9. 4.
    89)—to lengthen the pronunciation of a syllable
    or letter.

*haec vox longa syllaba terminatur, in longam syllabam
    cadit, exit*—this word ends in a long syllable.

*oriri a longa* (De Or. 1. 55. 236)—to begin with a long
    syllable.

---

[1] Compound words = *verba copulata, iuncta* (Or. 48. 159),
*coniuncta,* cf. Cic. De Or. 3. 38. 154.

*syllabarum auceps*—a verbal, petty critic ; a caviller.

*verborum aucupium* or *captatio*—minute, pedantic carping at words.

*litteras exprimere* (opp. *obscurare*) — to pronounce the syllables distinctly.

*ad litteram, litterate*—to the letter ; literally.

*litterarum* [1] *ordo* ⎱
*litterae, elementa* ⎰ the alphabet.

*ad litteram* or *litterarum ordine digerere*—to arrange in alphabetical order.

## 9. WRITING—WRITERS—BOOKS

*litteris mandare* or *consignare aliquid* (Acad. 2. 1. 2)—to put down in writing.

*litteris persequi* (*vid.* p. 127, note) *aliquid*—to treat in writing.

*scriptor* (not *auctor* = guarantor)—the writer, author.

*scribere*—to take to writing, become an author.

*ad scribendum* or *ad scribendi* ⎫
  *studium se conferre*       ⎪ to become a writer, em-
*animum ad scribendum appel-* ⎬  brace a literary career.
  *lere, applicare*           ⎭

*librum scribere, conscribere*—to write a book.

*librum conficere, componere* (De Sen. 1. 2)—to compose, compile a book.

*librum edere* (Div. 1. 3. 6)—to publish a book.

*librum evolvere, volvere* ⎱
*volumen explicare*        ⎰ to open a book.

---

[1] Cf. *quarta elementorum littera*, the fourth letter of the alphabet (Suet. Iul. 56).

*librum mittere ad aliquem* (Fin. 1. 3. 8)—to dedicate a book to some one.

*index, inscriptio*[1] *libri*—the title of a book.

*liber inscribitur*[2] *Laelius* (Off. 2. 9. 30)—the book is entitled "Laelius."

*Cicero dicit in Laelio* (*suo*) or *in eo* (not *suo*) *libro, qui inscribitur Laelius*—Cicero says in his "Laelius."

*est liber de . . .*—there exists a book on . . .

*exstat liber* (notice the order of the words)—the book is still extant.

*liber intercidit, periit*—the book has been lost.

*liber deperditus*—a book which has been entirely lost sight of.

*liber perditus*—a lost book of which fragments (*relliquiae*, not *fragmenta*) remain.

*liber qui fertur alicuius*—a book which is attributed to some one.

*nescio quis*—an anonymous writer.

*liber refertur ad nescio quem auctorem*—the book is attributed to an unknown writer.

*hic liber est de amicitia* (not *agit*) or *hoc libro agitur de am.*—the book treats of friendship.

*libro continetur aliquid*
*libro scriptor complexus est aliquid* ⎱ the book contains something . . . (not *continet aliquid*).

*in extremo libro* (Q. Fr. 2. 7. 1)—at the end of the book.

---

[1] Not *titulus* which means—(1) an inscription on a tomb, monument ; (2) public notice, e.g. an advertisement of a sale, *sub titulum misit lares* (Ov.) ; (3) metaph. title, honour, e.g. *consulatus, coniugis*. It is only in very late writers that it = a title of a book.

[2] The perfect *inscriptus est* is only used when the writer himself is speaking of his book, e.g. *de senectute disputavi eo libro, qui Cato maior inscriptus est*, ". . . which I have entitled *Cato maior*."

*liber mihi est in manibus*⎫
*librum in manibus habere* ⎬to be engaged on a book.
　(Acad. 1. 1. 2)　　⎭

*liber, oratio in manibus est*—the book, speech can easily be obtained.

*librum in manus sumere*—to take up a book in one's hands.

*librum de manibus ponere* [1]—to lay down a book (*vid.* p. 189, note).

*perpolire, limare diligenter librum, opus*—to polish, finish a work with the greatest care.

*extrema manus accēdit operi* (active *extremam manum imponere operi*)—to put the finishing touch to a work.

*liber accurate, diligenter scriptus*—a carefully written book.

*aliquid, multa ex Ciceronis libris excerpere* (not *excerpere librum*)—to make extracts from Cicero's writings.

*aliquid in commentarios suos referre* (Tusc. 3. 22. 54)—to enter a thing in one's note-book.

*librum annotare, interpolare, distinguere*—to furnish a book with notes, additional extracts, marks of punctuation.

*se abdere in bibliothecam suam*—to bury oneself in one's library.

*Platonem legere, lectitare*—to read Plato.

*locum Platonis afferre, proferre* (not *citare*)—to quote a passage of Plato.

*scriptor hoc loco dicit*—our (not *noster*) author tells us at this point.

*Cicero loco quodam haec dicit*—Cicero says this somewhere.

---

[1] Distinguish the two verbs *ponere*=to set down for a moment temporarily, and *deponere* to lay aside, abandon altogether. Cf. *vincere* and *devincere, perdere* and *deperdere.*

*Platonem legere et cognoscere*—to study Plato.

*legendo percurrere aliquid*—to read cursorily.

*apud Platonem scriptum videmus,*[1] *scriptum est* or simply *est* —we read in Plato.

*in Platonis Phaedone scriptum est*—in Plato's "Phaedo" we read.

*verba, oratio, exemplum scriptoris*—the text of the author (not *textus*).

*legentes, ii qui legunt*[2]—the reader.

*languorem, molestiam legentium animis afferre*—to weary, bore the reader.

*liber plenus delectationis*—a very charming book.

*alicuius mens in scriptis spirat*—a man's soul breathes through his writings.

*mendum (scripturae)* (Fam. 6. 7. 1)—a clerical error, copyist's mistake.

*mendose scriptum*—full of orthographical errors.

*labi in scribendo*—to make a mistake in writing.

*mendosum esse* (Verr. 2. 4. 77)—(1) to make frequent mistakes in writing ; (2) to be full of mistakes (speaking of a passage).

*inducere verbum* (Phil. 13. 19. 43)—to strike out, delete a word.

[1] *legere* in this connection only in the perfect.

[2] Not *lector*, which means a professional reader, cf. De Or. 2. 55. 223. Similarly "audience "=*ii qui audiunt* or *audientes* (usually in the oblique cases). Words in *-tor* and *-trix* always denote those who do something habitually or for some permanent object. Thus of functionaries—*censor, dictator, quaestor ;* of artisans—*fictor* sculptor, *institor* retail dealer, *mercator* wholesale merchant, *structor* mason ; of people who are always showing some distinguishing quality or defect—*calumniator, ratiocinator ;* of those who have performed a feat so remarkable as to confer on them a durable characteristic—*creator urbis* (Romulus), *servator Graeciae* (Themistocles), *Cimbrorum victor* (Marius), etc.

## 10. LETTERS

*epistulam (litteras) dare, scribere, mittere ad aliquem*—to write a letter to some one.

*epistula ad Atticum data, scripta, missa* or *quae ad A. scripta est*—a letter to Atticus.

*epistulam dare alicui ad aliquem*—to charge some one with a letter for some one else.

*epistulam reddere alicui* (Att. 5. 21. 4)—to deliver a letter to some one (used of the messenger).

*epistularum commercium* ⎱
*litterae missae et allatae* ⎰correspondence.

*colloqui cum aliquo per litteras*—to correspond with some one.

*litteras inter se dare et accipere*—to be in correspondence with . . .

*litteras perferre aliquo*—to take a letter somewhere.

*epistulam signare, obsignare*—to seal, fasten a letter.

*epistulam solvere, aperire, resignare* (of Romans also *linum incīdere*)—to open a letter.

*epistulam intercipere* (Att. 1. 13. 2)—to intercept a letter.

*epistulam deprehendere*—to take forcible possession of a letter.

*litteras recitare* (Att. 8. 9. 2)—to read a letter aloud (in public).

*litterae hoc exemplo* (Att. 9. 6. 3)—a letter, the tenor of which is . . .

*litterae in hanc sententiam* or *his verbis scriptae sunt*—the terms, contents of the letter are as follows.

*Kalendis Ianuariis Romā (dabam)*—Rome, January 1st.

*dies* (fem. in this sense)—the date.

*pater optime*[1] or *carissime, mi pater* (*vid.* p. 197)—my
    dear father.

*litteras reddere datas a. d. X. Kal. Octob.*—to deliver a
    letter dated September 22nd.

# IX. THE EMOTIONS

## 1. DISPOSITION—EMOTION IN GENERAL

*animi affectio* or *habitus* (De Inv. 2. 5)—humour;
    disposition.

*ita*[2] *animo affectum esse*—to be so disposed.

*animos tentare* (Cluent. 63. 176)—to try to divine a
    person's disposition.

*animum alicuius* or simply *aliquem flectere*—to make a
    person change his intention.

*animi motus, commotio, permotio*—the emotions, feelings.

*aliqua re moveri, commoveri*—to be moved by a thing.

*alicuius animum commovere*—to touch a person's heart,
    move him.

*alicuius animum pellere*—to make an impression on a
    person's mind.

*motus excitare in animo* (opp. *sedare, exstinguere*)—to
    excite emotion.

*commotum* or *concitatum esse*—to be moved, agitated.

*commotum perturbatumque esse*—to be greatly agitated.

*alicuius mentem turbare, conturbare, perturbare*—to upset
    a person.

*quid tibi animi est?*—what sort of humour are you in?

---

[1] Neither *amatus* nor *dilectus* can be used in this connection.

[2] But not *magno, laeto*, etc., *animo affici*.

## 2. JOY—PAIN.

*afficere aliquem gaudio, laetitia* } to give pleasure to some
*afferre alicui laetitiam* } one.

*laetitiam capere* or *percipere ex*
  *aliqua re* } to take pleasure in a
*delectari aliqua re* } thing.

*in sinu gaudere* (Tusc. 3. 21. 51)—to rejoice in secret.
*gaudio perfundi*[1]—to be filled with delight.
*cumulum gaudii alicui afferre* (*vid.* p. 50) (Fam. 16. 21. 1)
  —to add the crowning point to a person's joy.
*gaudio, laetitia exsultare*—to utter cries of joy.
*laetitia gestire* (Tusc. 4. 6. 13)—to be transported with
  joy.

*effusa*[2] *laetitia*
*laetitia gestiens* } a transport of joy.

*gaudio, laetitia efferri*—to be beside oneself with joy.
*animum alicuius ad laetitiam excitare*—to put a man in a
  pleasurable frame of mind.
*nimio gaudio paene desipere*—to almost lose one's reason
  from excess of joy.

*doleo aliquid, aliqua re, de* and
  *ex aliqua re*
*aegre, graviter, moleste fero* } I am pained, vexed, sorry.
  *aliquid* (or with Acc. c. Inf.
  or *quod*)

---

[1] *gaudio compleri* (Fin. 5. 14. 69) is rare in Cicero; *gaudio impleri* does not occur. Speaking generally, *complere, implere, replere,* should not be used of the emotions.

[2] Cf. *effusa fuga,* headlong flight; *effusi sumptus,* lavish expenditúre (Rosc. Am. 24. 68), *cursus effusus* (Liv. 9. 41. 17).

*tuam vicem*[1] *doleo*—I am sorry for you.

*dolore affici*—to feel pain.

*dolorem capere (percipere) ex aliqua re*—to be vexed about a thing.

*doloribus premi, angi, ardere, cruciari, distineri et divelli*—to feel acute pain.

*dolorem alicui facere, afferre, commovere*—to cause a person pain.

*acerbum dolorem alicui inurere*—to cause any one very acute pain.

*acer morsus doloris est* (Tusc. 2. 22. 53)—the pain is very severe.

*dolorem in lacrimas effundere* — to find relief in tears.

*dolori indulgere*—to give way to grief.

*dolor infixus animo haeret* (Phil. 2. 26)—grief has struck deep into his soul.

*dolore confici, tabescere*—to be wasted with grief; to die of grief.

*dolores remittunt, relaxant*—the pain grows less.

*dolori resistere*—to struggle against grief.

*callum obducere*[2] *dolori* (Tusc. 2. 15. 36)—to render insensible to pain.

*animus meus ad dolorem obduruit* (Fam. 2. 16. 1)—I have become callous to all pain.

*dolorem abicere, deponere, depellere*—to banish grief.

---

[1] *vicem* with a genitive or a possessive pronoun has the meaning "on account of," "with regard to," especially with verbs expressing the emotions, e.g. *doleo, timeo, irascor.*

[2] Note too *consuetudo callum obduxit stomacho meo* (Fam. 9. 2. 3), habit has made me callous. *callum* properly is the thick nerveless skin which covers the bodies of animals.

*dolorem alicui eripere* (Att. 9. 6. 4)—to free a person from
  his pain.

*cum magno meo dolore*—to my sorrow.


### 3. VEXATION—CARE—EQUANIMITY— CONTENTMENT—AFFLICTION

*in aegritudine, sollicitudine esse*
*aegritudine, sollicitudine affici* } to be vexed, mortified,
*sollicitum esse* anxious.

*nihil omnino curare* } not to trouble oneself about a
*non laborare de aliqua re* thing.

*aliquid me sollicitat, me sollicitum habet, mihi sollicitudini
  est, mihi sollicitudinem affert*—something harasses
  me, makes me anxious.

*aegritudo exest animum planeque conficit* (Tusc. 3. 13. 27)
  —anxiety gnaws at the heart and incapacitates it.

*aegritudine, curis confici*—to be wasting away with grief.

*aegritudine afflictum, debilitatum esse, iacēre*—to be bowed
  down, prostrated by grief.

*aegritudinem alicuius elevare* } to comfort another in his
*aliquem aegritudine levare* trouble.

*quieto, tranquillo, securo animo esse*—to enjoy peace of mind.

*rebus suis, sorte sua contentum esse*—to be contented.

*satis habeo, satis mihi est* c. Inf.—I am content to . . .

*paucis, parvo contentum esse*—to be satisfied with a little.

*fortunae meae me paenitet*[1]—I am discontented with my
  lot.

---

[1] The evidence of inscriptions and the best MSS. seems to point
to the derivation of *paenitet*, not from *poena* (cf. *punire, impunis*),
but from the root contained in *penes, penetrare, penitus ;* its original
meaning would thus be, " to be touched, affected within, at heart "
(Bréal).

*non me paenitet, quantum profecerim*—I am not dissatisfied
　　with my progress.

*in luctu esse* (Sest. 14. 32)—to suffer affliction.

*in sordibus luctuque iacēre*—to be in great trouble,
　　affliction.

*mors alicuius luctum mihi attulit*—some one's death has
　　plunged me in grief.

*in maximos luctus incidere*—to be overwhelmed by a
　　great affliction.

*magnum luctum haurire* (without *ex-*)—to undergo severe
　　trouble, trials.

*luctum percipere ex aliqua re*—to feel sorrow about a thing.

*omnem luctum plane abstergere*—to banish all sad
　　thoughts.

*luctum deponere* (Phil. 14. 13. 34)—to lay aside one's
　　grief.

*vel maximos luctus vetustate tollit diuturnitas* (Fam. 5. 16.
　　5)—time assuages the most violent grief.


## 4. FEAR—TERROR—ANXIETY

*timorem, terrorem alicui inicere*, more strongly *incutere*—to
　　inspire fear, terror.

*timor aliquem occupat* (B. G. 1. 39)—fear comes upon
　　some one.

*in timore esse, versari*—to be in fear.

*in timorem venire, pervenire*—to become frightened.

*metus aliquem exanimat* (Mil. 24. 65)—a man is paralysed
　　with fear.

*exalbescere metu*—to grow pale with fear.

*metu fractum et debilitatum, perculsum esse*—to be com-
　　pletely prostrated by fear.

*abicere, omittere timorem*—to banish one's fears.

*a metu respirare* (Cluent. 70. 200)⎱ to recover from one's
*ex metu se recreare, se colligere* ⎰ fright.

*respirandi spatium dare*—to give time for recovery.

*terror incidit alicui*⎫
*terror invadit in aliquem* (rarely ⎬ terror, panic seizes some
 *alicui*, after Livy *aliquem*)⎭ one.

*in terrorem conicere aliquem*—to overwhelm some one with
 terror.

(*animo*) *angi* (Brut. 27)—to be very uneasy; to fret.

*cura sollicitat angitque aliquem*—anxiety troubles and
 torments one.

*angoribus premi*—to be tormented with anxiety.

*angoribus confici* (Phil. 2. 15. 37)—to be worn out, almost
 dead with anxiety.


## 5. COURAGE—DISCOURAGEMENT— PUSILLANIMITY—PRIDE—ARROGANCE— INSOLENCE

*bono animo esse*⎫
*bonum animum habere*⎰ to be brave, courageous.

*animus alicui accedit, crescit*⎫
*animum capere, colligere*⎰ to take courage.

*animum recipere* (Liv. 2. 50)—to take courage again.

*animo forti esse*—to be brave by nature.

*fortem te praebe*—be brave!

*alacri et erecto animo esse*—to show a brisk and cheerful
 spirit.

*animum facere, addere alicui*—to succeed in encouraging
 a person

*animum alicuius confirmare*—to strengthen, confirm a person's courage.

*animum alicui augere* (B. G. 7. 70)—to increase a person's courage.

*animum alicuius redintegrare*—to re-inspire courage.

*animus frangitur, affligitur, percellitur, debilitatur*—their spirits are broken.

*animos militum accendere*—to fire with courage.

*animi cadunt*—their courage is ebbing.

*animo cadere, deficere* } *animum demittere* }—to lose courage ; to despair.

*erigere alicuius animum* or *aliquem*—to encourage a person.

*excitare animum iacentem et afflictum* (opp. *frangere animum*)—to inspire the spiritless and prostrate with new vigour.

*animo esse humili, demisso* (more strongly *animo esse fracto, perculso et abiecto*) (Att. 3. 2)—to be cast down, discouraged, in despair.

*inflatum, elatum esse aliqua re*—to be proud, arrogant by reason of something.

*insolentia, superbia inflatum esse*—to be puffed up with pride.

*magnos spiritus sibi sumere* (B. G. 1. 33)—to be haughty.

*spiritus alicuius reprimere*—to lower a person's pride.

*insolentius se efferre*—to behave arrogantly.

*elatius se gerere*—to give oneself airs.

*sibi sumere aliquid* (Planc. 1. 3)—to take upon oneself.

*contumacius se gerere*—to display a proud obstinacy.

*libera contumacia Socratis* (Tusc. 1. 29. 71)—the frank but defiant demeanour of Socrates (before his judges).

## 6. PRESENCE OF MIND—COMPOSURE—
### DESPAIR

*praesenti animo uti* (*vid.* p. 84, note)—to possess presence of mind.

*aequo* (*aequissimo*) *animo ferre aliquid*—to endure a thing with (the greatest) sang-froid.

*humane, modice, moderate, sapienter, constanter ferre aliquid* —to bear a thing with resignation, composure.

(*animo*) *paratum esse ad aliquid*—to be resigned to a thing.

*omnia perpeti paratum esse*—to be ready to endure anything.

*ad omnes casus se comparare*—to prepare oneself for all contingencies.

*animum alicuius de statu, de gradu demovere* (more strongly *depellere, deturbare*) — to disconcert a person.

*de statu suo* or *mentis deici*
   (Att. 16. 15)
*de gradu deici, ut dicitur*[1] } to lose one's composure; to
*perturbari* (*animo*) be disconcerted.

*sui* (*mentis*) *compŏtem non esse*
*non esse apud se*[2] (Plaut. Mil. } to lose one's head, be
  4. 8. 26) beside oneself.

*mente vix constare* (Tusc. 4. 17. 39)—to compose oneself with difficulty.

*animo adesse* (Sull. 11. 33)—to be quite unconcerned.

---

[1] These expressions are metaphors from the fencing-school. *gradus* is the position taken up by a combatant, so *gradu depelli, deici* = to be driven out of one's ground.

[2] Used especially in the comic poets.

*ad se redire*—to regain one's self-possession.

*constantiam servare*⎫
*mente consistere*    ⎬ to be calm, self-possessed.

*desperare* [1] *suis rebus*—to despair of one's position.

*ad (summam) desperationem pervenire, adduci* (B. C. 2. 42)
      —to be plunged into the depths of despair.

*desperatio rerum (omnium)* (Catil. 2. 11. 25)—absolute
      despair; a hopeless situation.

*quid (de) me fiet?* (Ter. Heaut. 4. 3. 37)—what will
      become of me?

*actum est de me*—it's all over with me; I'm a lost man.


## 7. HOPE—EXPECTATION

*spem habere*           ⎫
*spe duci, niti, teneri* ⎬ to cherish a hope.

*magna me spes tenet* (with Acc. c. Inf.) (Tusc. 1. 41. 97)
      —I have great hopes that . . .

*sperare videor*—I flatter myself with the hope . . .

*bene, optime (meliora) sperare de aliquo* (Nep. Milt. 1. 1)—
      to hope well of a person.

*in spem venire, ingredi, adduci* ⎫
*spem concipere animo*            ⎬ to conceive a hope.

*spem redintegrare* (B. G. 7. 25)—to revive a hope.

*spem alicui facere, afferre, inicere*—to inspire any one with
      hope.

---

[1] *desperare* is used, generally with *de*, more rarely with the accusative, in the meaning "to no longer count upon a thing," e.g. *reditum, pacem ;* or with the dative, especially with *sibi, suis rebus, saluti, fortunae suae.* Note the use of *desperatus*, "abandoned," "given up," "despaired of," e.g. *desperati morbi* (Cic.), *aegrota ac paene desperata res publica* (Cic.)

*ad spem aliquem excitare, erigere*—to awaken new hope in some one.

*in maximam spem aliquem adducere* (Att. 2. 22. 3)—to inspire some one with the most brilliant hopes.

*in meliorem spem, cogitationem aliquem inducere* (Off. 2. 15. 53)—to induce some one to take a brighter view of things.

*spem proponere alicui*—to lead some one to expect . . .

*spes affulget* (Liv. 27. 28)—a ray of hope shines on us.

*spem falsam alicui ostendere*—to rouse a vain, groundless hope in some one's mind.

*spem alicui adimere, tollere, auferre, eripere*—to deprive a person of hope.

*spem praecīdere, incidere* (Liv. 2. 15)—to cut off all hope.

*spem perdere*
*spe deici, depelli, deturbari* } to lose hope.

*spes ad irritum cadit, ad irritum redigitur*—expectation is overthrown.

*spem abicere, deponere*—to give up hoping.

*inani, falsa spe duci, induci*—to be misled by a vain hope.

*spes me frustratur*—hope has played me false.

*spes extenuatur et evanescit*—hope is vanishing by degrees.

*spem alicuius fallere* (Catil. 4. 11. 23)—to deceive a person's hopes.

*spem alicui* or *alicuius minuere*—to weaken, diminish a person's hope.

*spem alicuius confirmare*—to strengthen a person in his hopes.

*spem alere*—to entertain a hope.

*spem habere in aliquo*
*spem suam ponere, collocare in aliquo* } to set one's hope on some one.

*inter spem metumque suspensum esse*—to hover between hope and fear.

*praeter spem, exspectationem*—contrary to expectation.

*exspectationem* [1] *sui facere, commovere*—to cause oneself to be expected.

*exspectationem explere* (De Or. 1. 47. 205)—to fulfil expectation.

*exspectationi satisfacere, respondere*—to respond to expectations.

*exspectatione alicuius rei pendēre* (*animi*) (Leg. Agr. 2. 25. 66)—to be in suspense, waiting for a thing.

*exspectatione torqueri, cruciari*—to suffer torments of expectation, delay.

*suspenso animo exspectare aliquid*—to be waiting in suspense for . . .

*aliquem in summam exspectationem adducere* (Tusc. 1. 17. 39)—to rouse a person's expectation, curiosity to the highest pitch.

## 8. PITY—PARDON—WANT OF FEELING— CRUELTY

*misericordiam alicui commovere*  
*misericordiam alicuius concitare* }to excite some one's pity.

*ad misericordiam aliquem allicere, adducere, inducere*—to arouse feelings of compassion in some one.

*misericordia moveri, capi* (De Or. 2. 47)—to be touched with pity.

*misericordiam implorare*—to implore a person's sympathy, pity.

---

[1] Att. 1. 4. 5 *crebras exspectationes tui commoves*—i.e. you are leading us to expect your arrival.

*indulgere vitiis alicuius*—to be indulgent to a person's faults.

*alicui veniam dare (alicuius rei)* — to pardon some one.

*omnem humanitatem exuisse, abiecisse* (Lig. 5. 14)
*omnem humanitatis sensum amisisse*
} to be quite insensible to all feelings of humanity.

*omnis humanitatis expertem esse*—to be absolutely wanting in sympathy.

*omnem humanitatem ex animo exstirpare* (Amic. 13. 48) —to stifle, repress all humane sentiments in one's mind.

*nullam partem sensus habere*—to possess not the least spark of feeling.

*crudelitate uti (vid.* p. 84, note)—to behave with cruelty.

*crudelitatem exercere in aliquo*
*crudelitatem adhibere in aliquem*
} to exercise one's cruelty on some one.

*animadvertere in aliquem*—to inflict punishment on a person.

## 9. LOVE—LONGING—ADMIRATION— ENTHUSIASM

*carum habere aliquem*
*in amore habere aliquem*
*amore prosequi, amplecti aliquem*
} to feel affection for a person.

*carum esse alicui*
*carum atque iucundum esse alicui*
} to be dear to some one.

*adamasse aliquem* (only in Perf. and Plup.) (Nep. Dion 2. 3)—to become devoted to some one.

*aliquem toto pectore,*[1] *ut dicitur, amare* (Leg. 18. 49)—to
    love some one very dearly, with all one's heart.

*aliquem ex animo* or *ex animi sententia amare* (Q. Fr. 1. 1.
    5)—to love deeply.

*amore captum, incensum, inflammatum esse, ardere*—to be
    fired with love.

*amorem ex animo eicere* — to banish love from one's
    mind.

*mel ac deliciae alicuius* (Fam. 8. 8. 1)⎫
*amores et deliciae alicuius*         ⎬somebody's darling.

*in amore et deliciis esse alicui* (active *in deliciis habere
    aliquem*)—to be some one's favourite.

*aliquem in sinu gestare (aliquis est in sinu alicuius)* (Ter.
    Ad. 4. 5. 75)—to love and make a bosom friend of
    a person.

*aliquis, aliquid mihi curae* or *cordi*[1] *est*—somebody,
    something is never absent from my thoughts.

*curae habere aliquid*—to have laid something to heart ; to
    take an interest in a thing.

*nihil antiquius* or *prius habeo quam ut (nihil mihi antiquius*
    or *potius est, quam ut*)—there is nothing I am more
    interested in than . . .

*desiderio alicuius rei teneri, affici* (more strongly *flagrare,
    incensum esse*)—to long for a thing, yearn for it.

*desiderio exardescere*—to be consumed with longing.

*admirationi esse* ⎫
*admiratione affici*[2]                   ⎬to be admired.
*admirationem habere* (Quintil. 8. 2. 6)⎭

---

[1] *pectus* metaphorically only occurs in isolated phrases, e.g. *toto
pectore, cogitare, tremere.* Its commonest substitute is *animus.*
Similarly *cor* metaphorically is only used in the phrase *cordi est.*

[2] *admiratione affici* also means " to be filled with admiration."

*magna est admiratio alicuius*—some one is the object of much admiration.

*admirationem alicui movere*—to fill a person with astonishment.

*admiratione incensum esse*—to be fired with admiration.

*admirabilia* ( = παράδοξα)—paradoxes; surprising things.

*studio ardere alicuius* or *alicuius rei* (De Or. 2. 1. 1)—to have enthusiasm for a person or thing.

*studio alicuius rei aliquem incendere*—to make some one enthusiastic for a thing.

*ardor, inflammatio animi, incitatio mentis, mentis vis incitatior*—enthusiasm.

*ardorem animi restinguere*—to damp, chill enthusiasm.

*ardor animi resēdit, consedit*—his enthusiasm has abated, cooled down.

## 10. BELIEF—CONFIDENCE—LOYALTY—PROTECTION—PROMISE—VERACITY

### (*fides, fiducia*)

*fidem*[1] *habere alicui*—to believe a person.

*fidem alicuius rei facere alicui*—to make some one believe a thing.

*fidem tribuere, adiungere alicui rei*—to believe in, trust in a thing.

---

[1] *fides* has six principal meanings : A. subjectively—(1) in an active sense, belief, confidence, which some one holds ; (2) passive, veracity, credit which one enjoys ; (3) neutral, good faith, sincerity, loyalty, conscientiousness, and especially of the protection which one expects by appealing to a man's loyalty. B. (4) active, ratification, sanction ; (5) passive, the thing promised, surety, guarantee ; (6) neutral, authenticity, certitude, truth of a thing. Cf. Haacke, Lat Stil. 40-41.

*fidem abrogare, derogare alicui*—to rob a person of his credit.

*fidem alicuius imminuere, infirmare* (opp. *confirmare*)—to weaken, destroy a man's credit.

*fiduciam in aliquo ponere, collocare*⎫ to put confidence in
*confidere alicui* (but *aliqua re*) ⎭ some one.

*fiduciam* (*alicuius rei*) *habere*—to have great confidence in a thing.

*fiducia sui* (Liv. 25. 37)—self-confidence.

*committere aliquid alicui* or *alicuius fidei*—to entrust a thing to a person's good faith.

*totum se committere, tradere alicui*—to put oneself entirely in some one's hands.

*fidem colere, servare*—to preserve one's loyalty.

*fidem praestare alicui*—to keep faith with a person, keep one's word.

*in fide manere* (B. G. 7. 4. 5)—to remain loyal.

*fidem laedere, violare, frangere*—to break one's word.

*fidem alicuius labefactare* (Cluent. 60. 194)—to make a person waver in his loyalty.

*de fide deducere* or *a fide abducere aliquem*—to undermine a person's loyalty.

*fide data et accepta* (Sall. Iug. 81. 1)—having exchanged pledges, promises.

*se conferre, se tradere, se permittere in alicuius fidem*—to put oneself under some one's protection.

*confugere ad aliquem, ad fidem alicuius*—to flee for refuge to some one.

*in fidem recipere aliquem* (B. G. 2. 15. 1)—to take a person under one's protection.

*fidem alicuius obsecrare, implorare*—to implore some's one protection.

*fidem addere alicui rei*—to confirm, ratify, sanction something.

*fidem publicam dare, interponere* (Sall. Iug. 32. 1)—to guarantee the protection of the state ; to promise a safe-conduct.

*fidem dare alicui* (opp. *accipere*) (c. Acc. c. Inf.)—to give one's word that . . .

*fidem servare* (opp. *fallere*)—to keep one's word (not *tenere*).

*fidem persolvere*
*fidem (promissum) praestare* } to fulfil a promise.

*fidem interponere* (Sall. Iug. 32. 5)—to pledge one's word to . . .

*fidem prodere*
*fidem frangere* } to break one's word.

*promisso stare*—to abide by one's undertaking.

*fide obstrictum teneri* (Pis. 13. 29)—to be bound by one's word ; to be on one's honour.

*fidem facere, afferre alicui rei* (opp. *demere, de-, abrogare fidem*)—to make a thing credible.

*aliquid fidem habet* (*vid.* also *fides* under History, p. 112) —a thing finds credence, is credible.

*sponsionem facere, sponsorem esse pro aliquo*—to be security for some one.

*praestare aliquem, aliquid, de aliqua re* or Acc. c. Inf.— to be answerable for a person, a thing.

## 11. SUSPICION—PRESENTIMENT

*suspicionem movere, excitare, inicere, dare alicui*—to rouse a person's suspicions.

*suspicionem habere de aliquo*—to suspect a person.

*suspicionem alicuius rei habere*—to be suspected of a thing.

*suspicio (alicuius rei) cadit in aliquem, pertinet ad aliquem* —suspicion falls on some one.

*aliquem in suspicionem adducere (alicui), aliquem suspectum reddere*—to make a person suspected.

*in suspicionem vocari, cadere*—to become the object of suspicion.

*in suspicionem alicui venire*—to be suspected by some one.

*suspicionem a se removere, depellere, propulsare* (Verr. 3. 60. 140)—to clear oneself of a suspicion.

*suspicionem ex animo delere*—to banish all feeling of prejudice from the mind.

*suspicio insidet in animo ejus* } *suspicio ei penitus inhaeret* } he is in a suspicious mood.

*suspicio tenuissima, minima*—the faintest suspicion.

*a suspicione alicuius rei abhorrere*—to have no presentiment of a thing.

*animus praesāgit malum* } *animo praesagio malum* } my mind forebodes misfortune.

## 12. HATRED—JEALOUSY—ENVY

*invisum esse alicui* *odio, invidiae esse alicui* *in invidia esse alicui* *in odio esse apud aliquem* } to be hated by some one.

*invidia flagrare, premi*—to be detested.

*in odium, in invidiam venire alicui* *invidiam colligere (aliqua re)* *alicuius odium subire, suscipere, in se convertere, sibi conflare* *in alicuius odium incurrere* } to incur a person's hatred.

*in invidiam, odium (alicuius) vocare aliquem* ⎫
*in invidiam adducere aliquem* ⎪ to make a person
*invidiam alicui conflare* (Catil. 1. 9. 23) ⎬ odious, unpop-
*invidiam, odium ex-, concitare alicui, in aliquem* ⎭ ular.

*capitali odio dissidere ab aliquo* (De Am. 1. 2)—to be separated by a deadly hatred.

*odium explere aliqua re* (Liv. 4. 32) — to glut one's hatred.

*odium implacabile suscipere in aliquem*—to conceive an implacable hatred against a man.

*odio* or *invidia alicuius ardere*—to be consumed with hatred.

*odium inveteratum habere in aliquem* (Vat. 3. 6) — to cherish an inveterate animosity against some one.

*odio inflammatum, accensum esse* — to be fired with a passionate hatred.

*odium alicuius inflammare*—to kindle hatred in a person's heart; to fill some one with hatred (not *implere, vid.* p. 146, note).

*odium restinguere, exstinguere* — to stifle, drown one's hatred.


## 13. DISCONTENT—ANGER—REVENGE—FURY

*aegre, graviter, moleste, indigne ferre aliquid*—to be discontented, vexed at a thing; to chafe.

*indignitas, atrocitas rei* (Mur. 25. 51) — the revolting nature of an action.

*o facinus indignum!* (Ter. Andr. 1. 1. 118)—monstrous!

*ira incensum esse*
*iracundia inflammatum esse* }to be fired with rage.
*ira ardere* (Flacc. 35. 88)

*iracundia exardescere, effervescere*—to be transported with
    passion.

*iracundia efferri*—to be carried away by one's anger.

*ira defervescit* (Tusc. 4. 36. 78)—his anger cools.

*virus acerbitatis suae effundere in*
  *aliquem* (De Amic. 23. 87) }to vent one's anger,
*iram in aliquem effundere* }spite on some one.
*iram, bilem evomere in aliquem*

*irae indulgere* (Liv. 23. 3)—to give free play to one's
    anger.

*praecipitem in iram esse* (Liv. 23. 7)—to be short-tempered ;
    to be prone to anger.

*animum explere*—to cool one's anger.

*iracundiam continere, cohibere, reprimere* — to restrain,
    master one's passion.

*iram restinguere, sedare*—to calm one's anger.

*animum alicuius ab iracundia revocare*—to prevent some
    one from growing angry, appease his anger,

*stomachum, bilem alicui movere*—to excite a person's wrath.

*ulcisci aliquem,*[1] *poenas expetere ab aliquo*—to revenge
    oneself on some one.

*ulcisci aliquid, poenas alicuius rei expetere*—to revenge
    oneself for a thing.

*ulcisci aliquem pro aliquo* or *pro* }to revenge oneself on
  *aliqua re* }another for a thing
*poenas alicuius* or *alicuius rei* }or on some one's be-
  *repetere ab aliquo* }half.

[1] *ulcisci aliquem* also means to avenge some one ; to exact
satisfaction on his behalf.

*iniurias persequi* (Verr. 2. 3. 9)—to avenge an insult.

*impellere aliquem in furorem*—to make some one furious.

*furore inflammari, incendi*—to become furious.

*furore incensus, abreptus, impulsus*—in a transport of rage.

*indignatio aliquem incedit*—to be filled with indignation.

*indignationes* (Liv. 25. 1. 9) — signs of irritation, of discontent.


# X. VIRTUES AND VICES

## 1. VIRTUE—MORALITY

*vita honesta (turpis)*—a virtuous (immoral) life.

*honesta expetere ; turpia fugere*—to follow virtue ; to flee from vice.

*virtute praeditum, ornatum esse* (opp. *vitiis obrŭtum esse*)— to be virtuous.

*virtutem (iustitiam, pietatem) colere*—to cultivate virtue.

*viam virtutis ingredi* (Off. 1. 32. 118)—to walk in the ways of virtue.

*omnia consilia et facta ad virtutem referre* [1] (Phil. 10. 10. 20)—to make virtue the standard in every thought and act.

*virtutem sequi, virtutis studiosum esse*—to strive to attain virtue.

*virtutis perfectae perfecto munere fungi* (Tusc. 1. 45. 109) —to live·a perfect life.

---

[1] For "thoughts and deeds," cf. Or. 3. 43. 182 *mores instituta et facta ;* Prov. Cons. 8. 20 *consilia et facta ;* Fin. 2. 14. 5 *studia et facta ;* Verr. 5. 14. 35 *mentes hominum et cogitationes.*

*virtutem pristĭnam retinere* ⎫ to live as scrupulously
*nihil ex pristina virtute remittere* ⎭ moral a life as ever.

*summum bonum* [1] *in virtute ponere*—to consider virtue the
highest good.

*virtus hoc habet, ut . . .*—this is a characteristic of
virtue, it . . .

*a virtute discedere* or *deficere* ⎫ to deviate from the path of
*honestatem deserere* ⎭ virtue.

*a maiorum virtute desciscere, degenerare, deflectere* — to
deteriorate.

*a parentibus degenerare*—to degenerate (from one's ancestors).

*corrumpi, depravari*—to be demoralised, corrupted.

*excitare aliquem ad virtutem*—to rouse in some one an
enthusiasm for virtue.

*bonitas* (Fin. 5. 29. 65)—kindheartedness.

*naturae bonitas* (Off. 1. 32. 118)—innate goodness, kindness.

*naturae bona*—natural advantages.


## 2. VICE—CRIME

*omni vitio carere*—to be free from faults.

*vitia erumpunt* (*in aliquem*) (De Amic. 21. 76)—his vices
betray themselves.

*animum vitiis dedere*—to abandon oneself to vice.

*vitiis, sceleribus contaminari* or *se contaminare* (Off. 3. 8.
37)—to be tainted with vice.

*vitiis, sceleribus inquinatum, contaminatum, obrutum esse*—
to be vicious, criminal.

[1] Note too *finis bonorum et malorum* = the highest good and the
greatest evil.

*vitia exstirpare et funditus tollere*—to eradicate vice.

*vita omnibus flagitiis,*[1] *vitiis dedita* \
*vita omnibus flagitiis inquinata* } a life defiled by every crime.

*natura proclivem esse ad vitia*—to have a natural propensity to vice.

*scelera moliri* (Att. 7. 11)—to meditate crime.

*scelus facere, committere, admittere*—to commit crime.

*facinus facere, committere*—to do a criminal deed.

*scelere se devincire, se obstringere,* \
  *astringi* \
*scelus (in se) concipere, suscipere* } to commit a crime and so make oneself liable to the consequences of it.

*scelus edere in aliquem* (Sest. 26. 58)—to commit a crime against some one.

*scelus scelere cumulare* (Catil. 1. 6. 14)—to heap crime on crime.

*scelus*[1] *supplicio expiare*—to expiate a crime by punishment.


## 3. DESIRE—PASSION—SELF-CONTROL

*cupiditate alicuius rei accensum, inflammatum esse*—to be fired with desire of a thing.

*cupiditate alicuius rei ardere, flagrare*—to have an ardent longing for a thing.

*cupiditatem alicuius accendere* \
*aliquem ad cupiditatem incitare* \
*aliquem cupiditate inflammare* } to rouse a person's interest, cupidity.

---

[1] *flagitium* is a crime against oneself, e.g. drunkenness. *scelus* is a sin against society at large, e.g. theft, murder. *nefas* a sin against God, e.g. sacrilege, parricide. *facinus* any unusual action, then generally a crime, outrage.

*cupiditatibus occaecari* (Fin. I. 10. 33)—to be blinded by passions.

*libidine ferri*—to be carried away by one's passions.

*se (totum) libidinibus dedere*—to abandon oneself (entirely) to debauchery.

*cupiditatibus servire, pārēre*—to be the slave of one's desires.

*praecipitem ferri aliqua re* (Verr. 5. 46. 121)—to be carried away by something.

*homo impotens sui*  
*homo effrenatus, intemperans*  } a man of no self-control, self-indulgent.

*sibi imperare* or *continere et coërcere se ipsum*  
*animum regere, coërcere, cohibere*  
*animum vincere* (Marcell. 3. 8)  } to have self-control; to restrain oneself, master one's inclinations.

*imperare cupiditatibus*  
*coërcere, cohibere, continere,*  
*domitas habere cupiditates*  } to overcome one's passions.

*refrenare cupiditates, libidines*—to bridle one's desires.

*effrenatae cupiditates*  
*indomitae animi cupiditates*  } unrestrained, unbridled lust.

*cupiditates explere, satiare*—to satisfy one's desires.

*libidinem alicuius excitare*—to arouse some one's lust.

*libido dominatur* (Or. 65. 219)—the passions win the day.

*libido consēdit*—the storm of passion has abated.

*cupiditates deferbuerunt* (Cael. 18. 43)—the passions have cooled down.

*animi perturbationes exstirpare*—to eradicate passion from the mind.

## 4. WRONG—INSULT—OUTRAGE—OFFENCE
### (cf. p. 57)

*iniuriam inferre, facere alicui*
*iniuria afficere aliquem* } to wrong a person.

*iniuria lacessere aliquem*—to provoke a person by a gratuitous insult.

*iniuria abstinere* (Off. 3. 17. 72)—to refrain from doing a wrong, an injustice.

*iniuriam accipere*—to be the victim of an injustice.

*iniuriam ferre, pati*—to suffer wrong.

*iniurias defendere, repellere, propulsare*—to repel an injury.

*iniurias neglegere*—to leave a wrong unpunished, to ignore it.

*ab iniuria aliquem defendere*—to protect any one from wrong.

*satisfacere alicui pro* (*de*) *iniuriis*—to give some one satisfaction for an injury.

*contumelia aliquem afficere*—to insult some one.

*voces* (*verba*) *contumeliosae*
*verborum contumeliae* } insulting expressions.

*contumeliosis vocibus prosequi aliquem* (*vid.* p. 88, note)— to use insulting expressions to any one.

*maledictis aliquem onerare, lacerare*—to heap abuse on some one.

*offendere aliquem, alicuius animum*
*offendere apud aliquem* (Cluent. 23. 63)
*in offensionem alicuius incurrere* (Verr. 1. 12. 35) } to hurt some one's feelings.

*offendi aliqua re* (*animus offenditur*)—to feel hurt by something.

*offendere in aliquo* (Mil. 36. 99)—to have something to say against a person, to object to him.

*offendere* [1] *in aliqua re* (Cluent. 36. 98)—to take a false step in a thing; to commit an indiscretion.

*offensionem habere*—to give offence to, to shock a person (used of things, *vid.* p. 65).

*res habet aliquid offensionis*—there is something repulsive about the thing.

## 5. VIOLENCE—AMBUSCADE—THREATS

*vim adhibere, facere alicui*—to use violence against some one.

*vim inferre alicui*—to do violence to a person.

*vim et manus afferre alicui* (Catil. 1. 8. 21)—to kill with violence.

*vim vi depellere*
*vi vim illatam defendere* } to meet force by force.

*insidias collocare, locare* (Mil. 10. 27)—to set an ambuscade.

*insidias alicui parare, facere, struere, instruere, tendere*—to waylay a person.

*aliquem in insidiis locare, collocare, ponere*—to place some one in ambush.

*aliquem in insidias elicere, inducere*—to draw some one into an ambush.

*subsidĕre in insidiis* (Mil. 19. 49)—to place oneself in ambush.

---

[1] Notice too *offendere caput* (Quintil. 6. 3. 67), *pedem* (B. Hisp. 23), to strike one's head, foot against anything; *offendere aliquem imparatum* (Fam. 2. 3), to find some one unprepared, cf. καταλαμβάνειν.

*minitari (minari) alicui mortem, crucem et tormenta, bellum*
—to threaten some one with death, crucifixion,
torture, war.

*minitari alicui igni ferroque* (Phil. 13. 9. 21)—to threaten
with fire and sword.

*denuntiare*[1] *bellum, caedem* (Sest. 20. 46)—to threaten
war, carnage.

*minas iacĕre, iactare*⎫
⎬to use threats.
*minis uti*⎭

## 6. APPEARANCE—DECEIT—FALSEHOOD—DERISION

*speciem alicuius rei habere*—to have the appearance of
something.

*speciem alicuius rei praebere*⎫ to give the impression of . . .
*speciem prae se ferre*[2] ⎬ have the outward aspect
⎭ of . . .

*in speciem*⎫
*specie* (De Amic. 13. 47)⎬apparently ; to look at.
*per speciem (alicuius rei)*⎭

*per simulationem, simulatione alicuius rei*—under pretext,
pretence of . . .

*simulare morbum*—to pretend to be ill.

*dissimulare*[3] *morbum*—to pretend not to be ill.

---

[1] "Threaten" in the sense of to be at hand, to be imminent, is
rendered by some such word as *imminere, impendere, instare*, e.g.
*bellum imminet.* For the meaning to seem likely, to promise, cf.
*coniuratio rem publicam perversura videtur*, the conspiracy threatens
to overthrow the state.

[2] *prae se ferre* followed by Acc. and Inf. =to manifest, display,
e.g. *Romanum esse semper prae me tuli.*

[3] *simulo* = I pretend to be what I am not, cf. ἀλαζών, a braggart ;
*dissimulo* = I pretend not to be what I am, cf. εἴρων, a mock-modest
person. *Quae non sunt simulo, quae sunt ea dissimulantur.*

*aliquis simulat aegrum* or *se esse aegrum*—some one feigns
    illness.

*aliter sentire ac loqui* (*aliud sentire, aliud loqui*) — to
    think one thing, say another; to conceal one's
    opinions.

*per dolum* (B. G. 4. 13)—by craft.

*dolis et fallaciis* (Sall. Cat. 11. 2)—by the aid of fraud and
    lies.

*sine fuco ac fallaciis* (Att. 1. 1. 1)—without any disguise,
    frankly.

*verba dare alicui* (Att. 15. 16)—to deceive a person, throw
    dust in his eyes.

*mendacium dicere*
*falsa* (*pro veris*) *dicere*  }to tell lies.

*ludere, irridere, deridere aliquem*
*illudere alicui* or *in aliquem* }to make sport of, rally a
  (more rarely *aliquem*)   person.

*ludibrio esse alicui*—to serve as some one's butt.

*in ludibrium verti* (Tac. Ann. 12. 26)—to become an
    object of ridicule; to be laughed at.

*omnibus artibus aliquem ludificari, eludere*—to fool a person
    thoroughly.

*per ludibrium*—in sport, mockery.


## 7. DUTY—INCLINATION

*officium suum facere, servare,*
  *colere, tueri, exsequi, praestare*
*officio suo satisfacere* (Div. in }to do one's duty.
  Caec. 14. 47)
*officio suo fungi*

*omnes officii partes exsequi* } to fulfil one's duty in every
*nullam officii partem deserere* } detail.

*diligentem esse in retinendis officiis*—to be exact, punctual
in the performance of one's duty.

*officium suum deserere, neglegere*
*ab officio discedere*
*de, ab officio decedere* } to neglect one's duty.
*officio suo deesse* (Fam. 7. 3)

*ad officium redire*—to return to one's duties.

*in officio manere* (Att. 1. 3)—to remain faithful to one's
duty.

*contra officium est* c. Inf.—it is a breach of duty to . . .

*ab officio abduci, avocari*—to let oneself be perverted
from one's duty.

*salvo*[1] *officio* (Off. 3. 1. 4)—without violating, neglecting
one's duty.

*multa et magna inter nos officia*[2] *intercedunt* (Fam. 13. 65)
—we are united by many mutual obligations.

*in aliquem officia conferre*
*aliquem officiis suis complecti,* } to be courteous, obliging to
*prosequi* } some one.
*officiosum esse in aliquem*

*litterae officii* or *humanitatis plenae*—a most courteous
letter.

---

[1] Notice *salvis legibus* (Fam. 1. 4), without breaking the law ;
*salva fide* (Off. 3. 4. 44), without breaking one's word.

[2] *officium* is used of anything which one feels bound to do, either on
moral grounds or from a desire to please others (especially those in
authority). Thus the word denotes not merely duty, sense of duty,
faithful performance of duty, submissiveness (cf. xvi. 13), but also
courteous, obliging behaviour, complaisance, mark of respect.
Objectively it has the meaning of an office, service, command, e.g.
*officium maritimum.*

*studere alicui rei, studiosum esse*
   *alicuius rei*

*studio alicuius rei teneri*

*propensum, proclivem esse ad*
   *aliquid* (opp. *alienum, aversum*
   *esse, abhorrere ab aliqua re*)

to have an inclination for a thing.

*studiis suis obsequi* (De Or. 1. 1. 3)—to follow one's inclinations.

*sibi* or *ingenio suo indulgere* (Nep. Chabr. 3)—to indulge one's caprice.

## 8. REASON—CONSCIENCE—REMORSE

*rationis participem* (opp. *exper-*
   *tem*) *esse*

*ratione praeditum esse, uti*

to be endowed with reason.

*prudenter, considerate, consilio agere* (opp. *temere, nullo consilio, nulla ratione*)—to act reasonably, designedly.

*sapere* (Off. 2. 14. 48)—to be a man of sense, judgment.

*resipiscere* (Att. 4. 5. 2)

*ad sanitatem reverti, redire*

*ad bonam frugem se recipere*

to recover one's reason, be reasonable again.

*ad sanitatem adducere, revocare aliquem*—to bring some one back to his senses.

*satin* ( = *satisne*) *sanus es?*—are you in your right mind?

*rationi repugnare*—to be contrary to all reason.

*conscientia recta, recte facti* (*fac-*
   *torum*), *virtutis, bene actae*
   *vitae, rectae voluntatis*

*mens bene sibi conscia*

a good conscience.

*conscientia mala* or *peccatorum,*
  *culpae, sceleris, delicti*        ⎫a guilty conscience.
*animus male sibi conscius*          ⎭

*nullius culpae sibi conscium esse*—to be conscious of no
  ill deed.

*conscientia morderi* (Tusc. 4. 20. 45)—to be conscience-
  stricken.

*conscientiae maleficiorum stimulant aliquem*—his guilty
  conscience gives him no rest.

*conscientia mala angi, excruciari*⎫to be tormented by re-
*(mens scelerum furiis agitatur)* ⎭  morse.

*conscientia recte factorum erigi*—to congratulate oneself
  on one's clear conscience.

*Furiae agitant et vexant aliquem*—the Furies harass and
  torment some one.


## 9. MEASURE—STANDARD—LIMIT—
MODERATION

*modum tenere, retinere, servare, adhibere*—to observe
  moderation, be moderate.

*omnia modice agere*—to be moderate in all things, commit
  no excess.

*modum facere, statuere, constituere alicui rei* or *alicuius rei*
  —to set a limit to a thing.

*modum transire*             ⎫
*extra modum prodire*        ⎬to pass the limit.
*ultra modum* [1] *progredi* ⎭

---

[1] Only Livy and subsequent writers use *modum excedere,* and in
the same way *supra modum.*

| | |
|---|---|
| *metiri, ponderare, aestimare, iudicare aliquid (ex) aliqua re*<br>*dirigere* or *referre aliquid ad aliquam rem* | to measure something by the standard of something else ; to make something one's criterion. |

*fines certos terminosque constituere*—to impose fixed limitations.

*terminis circumscribere aliquid*—to set bounds to a thing, limit it.

| | |
|---|---|
| *moderatum, continentem esse*<br>*moderatum se praebere*<br>*temperantia uti* | to behave with moderation. |

| | |
|---|---|
| *moderationem, modum adhibere in aliqua re*<br>*moderari aliquid* (Flacc. 5. 12) | to show moderation in a matter. |

*modice ac sapienter*—with moderation and judgment.

*sine modo ; nullo modo adhibito*—with no moderation.

*extra, praeter modum*—beyond all measure.

*mediocritatem tenere* (Off. 1. 25. 89)—to observe the golden mean.


## 10. MORALS—IMMORALITY—PRINCIPLES— CHARACTER

*homo bene (male) moratus*—a moral (immoral) man.

*homo perditus*—a depraved, abandoned character.

*praecepta de moribus* or *de virtute*—moral precepts.

| | |
|---|---|
| *morum praecepta tradere alicui*<br>*de virtute praecipere alicui* | to give moral advice, rules of conduct. |

*mores corrupti* or *perditi*—moral corruption (not *corruptela morum*).

*tam perditis* or *corruptis moribus*—amongst such moral depravity.

*mores in dies magis labuntur* (also with *ad*, e.g. *ad mollitiem*)—immorality is daily gaining ground.

*severus morum castigator*—a stern critic of morals.

*aliquid abhorret a meis moribus* (opp. *insitum* [*atque innatum*] *est animo* or *in animo alicuius*)—something is contrary to my moral sense, goes against my principles.

*consilia et facta* (cf. p. 164, note)—thought and deed.

*institutum tenere*—to remain true to one's principles.

*ratione ; animi quodam iudicio*—on principle.

*vitae ratio bene ac sapienter instituta*—a sound and sensible system of conduct.

*meae vitae rationes ab ineunte aetate susceptae* (Imp. Pomp. 1. 1)—the principles which I have followed since I came to man's estate.

*certas rationes in agendo*[1] *sequi*—to follow fixed principles of conduct.

*omnia temere agere, nullo*
*    iudicio uti*                  }to have no principles.
*caeco impetu ferri*

*natura et mores ; vita moresque ; indoles animi ingeniique ;* or simply *ingenium, indoles, natura, mores*—character.

*vir constans, gravis* (opp. *homo inconstans, levis*)—a man of character, with a strong personality.

*sibi constare, constantem esse*—to be consistent.

---

[1] Do not translate "to act, behave, conduct oneself" by *agere* without an object or an accompanying adverb, e.g. *bene, recte agere ;* however, with the gerundive the adverb may be omitted, e.g. *agendum est, tempus agendi, celeritas in agendo.*

*animo mobili esse* (Fam. 5. 2. 10)—to be inconsistent, changeable.

*aliquid est proprium alicuius*—something is a characteristic of a man.

*mobilitas et levitas animi*—inconsistency ; changeability.

## XI. RELIGION

### 1. GOD—WORSHIP

*numen (deorum) divinum*—the sovereign power of the gods.

*dei propitii* (opp. *irati*)—the favour of heaven.

*superi ; inferi*—the gods of the upper, lower world.

*inferi (Orcus* and *Tartarus* only poetical)—the world below.

*ad inferos descendere*—to descend to the world below.

*apud inferos esse*—to be in the lower world.

*aliquem ab inferis* or *a mortuis evocare, excitare* (passive *ab inferis exsistere*)—to summon some one from the dead.

*deos sancte, pie venerari*—to be an earnest worshipper of the gods.

*deum rite (summa religione) colere*—to honour the gods with all due ceremonial (very devoutly).

*cultus dei, deorum* (N. D. 2. 3. 8)—worship of the gods ; divine service.

*sacra, res divinae, religiones, caerimoniae*—ritual ; ceremonial.

*rebus divinis interesse* (B. G. 6. 13)—to take part in divine service (of the priest).

*sacris adesse*—to be present at divine service (of the people).

*sacris initiari* (Quintil. 12. 10. 14)—to be initiated into the mysteries of a cult.

*templa deorum adire*—to make a pilgrimage to the shrines of the gods.

*numerum deorum obtinere* (N. D. 3. 20)—to be regarded as a god.

*aliquem in deorum numerum referre, reponere*—to deify a person.

*aliquem in deorum numerum referre*—to consider as a god.

*aliquem divino honore colere*
*alicui divinos honores tribuere,* } to pay divine honours to
  *habere* some one.

*propius ad deos accedere* (Mil. 22. 59)—to approach the gods.

*supera et caelestia ; humana et citeriora*—heavenly things ; earthly things.

*divinitus* (De Or. 1. 46. 202)—by divine inspiration (often = marvellously, excellently).

*divinitus accidit*—it happened miraculously.


## 2. RELIGION—RELIGIOUS SCRUPLE—OATH

*imbuere* (*vid.* p. 103, note) *pectora religione* [1]—to inspire with religious feeling, with the fear of God.

---

[1] *religio* (original meaning probably that which binds down, cf. *religo*, *leges*, *lictor*, etc.) denotes, subjectively, religious feeling, devotion, fear of God, religious scruple, conscientiousness. Objectively it means the object of religious fear, a sacred thing or place, also that which is contrary to the gods' will, a crime, sin, curse ; lastly in an active sense a religious obligation, an oath.

*audientium animos religione perfundere* (Liv. 10. 388) — to fill the souls of one's audience with devotion.

*religionem ex animis extrahere* (N. D. 1. 43. 121)—to banish devout sentiment from the minds of others.

*omnem religionem tollere, delere*—to annihilate all religious feeling.

*religionem labefactare* (*vid.* p. 50, note)—to shake the foundations of religion.

*religione obstrictos habere multitudinis animos* (Liv. 6. 1. 10) —to have power over the people by trading on their religious convictions.

*religionem alicui afferre, inicere, incutere*—to inspire some one with religious scruples.

*aliquid religioni habere* or *in religionem vertere*
*aliquid in religionem alicui venit*
} to make a thing a matter of conscience, be scrupulous about a thing.

*nulla religio*—absence of scruples, unconscientiousness.

*religionem externam suscipere*—to embrace a strange religion.

*novas religiones instituere*—to introduce a new religion, a new cult.

*bellum pro religionibus susceptum*—a religious war.

*violatas caerimonias inexpiabili religione sancire* (Tusc. 1. 12. 27)—to invoke an irrevocable curse on the profanation of sacred rites.

*iusiurandum dare alicui*[1]—to swear an oath to a person.

*ex animi mei sententia iuro*—I swear on my conscience.

*iureiurando aliquem astringere*—to bind some one by an oath.

---

[1] *sacramentum dicere alicui* and *apud aliquem*=to take in some one's presence an oath to the standard, a military oath.

*iureiurando aliquem adigere*—to make some one take an oath.

*iureiurando ac fide se obstringere, ut*—to promise an oath to . . .

*iureiurando teneri* (Off. 3. 27. 100)—to be bound by oath.

*iusiurandum (religionem) servare, conservare*—to keep one's oath.

*periurium facere ; peierare*—to commit perjury, perjure oneself.

*iusiurandum violare*—to break one's oath.


## 3. BELIEF—UNBELIEF—SUPERSTITION

*opinio dei*—belief in God.

*deum esse credimus*—we believe in the existence of a God.

*deos esse negare*—to deny the existence of the gods.

*insitas (innatas) dei cognitiones habere* (N. D. 1. 17. 44)—to have innate ideas of the Godhead ; to believe in the Deity by intuition.

*omnibus innatum est et in animo quasi insculptum esse deum*—belief in God is part of every one's nature.

*natura in omnium animis notionem dei impressit* (N. D. 1. 16. 43)—Nature has implanted in all men the idea of a God.

*impietas*—unbelief.

*qui deum esse negat*—an atheist.

*superstitio mentes occupavit* (Verr. 4. 51. 113)—superstition has taken possession of their souls.

*superstitione imbutum esse*—to be tinged with superstition.

*superstitione teneri, constrictum esse, obligatum esse*—to be the slave of superstition.

*superstitionem funditus tollere*—to absolutely annihilate superstition.

*superstitionem radicitus* or *penitus evellere*—to destroy superstition root and branch.

*formidines*—superstitious fears ; phantoms.

## 4. PRAYERS—WISHES—VOWS

*precari aliquid a deo*  
*precari deum, deos*  
*supplicare deo* (Sall. Iug. 63. 1) ⎫ to pray to God.  
*adhibere deo preces*

*praeire verba (carmen)* (Liv. 31. 17)—to read prayers for the congregation to repeat.

*(supinas) manus*[1] *ad caelum tendere*—to raise the hands to heaven (attitude of prayer).

*favete ore, linguis* = εὐφημεῖτε—maintain a devout silence (properly, utter no ill-omened word).

*preces facere*—to pray.

*grates, laudes agere dis immortalibus*—to thank, glorify the immortal gods.

*testari deos* (Sull. 31. 86)—to call the gods to witness.

*contestari deos hominesque*—to call gods and men to witness.

*dis bene iuvantibus* (Fam. 7. 20. 2)—with the help of the gods.

*quod deus bene vertat !*[2]—and may God grant success !

---

[1] *supinus* = ὕπτιος, bent backwards ; *supinae manus*, with the palms turned up. The opposite of *supinus* is *pronus*, e.g. *puerum imponere equo pronum in ventrem, postea sedentem* (Varr.) ; *pecora quae natura prona finxit* (Sall.)

[2] Note that these clauses with *quod* are parenthetical.

*quod di immortales omen avertant!* (Phil. 44. 11)—and
    may heaven avert the omen! heaven preserve us
    from this!

*quod abominor!* (*procul absit!*)—God forbid!

*di prohibeant, di meliora!*—heaven forfend!

*quod bonum, faustum, felix fortunatumque sit!* [1] (Div. 1.
    45. 102)—may heaven's blessing rest on it!

*precari alicui bene* (*male*) or *omnia bona* (*mala*), *salutem*—
    to bless (curse) a person.

*vota facere, nuncupare, suscipere, concipere*—to make a vow.

*vota solvere, persolvere, reddere*—to accomplish, pay a vow.

*voti damnari, compŏtem fieri*—to have to pay a vow; to
    obtain one's wish.


## 5. SACRIFICE—FESTIVAL

*sacra, sacrificium facere* (ἱερὰ
   ῥέζειν), *sacrificare* ⎫
              ⎬ to sacrifice.
*rem divinam facere* (*dis*) ⎭

*ture et odoribus incensis*—with incense and perfumes.

*rebus divinis* (*rite*) *perpetratis*—after having performed
    the sacrifice (with due ritual).

*sacrificium statum* (*solemne*) (Tusc. 1. 47. 113)—a period-
    ically recurring (annual) sacrifice.

*sacra polluere et violare*—to profane sacred rites.

*victimas* (oxen), *hostias* (smaller animals, especially sheep)
    *immolare, securi ferire, caedere, mactare*—to slaughter
    victims.

*deos placare* (B. G. 6. 15)—to appease the anger of the
    gods.

*manes expiare* (Pis. 7. 16)—to appease the manes, make
    sacrifice for departed souls.

[1] Sometimes abbreviated q. b. f. f. f. s.

*pro victimis homines immolare*—to sacrifice human victims.

*parentare* (Leg. 2. 21. 54)—to make a sacrifice on the tomb of one's ancestors.

*libare*—to offer libations.

*diem festum agere* (of an individual)
*diem festum celebrare* (of a larger number)
} to keep, celebrate a festival.

*supplicationem indicere ad omnia pulvinaria* (Liv. 27. 4)— to proclaim a public thanksgiving at all the street-shrines of the gods.

*supplicationem quindecim dierum decernere* (Phil. 14. 14. 37) —to decree a public thanksgiving for fifteen days.

*supplicationem habere* (Liv. 22. 1. 15)—to celebrate a festival of thanksgiving.

*lectisternium facere, habere* (Liv. 22. 1. 18)—to hold a lectisternium.

## 6. ORACLE—PRODIGIES—AUSPICES— PRESAGE

*oraculum consulere*—to consult an oracle.

*oraculum petere* (*ab aliquo*)—to ask for an oracular response.

*mittere Delphos consultum*—to send and consult the oracle at Delphi.

*oraculum dare, edere*
*responsum dare* (*vid.* p. 131, note), *respondere*
} to give an oracular response.

*oraculum Pythium* (*Pythicum*)
*vox Pythia* (*Pythica*) (Liv. 1. 56)
} an oracle given by the Delphian Apollo (Apollo Pythius).

*prodigia procurare* [1] (Liv. 22. 1)—to avert by expiatory
sacrifices the effect of ominous portents.

*libros Sibyllinos adire, consulere, inspicere*—to consult the
Sibylline books.

*augurium agere,* [2] *auspicari* (N. D. 2. 4. 11)—to take the
auspices, observe the flight of birds.

*de caelo servare* (Att. 4. 3. 3)—to observe the sky (*i.e.*
the flight of birds, lightning, thunder, etc.)

*aves* (*alites, oscines*) [3] *addicunt alicui* (opp. *abdicunt aliquid*)
—the omens are favourable to some one.

*augures obnuntiant* (*consuli*) (Phil. 2. 33. 83)—the augurs
announce an unfavourable sign.

*auspicato* (*rem gerere, urbem condere*)—after having duly
taken the auspices.

*omen accipere* (opp. *improbare*)—to accept as a happy
omen.

*accipere, vertere aliquid in omen*—to interpret something
as an omen.

*faustis ominibus*—with favourable omens.

*omen infaustum, triste*—an evil omen ; presage of ill.

---

[1] *procurare*, a technical term of religious ceremonial = to avert
by expiation ; to take the necessary measures, observe the proper
ceremony for appeasing the anger of the gods.

[2] Not *auspicia habere*, which means to have the right to take
the auspices. As this right was usually combined with the right to
command, we find such phrases as *ponere auspicia*, to give up a
command ; *imperio auspicioque alicuius, auspiciis alicuius*, under
some one's command.

[3] In the science of augury, *alites* denoted birds which gave omens
by their flight ; *oscines* those which gave them by their cries.

## XII. DOMESTIC LIFE

### 1. THE HOUSE AND ITS DIFFERENT PARTS

*domus necessariis rebus instructa*—a comfortably-furnished house.

*domus ruina*[1] *impendet*
*domus collapsura, corruitura*
*(esse) videtur* } the house threatens to fall in *(vid.* p. 170, note).

*domus subita ruina collapsa est*—the house suddenly fell in ruins.

*domum demoliri* (Top. 4. 22)—to demolish, raze a house.

*domus non omnes capit*[2] (χωρεῖν)—the house is not large enough for all.

*domum frequentare* (Sall. Cat. 14. 7)—to be a regular visitor at a house.

*domus rimas agit*—the house walls are beginning to crack.

*apud eum sic fui tamquam domi meae* (Fam. 13. 69)—I felt quite at home in his house.

*apud aliquem esse*—to be at some one's house.

*tectum subire*—to enter the house.

*tecto, (in) domum suam aliquem recipere* (opp. *prohibere aliquem tecto, domo*)—to welcome to one's house (opp. to shut one's door against some one).

*domo pedem non efferre*—to never set foot out of doors.

---

[1] *ruina* = fall, overthrow (metaphor. e.g. *ruina rei publicae, ruinae fortunarum,* Catil. 1. 6. 14). In plur. it is used of the ruins, débris resulting from an overthrow, e.g. *urbs strata ruinis,* a town in ruins ; *fumantes ruinae urbis.* For "ruins" in the sense of remains of old buildings use *parietinae.*

[2] Also metaph. e.g. *Macedonia te non capit.*

*pedem limine efferre*—to cross the threshold.

*foras exire* (Plaut. Amph. 1. 2. 35)—to go out of the house.

*foras mittere aliquem*—to turn some one out of the house.

*in publico*—in the streets.

*in publicum prodire* (Verr. 2. 1. 31)—to show oneself in the streets, in public.

*publico carere, se abstinere* ⎫
*domi se tenere* ⎬ to never appear in public.

*deducere*[1] *aliquem de domo*—to escort a person from his house.

*pro aris*[2] *et focis pugnare, certare, dimicare*— to fight for hearth and home.

*domi* (opp. *foris*)—at home ; in one's native country.

*ostium, fores pulsare*—to knock at the door.

*ostium, fores aperire, claudere*—to open, shut the door.

*fores obserare*—to bolt the door.

*ianuam effringere, revellere*—to burst open the door.

*valvas* (*portam*) *obstruere*—to barricade a door (a city-gate).

---

[1] Notice too *deducere coloniam ; deducere naves*, to launch ships, opposed to *subducere*=to beach a boat ; *deducere adulescentes ad virum clarissimum* (De Am. 1. 1) ; *deducere de sententia aliquem ; rem in eum locum deducere, ut . . . ; de capite deducere* (opp. *addere*) *quod pernumeratum est*=to subtract from the capital the amount paid ; *deducere aliquem*, to escort a person from his province to Rome.

[2] At Rome there were altars not only in the temples but also in the streets and in private houses. In a house there were usually two—one in the court, the altar of the *Penates ;* another in the *atrium* on a small hearth (*focus*), this was the altar of the *Lares.* Hence *arae focique*= the altars and hearths of the *Lares* and *Penates.*

## 2. DOMESTIC MATTERS—PROPERTY

*rem domesticam, familiarem administrare, regere, curare*—
   to keep house.

*rem* or *opes habere, bona possidere, in bonis esse*—to possess
   means ; to be well off.

*opibus, divitiis, bonis, facultatibus abundare*—to be very
   rich.

*rem bene (male) gerere* [1] (*vid.* ⎫ to manage one's affairs,
   p. 261) ⎬ household, property well
*rem familiarem tueri* ⎭ or ill.

*rem familiarem neglegere*—to neglect, mismanage one's
   household matters.

*diligentem, frugi esse*—to be economical.

*diligens paterfamilias*—a careful master of the house.

*frugi* [2] (opp. *nequam*) *servus*—a good, useful slave.

*severum imperium in suis exercere, tenere* (De Sen. 11. 37)—
   to be a strict disciplinarian in one's household.

*in possessionem alicuius rei venire*—to come into the
   possession of something.

*in possessionem alicuius rei invadere*—to take forcible
   possession of a thing.

*expellere aliquem domo, possessionibus pellere*—to turn a
   person out of his house, his property.

---

[1] *rem gerere*=generally to manage one's affairs. Then specially
—(1) to do business (of commercial men) ; (2) to administer one's
estate ; (3) to hold a command (of a general in the field). *res
gerere* plur. = to carry out, accomplish undertakings, used specially
of political activity.

[2] *frugi* is an old case-form (either locative or dative) from an
obsolete nominative *frux*. Cf. *bonae frugi esse*, to be useful ; *ad
bonam frugem se recipere*, to come to one's senses (Cael. 12. 28).

*demovere, deicere aliquem de possessione*—to dispossess a
person.

*exturbare aliquem omnibus*
   *fortunis, e possessionibus* ⎫ to drive a person out of house
*evertere aliquem bonis, for-* ⎬   and home.
   *tunis patriis* ⎭

*possessione alicuius rei cedere alicui* (Mil. 27. 75)—to give
up a thing to some one else.

*res, quae moveri possunt; res moventes*[1] (Liv. 5. 25. 6)—
movable, personal property.

*fundi*—property in land; real property.

## 3. HABITATION—CLOTHING

*habitare*[2] *in domo alicuius, apud aliquem* (Acad. 2. 36.
115)—to live in some one's house.

*domicilium (sedem ac domicilium) habere in aliquo loco*—to
dwell in a certain place.

*sedem collocare alicubi* (Rep. 2.
   19. 34) ⎫ to take up one's abode in
*sedem ac domicilium (fortunas* ⎬ a place, settle down
   *suas) constituere alicubi* ⎪ somewhere.
*considĕre alicubi* (Att. 5. 14. 1) ⎭

[1] *res moventes; movere* is apparently sometimes used intransitively,
e.g. *terra movet* (Liv. 35. 40; 40. 59), but here *moventes* is probably
the participle of the middle *moveri* (cf. *res quae* m o v e r i *possunt*).
For parallel examples of a middle verb with a participle present or
a gerundive cf. Fin. 2. 10. 31 *utra voluptate stante an movente?*
Suet. Claud. 28 *lectica per urbem vehendi ius;* Or. 2. 71. 287
*ceteris in campo exercentibus,* etc.

[2] *habitare locum* is not used, *locus habitatur* is. On the other
hand, we find *incolere Asiam,* etc., or with preps. *cis, trans, inter,
prope, circum*—*incolere* being used intransitively, e.g. B. G. 1. 1.
4 *Germani qui trans Rhenum incolunt. incolere* is used of a number of people, *habitare* of individuals.

*multitudinem in agris collocare*—to settle a large number
   of people in a country.

*domo emigrare* (B. G. 1. 31)—to emigrate.

*domo profŭgus* (Liv. 1. 1)—homeless.

*induere vestem* (without *sibi*)—to dress oneself.

*vestem mutare* (opp. *ad vestitum suum redire*) (Planc. 12.
   29)—to go into mourning.

*vestimenta (et calceos) mutare*—to change one's clothes
   (and shoes).

*vestitus obsoletus, tritus*—cast-off clothing.

*vestis stragula* or simply *vestis*—drapery.

*togatus,*[1] *palliatus*—with a toga, cloak on.

*pannis obsitus*—in rags.

*paludatus, sagatus*—in a military cloak (*paludamentum*,
   of a general ; *sagum*, of soldiers).

*togam virilem (puram) sumere*—to assume the *toga virilis*.

*vestem ponere*[2] *(exuere)*—to undress.


## 4. FOOD—DRINK

*cibum sumere, capere*—to take food.

*cibum concoquere, conficere*—to digest food.

*multi cibi esse, edacem esse*—to be a great eater.

*cibum apponere, ponere alicui*—to set food before a person.

*corpus curare (cibo, vino, somno)*—to refresh oneself,
   minister to one's bodily wants.

---

[1] *togatus* = a Roman citizen as opposed to—(1) a foreigner, (2) a
soldier, (3) *tunicatus*, which is used of the lower classes who actually
had no *toga* but simply *tunica*, cf. Hor. Ep. 1. 7. 65 *tunicatus popellus*.

[2] *vestem deponere* = to give up wearing a garment, never use it
again.   Notice too *ponere arma*, to put down one's weapons ; *ponere
librum (de manibus)*, to lay aside a book (not *deponere*, which would
mean to lay aside for good.   Cf. viii. 9).

*ventri deditum esse*—to be the slave of one's appetite.

*cibo se abstinere*—to abstain from all nourishment.

*ieiunium servare*—to fast.

*tantum cibi et potionis adhibere quantum satis est*—to take only enough food to support life.

*cibus delicatus*—delicacies.

*panis cibarius*—ordinary bread.

*vino deditum esse, indulgere*—to be given to drink.

*potare*—to drink to excess; to be a drunkard.

*alicui bibere dare*[1]—to give some one to drink.

*alicui bibere ministrare*—to serve some one with drink.

*propino tibi hoc (poculum, salutem)*—I drink your health.

*bene tibi* or *te !*—your health !

*inter pocula*—whilst drinking; at table.

*exhaurire poculum*—to empty a cup at a draught.


## 5. SUBSISTENCE IN GENERAL

*victus cotidianus*—daily bread.

*victus tenuis* (Fin. 2. 28. 90)—meagre diet.

*res ad vitam necessariae*⎫
*quae ad victum pertinent*⎭ the necessaries of life.

*res ad victum cultumque necessariae*—things indispensable to a life of comfort.

*vitae commoditas iucunditasque*—comfort.

*omnes ad vitam copias suppeditare alicui*—to provide some one with a livelihood.

---

[1] These forms *dare bibere*, etc., are not Graecisms but old usages which have survived in conversational language. For the infinitive (the dative of the verbal noun) used in this way compare Verg. Aen. I. 527 *non nos aut ferro Libycos populare penates venimus;* Plaut. Bacch. iv. 3. 18 *parasitus modo venerat aurum petere.*

*quae suppeditant ad victum* (Off. 1. 4. 12)—a livelihood.

*copiae cotidianis sumptibus suppetunt* (*vid.* p. 31, note)—his
means suffice to defray daily expenses.

*victum aliqua re quaerere*—to earn a livelihood by something.

*vivere carne, piscibus, rapto* (Liv. 7. 25)—to live on meat,
fish, by plunder.

*de suo* (opp. *alieno*) *vivere*—to live on one's means.

*vitam (inopem) tolerare* (B. G. 7. 77)—to endure a life
of privation.

*non habeo, qui (unde) vivam*—I have no means, no livelihood.

*laute vivere* [1] (Nep. Chab. 3. 2)—to live well.


## 6. EXPENDITURE—LUXURY—PRODIGALITY

*sumptum facere, insumere in aliquid*—to spend money on
an object.

*sumptus effusi* (*vid.* p. 146, note) or *profusi*—prodigal
expenditure.

*sumptui parcere* (Fam. 16. 4)—to incur few expenses.

*sumptibus modum statuere*—to limit one's expenditure.

*sumptum minuere*—to retrench.

*sumptus perpetui* (Off. 2. 12. 42)—current expenses.

*sumptus liberales* (Off. 2. 12. 42)—munificence.

*delicate ac molliter vivere*—to live a luxurious and effemin-
ate life.

*luxuria diffluere* (Off. 1. 30. 106)⎫ to be abandoned to a
*omnium rerum copia diffluere* ⎬ life of excess.

*in luxuriam effundi*—to plunge into excesses, a career of
excess.

---

[1] Not *bene vivere*, which is used of leading a moral life.

*effundere, profundere pecuniam, patrimonium*—to squander
one's money, one's patrimony.

*dissipare rem familiarem (suam)*    } to squander all one's
*lacerare bona sua* (Verr. 3. 70. 164) }    property.

## 7. HOSPITALITY

*convivium instruere, apparare, ornare (magnifice splendide)*
—to prepare, give a feast, dinner.

*mensas exquisitissimis epulis instruere* (Tusc. 5. 21. 62)—
to load the tables with the most exquisite viands.

*mensae exstructae*—a table bountifully spread.

*caput cenae* (Fin. 2. 8. 25)—the main dish.

*secunda mensa* (Att. 14. 6. 2)—the dessert.

*ab ovo usque ad mala* (proverb.) [1]—from beginning to end.

*aliquem vocare, invitare ad cenam*—to invite some one to
dinner.

*promittere (ad cenam)* (Off. 3. 14. 58)—to accept an invi-
tation to dinner.

*inter cenam, inter epulas*—during dinner ; at table.

*promittere ad aliquem*—to promise to dine with a person.

*condicere alicui (ad cenam)*—to invite oneself to some one's
house for dinner.

*adhibere aliquem cenae* or *ad cenam, convivio* or *in convivium*
—to welcome some one to one's table.

*cenam alicui apponere*—to set a repast before a person.

*convivia tempestiva* (Arch. 6. 13)—a repast which begins
in good time.

*accipere aliquem (bene, copiose, laute, eleganter, regio apparatu,
apparatis epulis)*—to entertain, regale a person.

---

[1] Lit. "from the egg to the apples," i.e. throughout the dinner ;
cf. *integram famem ad ovum affero* (Fam. 9. 20. 1).

*deverti ad aliquem* (*ad* [*in*] *villam*)—to go to a man's house as his guest.

*deversari apud aliquem* (Att. 6. 1. 25)—to stop with a person, be his guest for a short time when travelling.

*mihi cum illo hospitium est, intercedit*—my relations with him are most hospitable.

*hospitio alicuius uti*—to enjoy a person's hospitality.

*hospitium cum aliquo facere,* (*con-*)*iungere*—to become a friend and guest of a person.

*hospitio aliquem accipere* or *excipere* (*domum ad se*)—to welcome a man as a guest in one's house.

*hospitium renuntiare* (Liv. 25. 18)—to sever (previous) hospitable relations.

*domus patet, aperta est mihi*—I am always welcome at his house.

*invitare aliquem tecto ac domo* or *domum suam* (Liv. 3. 14. 5)—to invite some one to one's house.


## 8. SOCIABILITY—INTERCOURSE—ISOLATION

*vitae societas* [1]—social life.

*facilitas, faciles mores* (De Am. 3. 11)—a sociable, affable disposition.

*societatem inire, facere cum aliquo*—to associate with some one.

*dissipatos homines in* (*ad*) *societatem vitae convocare* (Tusc. 1. 25. 62) — to unite isolated individuals into a society.

---

[1] The adj. *socialis* in the sense of "sociable" only occurs in late Latin, e.g. *homo sociale animal* (Sen.)

*socium se adiungere alicui*—to attach oneself to a person's
society.

*aliquem socium admittere*—to admit a person into one's
society.

*assiduum esse cum aliquo*—to be always in some one's
company.

*uti aliquo (familiariter)* ⎫ to be on intimate terms with
*alicuius familiaritate uti* ⎭   some one.

*usu, familiaritate, consuetudine* ⎫
  *coniunctum esse cum aliquo* ⎪ to be on friendly terms
*est mihi consuetudo,* or *usus* ⎬   with a person.
  *cum aliquo* ⎪
*vivere cum aliquo* ⎭

*vetus usus inter nos intercedit*—we have known each other
well for several years.

*devincire aliquem consuetudine*—to attach a person to oneself.

*se dare in consuetudinem alicuius*—to devote oneself to a
person's society.

*se insinuare in consuetudinem alicuius* (Fam. 4. 13. 6)—to
insinuate oneself into a person's society.

*summa necessitudine aliquem contingere*—to stand in very
intimate relations to some one.

*in simultate cum aliquo sum* — relations are strained
between us.

*hominum coetus, congressus fugere*—to shun society.

*in solitudine vivere* (Fin. 3. 20. 65)—to live in solitude.

*secum vivere*—to live to oneself.

*vitam solitariam agere*—to live a lonely life.

## 9. CONVERSATION—AUDIENCE—CONFERENCE

*sermonem conferre,*[1] *instituere, ordiri cum aliquo* / *se dare in sermonem cum aliquo* — to enter into conversation with some one.

*sermonem inferre de aliqua re*—to turn the conversation on to a certain subject.

*in eum sermonem* [2] *incidere, qui tum fere multis erat in ore* —to talk of a subject which was then the common topic of conversation.

*sermo incidit de aliqua re*—the conversation turned on . . .

*in sermonem ingredi*—to begin a conversation.

*sermo ortus est ab aliqua re* — the conversation began with . . .

*sermonem alio transferre*—to turn the conversation to another topic.

*medium sermonem abrumpere* (Verg. Aen. 4. 388) — to break off in the middle of the conversation.

*sermonem producere in multam noctem* (Rep. 6. 10. 10)— to prolong a conversation far into the night.

*sermonem habere cum aliquo de aliqua re* (De Am. 1. 3)— to converse, talk with a person on a subject.

*hinc sermo ductus est* / *sermo inductus a tali exordio* — the conversation began in this way.

*multus sermo*—a long conversation.

*narratio, fabula*—a narrative, tale, story.

*narratiuncula, fabella* (Fin. 5. 15)—an anecdote.

*haec fabula docet*—this fable teaches us (without *nos*).

---

[1] *sermonem conserere* only in late Latin.

[2] Distinguish from such phrases as *incidere in sermonem* (*hominum*), to become common talk.

*convenire aliquem*—to meet a person (accidentally or intentionally) and talk with him.

*congredi cum aliquo*—to meet a person by arrangement, interview him.

*sui potestatem facere, praebere alicui*  
*colloquendi copiam facere, dare* } to give audience to some one.  
*conveniendi aditum*[1] *dare alicui*

*aditum conveniendi* or *colloquium*[2] *petere*—to ask a hearing, audience, interview.

*(ad colloquium) admitti* (B. C. 3. 57)  
*in congressum alicuius venire* } to obtain an audience of some one.

*velle aliquem* (Plaut. Capt. 5. 2. 24)—to wish to speak to some one.

*paucis te volo*  
*tribus verbis te volo* } a word with you.

*sermo cotidianus*, or simply *sermo*—conversational language.

*coram loqui (cum aliquo)*—to speak personally to . . .

*commercium loquendi et audiendi*—interchange of ideas; conversation.

*capita conferre* (Liv. 2. 45)—to put our heads together.

*remotis arbitris* or *secreto*—in private; tête-à-tête.

*intra parietes* (Brut. 8. 32)—within four walls.

---

[1] *audientia* is not used in this connection, but only in such phrases as *audientiam facere alicui* or *orationi alicuius*, to procure a hearing.

[2] *colloquium* as opposed to *sermo* means an interview specially arranged, usually for transaction of some business.

## 10. GREETING—FAREWELL

*salutem alicui dicere, impertire,*
  *nuntiare*
*aliquem salvere iubere* (Att. 4. 14) ⎱ to greet a person.

*quid agis ?*[1]—how are you?

*quid agitur? quid fit?*—what is going on? how are you getting on?

*Cicero Attico*[2] *S.D.P.* (*salutem dicit plurimam*)—Cicero sends cordial greeting to Atticus.

*tibi plurimam salutem*—my best wishes for your welfare.

*nuntia fratri tuo salutem verbis meis* (Fam. 7. 14)—remember me to your brother.

*adscribere alicui salutem* (Att. 5. 20. 9)—to add to one's letter good wishes to some one.

*salute data* (*accepta*) *redditaque*—after mutual greeting.

*inter se consalutare* (De Or. 2. 3. 13) — to exchange greetings.

*dextram alicui porrigere, dare*—to give one's right hand to some one.

*dextram iungere cum aliquo, dextras inter se iungere*—to shake hands with a person.

*te valere*[3] *iubeo*—I bid you good-bye, take my leave.

*vale* or *cura ut valeas*—good-bye; farewell.

*bene ambula et redambula*—a safe journey to you.

*gratulari alicui aliquid* or *de aliqua re*—to congratulate a person on something.

---

[1] *quid agis ?* is also used as an expression of surprise, "what are you thinking of?"

[2] This and the following phrase only epistolary.

[3] *valedicere alicui* is poetical.

## 11. BETROTHAL—MARRIAGE—DIVORCE

*filiam alicui despondere*—to betroth one's daughter to some one.

*sibi (aliquam) despondere* (of the man)—to betroth oneself, get engaged.

*nuptias conciliare* (Nep. Att. 5. 3)—to arrange a marriage.

*nuptias parare*—to make preparations for a marriage.

*condicio (uxoria)* (Phil. 2. 38. 99)—a match.

*ducere uxorem*
*ducere aliquam in matrimonium* } to marry (of the man).

*nubere alicui*—to marry (of the woman).

*nuptam esse cum aliquo* or *alicui*—to be married to some one.

*uxorem habere* (Verr. 3. 33. 76) — to be a married man.

*dotem filiae dare*—to give a dowry to one's daughter.

*filiam alicui in matrimonio* or
   *in matrimonium collocare* or
   simply *filiam alicui collocare*
*filiam alicui in matrimonium dare*
*filiam alicui nuptum dare* } to give one's daughter in marriage to some-one.

*nuntium remittere alicui* (De Or.
   1. 40)
*repudium dicere* or *scribere alicui* } to separate, be divorced (used of man or woman).

*divortium facere cum uxore*
*aliquam suas res sibi habere* [1]
   *iubere* (Phil. 2. 28. 69) } to separate from, divorce (of the man).

[1] The formula of divorce used by the man was *tuas res tibi habeto*, cf. Plaut. Trin. 266.

*repudium*[1] *remittere viro* (Dig. 24. 3)—to separate (of the woman).

## 12. WILL—INHERITANCE

*testamentum facere, conscribere*—to make a will.

*testamentum obsignare* (B. G. 1. 39)—to sign a will.

*testamentum resignare*—to open a will.

*testamentum rescindere*—to declare a will to be null and void.

*testamentum subicere, supponere*—to produce a false will.

*testamentum irritum facere, rumpere*—to annul, revoke a will.

*testamento aliquid cavere* (Fin. 2. 31)—to prescribe in one's will.

*pecuniam alicui legare*—to leave money to a person in one's will.

*aliquem heredem testamento scribere, facere*—to appoint some one as heir in one's will.

*alicuius mortui voluntas (suprema)*—the last wishes of a deceased person.

*heredem esse alicui*—to be some one's heir.

*hereditate aliquid accipere*—to inherit something.

*exheres paternorum bonorum* (De Or. 1. 38. 175)—disinherited.

*exheredari a patre*—to be disinherited.

*hereditate aliquid relictum est ab aliquo*—something has been left as a legacy by some one.

---

[1] Cicero uses *divortium* not *repudium*. *divortium (dis, vertere)* is a separation by mutual consent, *divortium est, quod in diversas partes eunt, qui discedunt* (Paul. Dig. L. 16. 1. 161). In *repudium* one party takes the initiative, usually the husband. The formula commonly used was *tua condicione non utar*.

*hereditas ad me* or *mihi venit ab aliquo* (Verr. 2. 1. 10)—I have received a legacy from a person.

*hereditatem adire, cernere*—to take possession of an inheritance.

*heres ex asse, ex dodrante*—sole heir; heir to three-quarters of the estate.

*heres ex besse*—heir to two-thirds of the property.

## 13. CUSTOM—USAGE

*assuefactus* [1] or *assuetus aliqua re*—accustomed to a thing.

*in consuetudinem* or *morem venire*—to become customary, the fashion.

*in nostros mores inducere aliquid* (De Or. 2. 28)—to introduce a thing into our customs; to familiarise us with a thing.

*consuetudinem suam tenere, retinere, servare*—to keep up a usage.

*consuetudo inveterascit* (B. G. 5. 41. 5)—a custom is taking root, growing up.

*res obsolescit*—a thing is going out of use, becoming obsolete.

*a vetere consuetudine discedere*
*a pristina consuetudine deflectere*}—to give up old customs.

*in pristinam consuetudinem revocare aliquid*—to return to ancient usage.

*aliquid est meae consuetudinis*
*aliquid cadit in meam consuetudinem*}—it is my custom.

*mos (moris) est, ut* (Brut. 21. 84)—it is customary to . . .

*more, usu receptum est*—it is traditional usage.

---

[1] Note *assuescere*, to accustom oneself to . . . . and *assuefacere aliquem*, to accustom some one else to . . .

*ut fit, ita ut fit, ut fere fit*⎱
*ut solet, ut fieri solet* ⎰ as usually happens.

*ita fert consuetudo*—so custom, fashion prescribes.

*ex consuetudine mea* (opp. *praeter consuetudinem*)—according to my custom.

*more institutoque maiorum* (Mur. 1. 1)—according to the custom and tradition of my fathers.

*ex instituto* (Liv. 6. 10. 6)—according to traditional usage.

# XIII. COMMERCE AND AGRICULTURE

## 1. COMMERCE IN GENERAL—PURCHASE—PRICE

*negotiatores*[1] (Verr. 2. 69. 168)⎱
*homines negotii* (always in sing.) *gerentes* ⎰ business-men.

*negotii bene gerentes* (Quint. 19. 62)—good men of business.

*negotium obire* or *exsequi*—to be engaged upon a transaction, carry it out.

*negotium (rem) conficere, absolvere*—to settle, finish a transaction.

*mercaturam facere*—to be engaged in commerce, wholesale business.

---

[1] The usual terms for men of business are *negotiator, mercator, caupo, institor.* The first two are used of merchants, wholesale dealers, *negotiator* especially when talking of the transactions (*negotia*) of business, *mercator* with reference to the profits (*merces*). *caupo* is a retail dealer, tradesman, shopkeeper; *institor*, a pedlar, commercial traveller.

*negotia habere* (*in Sicilia*)—to have commercial interests in Sicily.

*contrahere rem* or *negotium cum aliquo* (Cluent. 14. 41)—to have business relations with some one.

*transigere aliquid* (*de aliqua re*) *cum aliquo* or *inter se*—to transact, settle a matter with some one.

*nihil cum aliquo contrahere*—to do no business with a man.

*quaestum facere* (Fam. 15. 14)—to make money.

*quaestui aliquid habere* (Off. 2. 3. 13)—to make a profit out of something.

*res, quae importantur et exportantur*—imports and exports.

*exponere, proponere merces* (*venales*)—to set out goods for sale.

*parvo, vili pretio* or *bene emere*—to buy cheaply.

*magno* or *male emere*—to buy dearly.

*aliquid magno, parvo stat, constat*—a thing costs much, little.

*aliquid nihilo* or *gratis constat*—a thing costs nothing.

*pretium alicui rei statuere, constituere* (Att. 13. 22)—to fix a price for a thing.

## 2. MONEY—INTEREST—LOANS

*pecunia magna,*[1] *grandis* (*multum pecuniae*)—much money.

*pecunia exigua* or *tenuis*—little money.

*pecunia praesens* (*vid.* p. 54, note) or *numerata*—cash; ready money.

*aes* (*argentum*) *signatum*—coined money; bullion.

*argentum* (*factum*) (Verr. 5. 25. 63)—silver plate.

*nummi adulterini*—bad money; base coin.

*pecuniam erogare* (*in classem*)—to spend money.

---

[1] In plur. *magnae, multae pecuniae* = large sums of money.

*pecuniam insumere in aliquid* or *consumere in aliqua re*—
to devote money to a purpose.

*pecuniam numerare alicui* (Att. 16. 16)—to pay cash.

*pecuniam solvere*—to pay money.

*pecuniam alicui debere*—to owe some one money.

*pecuniam alicui credere* (*sine fenore, usuris*)—to lend some
one money (without interest).

*pecuniam fenori* (*fenore*) *alicui dare, accipere ab aliquo*—to
lend, borrow money at interest.

*pecuniam fenore occupare* (Flacc. 21. 54)—to put out
money at interest.

*pecuniam collocare*[1] *in aliqua re*—to put money in an
undertaking.

*pecunia iacet otiosa*—the money is bringing in no interest,
lies idle.

*pecuniam mutuari* or *sumere mutuam ab aliquo*—to borrow
money from some one.

*pecuniam alicui mutuam dare*—to lend money to some one.

*pecuniam creditam solvere*—to repay a loan.

*non solvendo*[2] *esse, decoquere, conturbare* (Phil. 2. 2. 4)—
to be bankrupt.

*pecuniam exigere* (*acerbe*)—to demand payment.

*magnas pecunias ex aliqua re* (e.g. *ex metallis*) *facere*—
to have a large income from a thing (e.g. from
mines).

*nummus iactatur* (Off. 3. 20. 80)—the bank-rate varies.

*versuram facere* (Att. 5. 21. 12)—to transfer a debt.

*nummulis acceptis* (Att. 1. 16. 6)—for a trifle, a beggarly
pittance.

---

[1] Sometimes absolutely, e.g. Cic. Off. 2. 25. 90 *pecuniam collocare*.

[2] *solvendo* is a predicative dative. For the development of such uses
cf. *nulli rei erimus postea* (Plaut. Stich. 718); Ovid Met. 15. 403
*dedit huic aetas vires onerique ferendo est*; Liv. 4. 35 *experiunda res
est sitne aliqui plebeius ferendo magno honori*.

## 3. MONEY-MATTERS—ACCOUNTS—AUDIT

*res nummaria* or *pecuniaria*, *ratio pecuniarum*—finance; money-matters.

*argentariam facere* (Verr. 5. 59. 155)—to be a banker.

*argentariam dissolvere* (Caecin. 4. 11)—to close one's bank, give up banking.

*codex* or *tabulae ratio accepti et expensi*—account-book; ledger.

*nomina facere* or *in tabulas referre*—to book a debt.

*pecunia in nominibus* [1] *est*—money is outstanding, unpaid.

*pecuniam in nominibus habeo*—I have money owing me.

*alicui expensum ferre aliquid*—to put a thing down to a man's account.

*alicui acceptum referre aliquid* [2] (Verr. 2. 70. 170)—to put down to a man's credit.

*rationem alicuius rei inire, subducere*, *ad calculos vocare aliquid* (Amic. 16. 58)—to go through accounts, make a valuation of a thing.

*inita subductaque ratione aliquid facere*—to do something after careful calculation.

*rationes putare* [3] *cum aliquo*—to balance accounts with some one.

[1] *nomina* are properly the sums entered in the ledger as due from a person. Hence *nomen solvere, dissolvere*, to pay a debt; *nomen expedire, exsolvere*, to get rid of a debt; *bonum nomen*, a safe investment (Cic. Fam. 5. 6. 2).

[2] Also used metaphorically to "owe a thing to another's instrumentality," e.g. *quod vivo tibi acceptum refero.*

[3] The original meaning of *putare* is to prune (cf. *purus, amputare*), cleanse by cutting off, then make clear, calculate, reckon. By a transference it became used of the result of calculation, i.e. thinking, believing. Compare the history of the French *raisonner* and the Italian *ragioneria.*

*ratio alicuius rei constat* (*convenit, par est*)—the accounts
  balance.

*ratio acceptorum et datorum* (*accepti et expensi*) (Amic. 16.
  58)—the account of receipts and expenditure.

*rationes diligenter conficere*—to keep the accounts (day-
  book) carefully.

*summam facere alicuius rei*—to compute the total of anything.

*de capite deducere* (*vid.* p. 186, note) *aliquid*—to subtract
  something from the capital.

*rationem alicuius rei reddere*—to render count of a matter ;
  to pass it for audit.

*rationem alicuius rei reposcere*⎫
  *aliquem* or *ab aliquo*           ⎬ to demand an account, an
*rationem ab aliquo repetere de* ⎰   audit of a matter.
  *aliqua re* (Cluent. 37. 104)⎭

## 4. RATE OF INTEREST

*centesimae* (sc. *usurae*) (Att. 5. 21. 11)—interest at 1 per
  cent per month, 12 per cent per annum.

*binis centesimis fenerari*—to lend at 24 per cent.

*ternae centesimae*—36 per cent per annum.

*quaternas centesimas postulare* (Att. 5. 21. 11)—to demand
  48 per cent.

*semisses*—6 per cent (i.e. if for 100 denarii, asses, one
  pays half a denarius, half an as per month).

*semissibus magna copia est*—money is plentiful at 6 per
  cent.

*usurae semissium* (Colum.)⎫
*usurae semisses* (Jurists)   ⎰6 per cent.

*quadrantes usurae*—3 per cent (a quarter of centesima).

*trientes* or *trientariae usurae* (Att. 4. 15)—4 per cent.

*quincunx* (Pers. 5. 149)⎫
*quincunces usurae*      ⎬5 per cent.

*fenus ex triente Id. Quint. factum erat bessibus* (Att. 4. 15. 7)
—the rate of interest has gone up from 4 per cent
to 8 per cent.

*perpetuum fenus* (Att. 5. 21. 13)—simple interest.

*fenus renovatum* ⎫
*anatocismus* (ἀνατοκισμός) ⎬compound interest.
   (Att. 5. 21. 11) ⎭

*fenus iniquissimum, grande, grave*—exorbitant rate of
interest.

*usura menstrua*—monthly interest.

*centesimis cum anatocismo contentum esse* (Att. 5. 21. 12)—to
be content with 12 per cent at compound interest.


## 5. PROFIT—CREDIT—DEBT

*lucrum facere* (opp. *damnum facere*) *ex aliqua re*—to make
profit out of a thing.

*in lucro ponere aliquid* (Flacc. 17. 40)—to consider a
thing as profit.

*debitor*, or *is qui debet*—the debtor.

*creditor*, or *is cui debeo*—the creditor.

*fides et ratio pecuniarum*—credit and financial position.

*fides* (*vid.* p. 158, note) *concidit*—credit is going down.

*fidem derogare alicui*—to rob a person of his credit.

*fides aliquem deficere coepit*—a man's credit begins to go
down.

*fides* (*de foro*) *sublata est* (Leg. Agr. 2. 3. 8)—credit has
disappeared.

*fides tota Italia est angusta*—credit is low throughout Italy.

*fidem moliri* (Liv. 6. 11. 8)—to shake credit.

*laborare de pecunia*—to have pecuniary difficulties.

*in summa difficultate nummaria versari* (Verr. 2. 28. 69)— to be in severe pecuniary straits.

*in maximas angustias (pecuniae) adduci*—to be reduced to extreme financial embarrassment.

*aes alienum* (always in sing.) *facere, contrahere*—to incur debts.

*grande, magnum* (opp. *exiguum*) *aes alienum conflare*—to incur debts on a large scale.

*incidere in aes alienum*—to get into debt.

*aes alienum habere*⎱
*in aere alieno esse*⎰ to be in debt.

*in suis nummis versari* (Verr. 4. 6. 11)—to have no debts.

*aere alieno obrutum, demersum esse*—to be deeply in debt.

*aere alieno oppressum esse*—to have pressing debts.

*aes alienum dissolvere, exsolvere*⎱
*nomina* (cf. p. 204), *solvere, dis-*⎰ to pay one's debts.
*solvere, exsolvere*

*nomina exigere* (Verr. 3. 10. 28)—to demand payment of, recover debts.

*ex aere alieno exire*⎱
*aere alieno liberari*⎰ to get out of debt.

*versurâ solvere, dissolvere* (Att. 5. 15. 2)—to pay one's old debts by making new.

## 6. BUILDING

*opus locare*—to contract for the building of something.

*opus redimere, conducere*—to undertake the contract for a work.

*domum aedificandam locare, conducere*—to give, undertake a contract for building a house.

*aedificatorem esse* (Nep. Att. 13. 1)—to be fond of building.

*exstruere aedificium, monumentum*—to erect a building, a monument.

*fundamenta iacĕre, agere*—to lay the foundations.

*turrim excitare, erigere, facere*—to build a tower.

*oppidum constituere, condere*—to build, found a city.

*pontem facere in flumine*
*inicere pontem*　　　　　}—to build a bridge over a river.
*flumen ponte iungere*

*pons est in flumine*—there is a bridge over the river.

*pontem dissolvere, rescindere, interscindere* (B. G. 2. 9. 4)—to break down a bridge.

*luminibus alicuius obstruere, officere*[1]—to obstruct a person's view, shut out his light by building.


## 7. AGRICULTURE—MANAGEMENT OF STOCK

*agrum colere* (Leg. Agr. 2. 25. 67)—to till the ground.

*agros fertiles deserere*—to leave fertile ground untilled.

*agriculturae studere* (opp. *agriculturam deserere*)—to have a taste for agriculture.

---

[1] Also used metaphorically to overshadow, eclipse a person, cf. vi. 1.

*opus rusticum*—tillage ; cultivation.

*in agris esse, habitare*—to live in the country.

*serere ; semen spargere*—to sow.

*sementem facere* (B. G. 1. 3. 1)—to look after the sowing.

*ut sementem feceris, ita metes* (proverb.) (De Or. 2. 65)—as you sow, so will you reap.

*laetae segetes*—the laughing cornfields.

*laetissimi flores* (Verr. 4. 48. 107)—a glorious expanse of flowers.

*odores, qui efflantur e floribus*—the perfume exhaled by flowers.

*messis in herbis est* (Liv. 25. 15)—the crop is in the blade.

*adhuc tua messis in herba est* (proverb.)—your crop is still green, *i.e.* you are still far from your ambition.

*frumenta in agris matura non sunt* (B. G. 1. 16. 2)—the corn is not yet ripe.

*messem facere*
*fructus demetere* or *percipere* } to reap.

*fructus condere* (N. D. 2. 62. 156)—to harvest crops.

*messis opīma* (opp. *ingrata*)—a good harvest.

*arbores serere* (De Sen. 7. 24)—to plant trees.

*arbores caedere*—to fell trees.

*inopia* (opp. *copia*) *rei frumentariae*
*difficultas annonae* (Imp. Pomp. 15. 44) } want of corn; scarcity in the corn-market.

*annona ingravescit, crescit*—the price of corn is going up.

*annona laxatur, levatur, vilior fit*—the price of corn is going down.

*caritas annonae* (opp. *vilitas*), also simply *annona*—dearth of corn ; high prices.

*ad denarios* [1] *L in singulos modiòs annona pervenerat*—corn had gone up to 50 denarii the bushel.

*annona cara est*—corn is dear.

*hac annona* (Plaut. Trin. 2. 4. 83)—when corn is as dear as it is.

*rem pecuariam facere, exercere* (cf. Varro R. R. 2. 1)—to rear stock.

*pastum agere*—to drive to pasture.

*pastum ire*—to go to pasture.

*pascere gregem*—to feed a flock (of goats).

*greges pascuntur* [2] (Verg. G. 3. 162)—the herds are grazing.

*alere equos, canes*—to keep horses, dogs.

*animalia quae nobiscum degunt* (Plin. 8. 40)—domestic animals.

## XIV. THE STATE

### 1. CONSTITUTION—ADMINISTRATION—GOVERNMENT

*forma rei publicae*
*discriptio civitatis* ⎬ the constitution.
*instituta et leges*

*rem publicam constituere* [3]
*rem publicam legibus et insti-*
  *tutis temperare* (Tusc. 1. 1. 2) ⎬ to give the state a consitution.
*civitati leges, iudicia, iura de-*
  *. scribere*

---

[1] *denarius*=about 9½d., *vid.* Gow, Companion to School Classics, p. 149.

[2] *pascere* and *pasci* are also used metaphorically, *vid.* iii. s. v. *oculi*.

[3] Cf. *tres viri rei publicae constituendae.*

*suis legibus utitur* (B. G. 1. 45. 3)—(a state) has its own laws, is autonomous.

*nullam habere rem publicam*—to have no constitution, be in anarchy.

*rem publicam in pristĭnum statum restituere*—to restore the ancient constitution.

*optima re publica*—at the time of a most satisfactory government.

*libera res publica, liber populus*—the Republic.

*rem publicam gerere, administrare, regere, tractare, gubernare* —to govern, administer the state.

*rei publicae praeesse*—to have the management of the state.

*ad gubernacula* (metaph. only in plur.) *rei publicae sedere*  
*clavum rei publicae tenere*  
*gubernacula rei publicae tractare* } to hold the reins of government.

*principem civitatis esse*—to be the chief man in the state.

*principem in re publica locum obtinere*—to hold the first position in the state.

*negotia publica* (Off. 1. 20. 69)—public affairs.

*vita occupata* (*vid.* p. 94)—the busy life of a statesman.

*accedere, se conferre ad rem publicam*  
*rem publicam capessere* (Off. 1. 21. 71) } to devote oneself to politics, a political career.

*in re publica* or *in rebus publicis versari*—to take part in politics.

*rei publicae deesse* (opp. *adesse*)—to take no part in politics.

*a negotiis publicis se removere*  
*a re publica recedere* } to retire from public life.

*in otium se referre* (Fam. 99)—to retire into private life.

*vita privata* (Senect. 7. 22)—private life.

*publico carere, forum ac lucem fugere*
*forensi luce carere* }—to shun publicity.

*rem publicam tueri, stabilire*—to defend, strengthen the state.

*res publica stat* (opp. *iacet*)—the state is secure.

*rem publicam augere, amplificare*—to aggrandise, extend the power of the state.

*saluti rei publicae non deesse*—to further the common weal.

*rei publicae* [1] *causa* (Sest. 47. 101)—for political reasons.

*e re publica* (opp. *contra rem p.*)—for the advantage of the state; in the interests of the state.

*summa res publica* (or *summa rei publicae*)—the welfare of the state.

*commoda publica* or *rei publicae rationes*—the interests of the state.

*rei publicae rationibus* or simply *rei publicae consulere*—to further the public interests.

*ad rei publicae rationes aliquid referre*—to consider a thing from a political point of view.

*in rem publicam omni cogitatione*
*curaque incumbere* (Fam. 10. 1. 2)
*omnes curas et cogitationes in rem* }—to devote one's every
*publicam conferre* thought to the
*omnes curas in rei publicae salute* state's welfare.
*defigere* (Phil. 14. 5. 13)

---

[1] There being no adjective in Latin for "political," we have to make use of periphrasis with such words as *res publica, civilis, popularis,* etc.

*totum et animo et corpore in salutem rei publicae se conferre*
—to devote oneself body and soul to the good of
the state.

*bene, optime sentire de re publica* ⎫
*omnia de re publica praeclara* ⎬ to have the good of the
*atque egregia sentire* ⎭ state at heart.

*rector civitatis* (De Or. 1. 48. 211)—the head of the state.

*viri rerum civilium, rei publicae* ⎫
  *gerendae periti* or *viri in re* ⎪
  *publica prudentes* ⎪
*auctores consilii publici* ⎬statesmen.
*principes rem publicam admini-* ⎪
  *strantes* or simply *principes* ⎭

*prudentia* (*civilis*) (De Or. 1. 19. 85)—statesmanship ;
political wisdom.

*homo in re publica exercitatus*—an experienced politician.

*res civiles*—political questions.

*plus in re publica videre*—to possess great political in-
sight.

*longe prospicere futuros casus rei publicae* (De Amic. 12. 40)
—to foresee political events long before.

*alicuius in re publica* or *capessendae rei publicae consilia eo*
*spectant, ut . . .*—a man's policy is aiming at,
directed towards . . .

*rei publicae muneribus orbatus* ⎫
*gerendis negotiis orbatus* (Fin. ⎬banished from public life.
  5. 20. 57) ⎭


## 2. CIVIL RIGHTS—RANK

*civitate donare aliquem* (Balb. 3. 7)—to make a man a
citizen.

*in civitatem recipere, ascribere, asciscere aliquem*—to enroll
  as a citizen, burgess.

*civitatem alicui dare, tribuere, impertire*—to present a person with the freedom of the city.

*civitatem mutare* (Balb. 11. 27)—to naturalise oneself
  as a citizen of another country.

*generis antiquitate florere*—to be of noble family.

*nobilitati favere* (Sest. 9. 21) } to be a friend of the
*nobilitatis fautorem, studiosum esse* } aristocracy.

*homo novus* [1]—a parvenu (a man no member of whose
  family has held curule office).

*ordo senatorius* (*amplissimus*)—the senatorial order.

*ordo equester* (*splendidissimus*)—the equestrian order; the
  knights.

*summo loco natus*—of high rank.

*nobili, honesto, illustri loco* or *genere natus*—of illustrious
  family.

*humili, obscuro loco natus*
*humilibus* (*obscuris*) *parentibus* } of humble, obscure origin.
  *natus*

*infimo loco natus*—from the lowest classes.

*equestri loco natus* or *ortus*—a knight by birth.

*summi* (*et*) *infimi* (Rep. 1. 34. 53)—high and low.

*homines omnis generis*—people of every rank.

*homines omnium ordinum et aetatum*—people of every
  rank and age.

*homo plebeius, de plebe*—one of the people.

*traduci ad plebem* (Att. 1. 18. 4)—to get oneself admitted
  as a plebeian.

---

[1] A *novus homo* by taking office becomes for his descendants
*princeps nobilitatis* (Cic. Brut. 14) or *auctor generis* (Leg. Agr. 2.
35).

*transitio ad plebem* (Brut. 16. 62)  
*traductio ad plebem*  
}  to transfer oneself from the patrician to the plebeian order.

*unus de* or *e multis*—one of the crowd ; a mere individual.

*faex populi, plebis, civitatis*—the dregs of the people.

*infima fortuna* or *condicio servorum*—a degraded, servile condition.

*unus e togatorum numero*—an ordinary, average Roman citizen.

## 3. DIGNITY—POSITION—HONOURS—PRE-EMINENCE—(cf. p. 64)

*dignitatem suam tueri, defendere, retinere, obtinere*—to guard, maintain one's dignity.

*dignitati suae servire, consulere*—to be careful of one's dignity.

*aliquem ad summam dignitatem perducere* (B. G. 7. 39)—to elevate to the highest dignity

*principem (primum), secundum locum dignitatis obtinere*—to occupy the first, second position in the state.

*in altissimo dignitatis gradu collocatum, locatum, positum esse*—to occupy a very high position in the state.

*aliquem ex altissimo dignitatis gradu praecipitare* (Dom. 37. 98)—to depose, bring down a person from his elevated position.

*aliquem de dignitatis gradu demovere*  
*aliquem gradu movere, depellere* or *de gradu (statu) deicere*  
}  to overthrow a person (cf. p. 152).

*dignitatis gradum ascendere* — to attain a position of dignity.

*ad honores ascendere*—to rise, mount to the honours of office.

*amplissimos honorum gradus assequi, adipisci*—to reach the highest grade of office.

*ad summos honores pervenire* (cf. also p. 64)—to attain to the highest offices.

*vir defunctus honoribus*—a man who has held every office (up to the consulship).

*principatum tenere, obtinere*—to occupy the leading position.

*de principatu deiectus* (B. G. 7. 63)—deposed from one's high position.

*principatum alicui* or *ad aliquem deferre*—to assign the first place to some one.

*contendere cum aliquo de principatu* (Nep. Arist. 1)—to contend with some one for the pre-eminence.

*primas* (e.g. *sapientiae*) *alicui deferre, tribuere, concedere*— to give the palm, the first place (for wisdom) to some one.


## 4. PUBLIC MEETINGS—SUFFRAGE

*convocare populi concilium* and⎱
   *populum ad concilium*       to summon an assem-
*contionem advocare* (Sall. Iug. 33. 3)⎰  bly of the people.

*agere cum populo*[1] (Leg. 3. 4. 10)—to submit a formal proposition to the people.

[1] Aulus Gellius (13. 16. 3) explains the difference between *cum populo agere* and *contionem habere ;* the former = *rogare quid populum quod suffragiis suis aut iubeat aut vetet.* Cf. Liv. 22. 10. 2 *velitis iubeatisne haec sic fieri?* also 21. 17. 4. *habere contionem* (*coventio = countio = contio*) is equivalent to *verba facere ad populum sine ulla rogatione.*

*concilium indicere, habere, dimittere*—to fix the day for, to hold, to dismiss a meeting.

*comitia habere*—to hold a meeting of the people.

*comitia magistratibus creandis*—meetings for the election of officers.

*comitiis* (Abl.) *convenire*—to meet for elections.

*comitiis consulem creari*—to be chosen consul at the elections.

*suffragium ferre (vid.* p. 79, note, *sententiam dicere)*—to vote (in the popular assembly).

*multitudinis suffragiis rem permittere*—to leave a matter to be decided by popular vote.


## 5. LAWS—BILLS

*legem, rogationem* [1] *promulgare* (Liv. 33. 46)—to bring a bill before the notice of the people.

*legem ferre* or simply *ferre ad populum, ut . . .*—to propose a law in the popular assembly.

*legem suadere* (opp. *dissuadere*)⎫ to support a bill (before
*pro lege dicere*                    ⎭    the people).

*legem rogare* or *rogare populum* (cf. p. 216, note)—to formally propose a law to the people.

*legem perferre* (Liv. 33. 46)—to carry a law (said of the magistrate).

*lex perfertur*—a law is adopted.

*legem antiquare* [2] (opp. *accipere, iubere*)—to reject a bill.

---

[1] A *rogatio* had to be posted up in some public place for *trinum nundinum (tempus)* (Phil. 5. 3. 8), i.e. for seventeen days, *nundinae (novem, dies)* being a holiday, fair, held every ninth day.

[2] On the voting-tablets (*tabellae*) used in the *comitia* was written either A (*antiquo*) to reject the bill, V · R (*uti rogas*) to pass it; in judicial questions A (*absolvo*), C (*condemno*), N · L (*non liquet*).

*legem sciscere* (Planc. 14. 35)—to vote for a law.

*legem iubere*—to ratify a law (used of the people).

*legem sancire*—to let a bill become law (of people and senate).

*Solo lege sanxit, ut* or *ne*—Solon ordained by law that . . .

*Solonis legibus sanctum erat, ut* or *ne*—the laws of Solon ordained that . . .

*legem abrogare*[1] (Att. 3. 23. 2)—to replace an old law by a new.

*legem tollere* (Leg. 2. 12. 31)—to abolish a law.

*legi intercedere*—to protest against a law (used of the veto, *intercessio*, of plebeian tribunes).

*legem proponere in publicum*—to bring a law before the notice of the people.

*edictum proponere* (Att. 2. 21. 4)—to publish, post up an edict.

*legem in aes incīdere*—to engrave a law upon a brazen tablet.

*lex rata est* (opp. *irrita*)—a law is valid.

*legem ratam esse iubere*—to declare a law valid.

*a lege discedere*—to transgress a law.

*salvis legibus* (*vid.* p. 172, note)—without breaking the law.

*lex*[2] *iubet, vetat* (*dilucide, planissime*)—the law orders, forbids (expressly, distinctly).

*in lege scriptum est*, or simply *est*—the law says . . .

*sententia* or *voluntas legis*—the spirit of the law.

---

[1] *legi* or *de lege derogare* = to reject a clause in it ; *legem abrogare*, to nullify a law by passing another which contradicts it ; *multam, poenam inrogare alicui*, to inflict a fine on some one with the approval of the people ; *pecuniam erogare* (*ex aerario in classem*), to draw money from the treasury and distribute it according to the wishes of the people.

[2] *lex* is often personified in this way.

*leges scribere, facere, condere, constituere* (not *dare*)—to make
 laws (of a legislator).

*legum scriptor, conditor, inventor*
*qui leges scribit* (not *legum* }a legislator.
 *lator*)[1]

*in legem iurare* (Sest. 16. 37)—to swear obedience to a
 law.

*lege teneri*—to be bound by a law.

*legibus solvere*—to free from legal obligations.

*ea lege, ut*—on condition of . . .

*aliquid contra legem est*—a thing is illegal.

*acta rescindere, dissolvere* (Phil. 13. 3. 5)—to declare a
 magistrate's decisions null and void.

*in album referre* (De Or. 2. 12. 52)—to record in the
 official tablets (*Annales maximi*).

## 6. POPULAR FAVOUR—INFLUENCE— UNPOPULARITY

*aura favoris popularis* (Liv. 22.
 26)
*populi favor, gratia popularis* }popular favour; popular-
*aura popularis* (Harusp. 18. 43) ity.

*auram popularem captare* (Liv.
 3. 33)
*gratiam populi quaerere* }to court popularity.

*aurae popularis homo* (Liv. 42. 30)—a popular man.

*ventum popularem quendam* (*in aliqua re*) *quaerere*—to
 strive to gain popular favour by certain means.

*gratiosum esse* (opp. *invisum esse*)—to be popular, influential.

---

[1] *legis lator* = the man who proposes a law.

*opibus, gratia, auctoritate valere, florere*—to have great influence.

*opes, gratiam, potentiam consequi*—to acquire influence.

*gratiam inire apud aliquem, ab aliquo* (cf. p. 58)—to gain some one's favour.

*gratiam, opes alicuius imminuere* (opp. *augere*)—to weaken a person's influence.

*crescere ex aliquo*—to raise oneself by another's fall.

*crescere ex invidia senatoria*—to profit by the unpopularity of the senate to gain influence oneself.

*iacēre* (*vid.* p. 92, note)—to be politically annihilated.

*existimatio populi, hominum*—public opinion.

*multum communi hominum opinioni tribuere*—to be always considering what people think.

*invidia*
*offensio populi, popularis* }unpopularity.
*offensa populi voluntas*

*invidia dictatoria* (Liv. 22. 26)—the feeling against the dictator.

*ex invidia alicuius auram popularem petere* (Liv. 22. 26)— to use some one's unpopularity as a means of making oneself popular.


7. PARTY-SPIRIT—NEUTRALITY—POLITICS—
ARISTOCRACY—DEMOCRACY

*partes* (usually of plebeians) }a party ; faction.
*factio* (of aristocrats)

*partium studium*, also simply *studia*—party-spirit.

*partium studiosum esse*—to be a strong partisan.

*certamen partium*
*contentio partium* (Phil. 5. 12. 32) }party-strife

*partium studiis divisum esse*—to be torn by faction.

*consiliorum in re publica socius*—a political ally.

*alicuius partes (causam)* or simply ⎫
  *aliquem sequi* ⎬ to embrace the cause of . . ., be a partisan of . . .
*alicuius partibus studere* ⎭

*ab (cum) aliquo stare* (Brut. 79. 273)—to be on a person's side (not *ab alicuius partibus*).

*alicuius studiosum esse*—to be a follower of some one.

*cum aliquo facere* (Sull. 13. 36)—to take some one's side.

*nullius* or *neutrius* (of two) ⎫
  *partis esse* ⎪
*in neutris partibus esse* ⎬ to be neutral.
*neutram partem sequi* ⎪
*medium esse* ⎪
*medium se gerere* ⎭

*a partibus rei publicae animus liber* (Sall. Cat. 4. 2)—an independent spirit.

*idem de re publica sentire*—to have the same political opinions.

*ab aliquo in re publica dissentire*—to hold different views in politics.

*ex rei publicae dissensione* — owing to political dissension.

*in duas partes discedere* (Sall. Iug. 13. 1)—to divide into two factions.

*studio ad rem publicam ferri*—to throw oneself heart and soul into politics.

*se civilibus fluctibus committere*—to enter the whirlpool of political strife.

*imperium singulare, unius dominatus, regium imperium*—monarchy.

*optimatium dominatus*
*civitas, quae optimatium arbitrio regitur* } aristocracy (as a form of government).

*boni cives, optimi, optimates*, also simply *boni* (opp. *improbi*) ; *illi, qui optimatium causam agunt*—the aristocracy (as a party in politics).

*principes* or *primores*—the aristocracy (as a leading class in government).

*nobiles ; nobilitas ; qui nobilitate generis excellunt*—the aristocracy (as a social class).

*paucorum dominatio* or *potentia*—oligarchy.

*multitudinis dominatus* or *imperium*—government by the mob.

*spiritus patricii* (Liv. 4. 42)—patrician arrogance ; pride of caste.

*homines graves* (opp. *leves*)—men of sound opinions.

*homo popularis*—a democrat.

*homo vere popularis* (Catil. 4. 5. 9)—a man who genuinely wishes the people's good.

*homo florens in populari ratione*—a democratic leader.

*imperium populi* or *populare, civitas* or *res publica popularis* —democracy.

*causam popularem suscipere* or *defendere*—to take up the cause of the people, democratic principles.

*populi causam agere*—to be a leading spirit of the popular cause.

*patriae amantem (amantissimum) esse* (Att. 9. 22)—to be (very) patriotic.

*mundanus, mundi civis et incola* (Tusc. 5. 37)—a citizen of the world ; cosmopolitan.

## 8. DEMAGOGY—REVOLUTION—REBELLION—
### ANARCHY

*plebis dux, vulgi turbator, civis turbulentus, civis rerum
novarum cupidus*—a demagogue, agitator.

*iactatio, concitatio popularis*—popular agitation.

*artes populares*—tricks of a demagogue.

*populariter agere*—to play the demagogue.

*conversio rei publicae* (Div. 2. 2. 6)—revolution.

*homines seditiosi, turbulenti* or *novarum rerum cupidi*—re-
volutionists.

*novis rebus studere* ⎫ to    hold    revolutionary
*novarum rerum cupidum esse* ⎭    opinions.

*novas res moliri* (Verr. 2. 125)—to plot a revolution.

*contra rem publicam sentire*—to foster revolutionary projects.

*contra rem publicam facere*—to be guilty of high treason.

*a re publica deficere*—to betray the interests of the state.

*plebem concitare, sollicitare*—to stir up the lower classes.

*seditionem facere, concitare*—to cause a rebellion.

*seditio erumpit*[1]—a rebellion breaks out.

*coniurare (inter se) de* c. Gerund. ⎫
   or *ut . . .* ⎬ to form a conspiracy.
*coniurationem facere* (Catil. 2. 4. ⎭
   6)

*conspirare cum aliquo (contra aliquem)*—to conspire with
some one.

*rem publicam labefactare*—to shake the stability of the
state.

*rem publicam perturbare*—to throw the state into confusion.

---

[1] But *bellum exardescit*, war breaks out.

*statum rei publicae convellere*—to endanger the existence of the state.

*rem publicam vexare*—to damage the state.

*rem publicam funditus evertere*—to completely overthrow the government, the state.

*omnes leges confundere*—to upset the whole constitution.

*omnia turbare ac miscere*—to cause universal disorder.

*perturbatio omnium rerum* (Flacc. 37)—general confusion ; anarchy.

*omnia divina humanaque iura permiscentur* (B. C. 1. 6. 8)— anarchy reigns supreme.

*leges nullae* }
*iudicia nulla* } lawlessness ; anarchy.

*res fluit ad interregnum*—things seem tending towards an interregnum.

*non nullus odor est dictaturae* (Att. 4. 18)—there are whispers of the appointment of a dictator.

*tumultum sedare* (B. C. 3. 18. 3)—to quell an outbreak.

*concitatam multitudinem reprimere*—to allay the excitement of the mob.

*plebem continere*—to hold the people in one's power, in check.

## 9. PROSCRIPTION—CONFISCATION—BANISHMENT—AMNESTY

*proscribere aliquem* or *alicuius*
  *possessiones* } to proscribe a person,
*aqua et igni interdicere alicui* } declare him an outlaw.

*in proscriptorum numerum referre aliquem* (Rosc. Am. 11. 32)—to place a person's name on the list of the proscribed.

*e proscriptorum numero eximere aliquem* — to erase a person's name from the list of the proscribed.

*bona alicuius publicare* (B. G. 5. 54)—to confiscate a person's property.

*bona alicui restituere*—to restore to a person his confiscated property.

*in exsilium eicere* or *expellere aliquem*
*ex urbe (civitate) expellere, pellere aliquem*
*de, e civitate aliquem eicere*
} to banish a person, send him into exile.

*exterminare (ex) urbe, de civitate aliquem* (Mil. 37. 101)— to expel a person from the city, country.

*e patria exire iubere aliquem*—to banish a man from his native land.

*patria carere*—to be in exile.

*interdicere alicui Italiâ*—to banish a person from Italy.

*aliquem exsilio afficere, multare*—to punish by banishment.

*in exsilium ire, pergere, proficisci*
*exsulatum ire* or *abire*
} to go into exile.

*solum vertere, mutare* (Caecin. 34. 100)—to leave one's country (only used of exiles).

*exsulare* (Div. 2. 24. 52)
*in exsilio esse, exsulem esse*
} to live in exile.

*aliquem (in patriam) restituere*—to recall from exile.

*in patriam redire*—to return from exile.

*ante actarum (praeteritarum) rerum oblivio* or simply *oblivio* —amnesty (ἀμνηστία).

*omnem memoriam discordiarum oblivione sempiterna delere* (Phil. 1. 1. 1)—to proclaim a general amnesty.

*postliminium* (De Or. 1. 40. 181)—a returning from exile to one's former privileges.

## 10. POWER—MONARCHY—ROYALTY

*imperium, rerum summam deferre alicui*[1] — to confer supreme power on a person.

*rem publicam alicui permittere*—to give some one unlimited power in state affairs.

*imperium tenere (in aliquem)*—to have power over some one.

*imperium obtinere*—to maintain power, authority.

*principatu deici* (B. G. 7. 63)—to be deposed from one's leading position.

*cum imperio esse* (cf. p. 249)—to have unlimited power ; to be invested with *imperium*.

*in imperio esse*—to hold a high office (such as conferred *imperium*, i.e. *consulatus, dictatura, praetura*).

*imperium in annum prorogare*—to prolong the command for a year.

*imperium deponere* (Rep. 2. 12. 23)—to lay down one's power.

*imperium singulare*[2]—absolute power ; autocracy.

*dominari in aliquem*—to have unlimited power over a person.

*imperium, regnum, tyrannidem*[3] *occupare*—to take upon oneself absolute power.

---

[1] *deferre* in the sense " confer," " attribute," is also constructed with *ad ;* when it means to bring news, give information, it always takes *ad.*

[2] Cf. *certamen singulare,* a fight of one individual with another, a duel (cf. xvi. 10a). *singularis* also has the meaning "unique," "pre-eminent," e.g. *singularis virtus.*

[3] *tyrannus, tyrannis, tyrannicus* are rarely used in the Greek sense, irresponsible sovereign, etc., but usually mean despot, despotic, etc. The pure Latin equivalents are *rex, dominus, dominatio, imperium, regius,* or if there is emphasis on the cruelty of despots, *dominus saevus, crudelis et superba dominatio,* etc,

*rerum potiri*—(1) to usurp supreme power, (2) to be in a position of power.

*dominatio impotens*
*potestas immoderata, infinita* } despotic, tyrannous rule.

*tyrannidem concupiscere*—to aspire to a despotism.

*tyrannidem sibi parĕre aliqua re*—to establish oneself as despot, tyrant by some means.

*regnum appetere* (B. G. 7. 4)—to aspire to the sovereignty.

*regnum adipisci*—to obtain the sovereignty, kingly office.

*alicui regnum deferre, tradere*—to invest some one with royal power.

*aliquem regem, tyrannum constituere*—to establish some one as king, tyrant.

*regem restituere*
*aliquem in regnum restituere* } to restore a king to his throne (not *in solium*).

*aliquem regno spoliare* or *expellere* (Div. 1. 22. 74)—to depose a king.

*regios spiritus sibi sumere*—to assume a despotic tone.


## 11. SLAVERY—FREEDOM

*servitute premi* (Phil. 4. 1. 3)—to languish in slavery.

*liberum populum servitute afficere*—to enslave a free people.

*aliquem in servitutem redigere*—to reduce to slavery.

*alicui servitutem iniungere, imponere*—to lay the yoke of slavery on some one.

*civitatem servitute oppressam tenere* (Dom. 51. 131)—to keep the citizens in servile subjection.

*libertatem populo eripere*—to rob a people of its freedom.

*populum liberum esse, libertate uti, sui iuris essè pati*—to grant a people its independence.

*aliquem in servitutem abducere, abstrahere*—to carry off into slavery.

*aliquem sub corona, sub hasta, vendere* (B. G. 3. 16)—to sell a prisoner of war as a slave.

*iugum servitutis accipere*—to submit to the yoke of slavery.

*libertas, libertatis studium*—independent spirit.

*imperium oppugnare, percellere*—to attack, overthrow a tyranny.

*ad libertatem conclamare*—to summon to liberty.

*ad arma conclamare* (Liv. 3. 50)—to call to arms.

*vincula rumpere*—to burst one's chains.

*iugum servitutis excutere*
*iugum servile a cervicibus deicere* (Phil. 1. 2. 6)
*servitutem exuere* (Liv. 34. 7) } to shake off the yoke of slavery.

*iugum servile alicui demere*
*ab aliquo servitutem* or *servitutis iugum depellere* } to deliver some one from slavery.

*dominationem* or *dominatum refringere*
*regios spiritus reprimere* (Nep. Dion 5. 5) } to destroy a despotism, tyranny.

*libertatem recuperare*—to recover liberty.

*rem publicam in libertatem vindicare a* or *ex dominatione*—to deliver the state from a tyranny.


## 12. REVENUE—COLONIES—PROVINCES

*vectigalia redimere, conducere*—to farm the revenues.

*vectigalia exercere* (*vid.* p. 51, note)—to collect the taxes.

*vectigalia exigere* (*acerbe*)—to exact the taxes (with severity).

*pecuniam cogere a civitatibus*—to extort money from the communities.

*vectigalia, tributa*[1] *pendĕre*—to pay taxes.

*immunis* (*tributorum*) (Verr. 5. 21. 51)—exempt from taxation.

*immunitatem omnium rerum habere*—to enjoy absolute immunity.

*vectigalia, tributa alicui imponere*—to impose tribute on some one.

*tributorum multitudine premi*—to be crushed by numerous imposts.

*ager publicus*—public land ; state domain.

*agros assignare* (Leg. Agr. 1. 6. 17)—to allot land.

*pecunia publica, quae ex metallis redit*—the public income from the mines.

*avertere pecuniam* (Verr. 2. 1. 4)⎱ to embezzle money.
*peculatum facere* (Rab. Perd. 3. 8)⎰

*rem publicam quaestui habere*—to enrich oneself at the expense of the state.

*coloniam deducere in aliquem locum* (*vid.* p. 186, note)—to found a colony somewhere.

*colōnos mittere* (Div. 1. 1. 3)—to send out colonists.

*coloniam constituere* (Leg. Agr. 1. 5. 16)—to found a colony.

*provinciam*[2] *alicui decernere, mandare*—to entrust some one with an official duty, a province.

---

[1] *vectigalia*=indirect taxes, including, for example, *decumae*, the tenth, tithe of corn ; *scriptura*, the duty on pasturage ; *portorium*, harbour-toll. *tributum*=direct tax on incomes.

[2] *provincia* originally means a sphere of activity, an employ, especially of magistrates ; it then means the administration of a country outside Italy conquered in war, and lastly the country itself, a province. The senate each year determined on the countries to which magistrates were to be sent (*provincias nominare, decernere*).

*provincias sortiri* (Liv. 38. 35)—to draw lots for the provinces.

*alicui Syria (sorte) obvēnit, obtigit*—the province of Syria has fallen to some one's lot.

*provincias inter se comparant*—(the magistrates) arrange among themselves the administration of the provinces, the official spheres of duty.

*in provinciam proficisci* (Liv. 38. 35)—to set out for one's province.

*provincias permutare*—to exchange provinces.

*provinciam administrare, obtinere*—to manage, govern a province.

*provinciam obire*—to visit, traverse a province.

(*de* or *ex*) *provincia decedere* or simply *decedere* (*vid.* p. 14, note)—to leave a province (at the termination of one's term of office).

## 13. MAGISTRACIES

### (*a*) CANDIDATURE—ELECTION

*petere magistratum, honores*—to seek office.

*ambire*[1] *aliquem* (always with Acc. of person)—to solicit the vote or favour of some one.

*nomen profiteri* or simply *profiteri*—to become a candidate.

*manus prensare*[2] (De Or. 1. 24. 112)—to shake hands with voters in canvassing.

---

[1] Hence *ambitio*, legitimate canvassing; *ambitus*, illegal canvassing.

[2] Under the head of *ambitionis occupatio* (De Or. 1. 1. 1) are enumerated *salutare, rogare, supplicare, manus prensare, invitare ad prandium,* and sometimes *convivia tributim data.* For the whole subject *vid.* Q. Cicero's book *de petitione consulatus ad M. fratrem.*

*nomina appellat* (*nomenclator*) — the agent (*nomenclator*) mentions the names of constituents to the canvasser.

*competītor* (Brut. 30. 113)—a rival candidate.

*multa* (*pauca*) *puncta in centuria* (*tribu*) *aliqua ferre*[1]—to obtain many (few) votes in a century or tribe.

*centuriam, tribum ferre* (Planc. 49)—to gain the vote of a century or tribe.

*omnes centurias ferre* or *omnium suffragiis, cunctis centuriis creari*—to be elected unanimously.

*repulsam ferre consulatus* (*a populo*) (Tusc. 5. 19. 54)—to fail in one's candidature for the consulship.

*magistratus vitio creati*—magistrates elected irregularly (*i.e.* either when the auspices have been unfavourable or when some formality has been neglected).

*sufficere aliquem in alicuius locum* or *alicui*—to elect a man to fill the place of another who has died whilst in office.

*alicui* or *in alicuius locum succedere*—to succeed a person in an office.

*alicui imperatori succedere*—to succeed some one as general.

*suo* (*legitimo*) *anno creari* (opp. *ante annum*)—to be elected at the age required by law (*lex Villia annalis*).

*continuare magistratum* (Sall. Iug. 37. 2)—to continue one's office for another year.

*continuare alicui magistratum*—to prolong some one's office for another year.

---

[1] In counting the votes polled, a dot or mark was put opposite a candidate's name as often as a tablet (*tabella*) with his name on it came up. Hence *punctum ferre*, to be successful, e.g. Hor. A. P. 343 *omne tulit punctum qui miscuit utile dulci.*

*prorogare alicui imperium* (*in annum*)—to prolong a person's command.

*magistratus et imperia* (Sall. Iug. 3. 1)—civil and military offices.

*inire magistratum*—to enter into office.

*munus administrare, gerere*
*munere fungi, muneri praeesse*}to perform official duties.

*honores alicui mandare, deferre*—to invest a person with a position of dignity.

*muneri aliquem praeficere, praeponere*—to appoint some one to an office.

*munus explere, sustinere*—to fulfil the duties of one's position.

*abdicare se magistratu* (Div. 2. 35)—to resign one's post (before the expiry of the term of office).

*deponere* [1] *magistratum*⎫to give up, lay down office (usual-
*abire magistratu*　　　 ⎬ly at the end of one's term of
*de potestate decedere*　⎭office).

*res ad interregnum venit* or *adducitur*—an interregnum ensues.

*abrogare alicui munus* (Verr. 2. 57)—to remove a person from his office.

*abrogare alicui imperium*—to deprive a person of his position as commandant.

*viri clari et honorati* (De Sen. 7. 22)—men of rank and dignity.

*honoribus ac reipublicae muneribus*⎫
　*perfunctus* (De Or. 1. 45)　　　 ⎬a man who has held
*amplis honoribus usus* (Sall. Iug.⎜many offices.
　25. 4)　　　　　　　　　　　　 ⎭

---

[1] But *deponere* is also found in the sense of *abdicare*, e.g. B. G. 7. 33. 4 ; N. D. 2. 11 ; Liv. 2. 28. 9.

## (*b*) Particular Magistracies

*consulem creare* [1]—to elect a consul.

*aliquem consulem declarare* (Leg. Agr. 2. 2. 4)—to declare a person consul-elect.

*aliquem consulem renuntiare* (De Or. 2. 64. 260)—to officially proclaim (by the *praeco*, herald) a man elected consul ; to return a man consul.

*bis consul*—twice consul.

*iterum, tertium consul*—consul for the second, third time.

*sextum* (Pis. 9. 20), *septimum consul*—consul for the sixth, seventh time.

*videant* or *dent operam consules, ne quid res publica detrimenti capiat* [2] (Catil. 1. 2. 4)—let the consuls take measures for the protection of the state.

*in hoc praeclaro consulatu*—during this brilliant consulship.

*aetas consularis*—the consular age (43 years).

*pro consule in Ciliciam proficisci*—to go to Cilicia as proconsul.

*superiore consulatu*—in his former consulship.

*dictatorem dicere* (*creare*)—to name a person dictator.

*dictaturam gerere*—to be dictator.

*dictator dicit* (*legit*) *magistrum equitum*—a dictator appoints a *magister equitum.*

*potestatem habet in aliquem vitae necisque* (B. G. 1. 16. 5)—he has power over life and death.

*lictores summovent turbam* (Liv. 4. 50)—the lictors clear the way.

---

[1] *creare* is used of any magistrate regularly elected. The *locus classicus* on this subject is Cic. De Leg. 3. 3. 6-12.

[2] This formula conferred absolute power on the consuls. This was done only in cases of great emergency, and was somewhat similar to our " declaration of martial law."

*fasces praeferre, summittere* — to walk before with the fasces ; to lower the fasces.

*censores censent populum*—the censors hold a census of the people.

*censum habere, agere* (Liv. 3. 22)—to hold the census.

*censuram agere, gerere*—to perform censors' duties.

*locare aedes, vias faciendas* (Phil. 9. 7. 16)—to receive tenders for the construction of temples, highroads.

*locare opera publica*—to let out public works to contract.

*redimere, conducere porticum aedificandam* (Div. 2. 21. 47) —to undertake a contract for building a portico.

*nota, animadversio censoria*—the reprimand of a censor.

*notare aliquem ignominia* (Cluent. 43. 119)—to brand a person with infamy.

*censu prohibere, excludere*—to strike off the burgess-roll.

*tribu movere aliquem*—to expel some one from his tribe.

*e senatu eicere*⎱
*senatu movere*⎰ to expel from the senate.

*lustrum condere* (Liv. 1. 44. 2)—to complete the censorship (by certain formal purificatory ceremonies = *lustro faciendo*).

*tribuni plebis sacrosancti* (Liv. 3. 19. 10)—the plebeian tribunes, whose persons are inviolable.

*appellare*[1] *tribunos plebis* (*in aliqua re a praetore*) (Liv. 2. 55) —to appeal to the plebeian tribunes against a praetor's decision.

*provocare*[2] *ad populum* (Liv. 2. 55)—to appeal to the people.

*intercessio tribunicia* (cf. p. 218)—the tribunicial veto.

---

[1] *appellare* as a legal technical term only occurs in classical Latin in the formula *te, vos appello*.

[2] *provocare* only with proper names, e.g. *ad Catonem provocare*. To appeal to some one's pity, etc. = *implorare alicuius misericordiam, fidem*, etc.

## 14. THE SENATE

*publicum consilium* (Phil. 7. 7. 19)—the council of the
nation ; the senate.

*in senatum legere,*[1] *eligere*—to elect to the senate.

*senatum vocare, convocare*—to call a meeting of the senate.

*senatum cogere* (Liv. 3. 39)—to assemble the senate.

*edicere,*[2] *ut senatus frequens adsit* (Fam. 11. 6. 2)—to issue
a proclamation calling on the senators to assemble
in full force.

*senatum habere*—to hold a sitting of the senate.

*ad senatum referre*[3] (Cic. dom. 53. 136)—to bring a
question before the senate (of the presiding
magistrate).

*patres* (*senatum*) *consulere de aliqua re* (Sall. Iug. 28)—to
consult the senators on a matter.

*sententiam rogare, interrogare*—to ask the opinion of . . .

*sententiam dicere*—to give an opinion (also used of a
judge, cf. p. 79).

*senatus sententia inclīnat ad* . . . (De Sen. 6. 16)—the
senate inclines to the opinion, decides for . . .

*sententia vincit* (Liv. 2. 4. 3)—the majority were of the
opinion . . .

*maior pars*—the majority.

[1] Distinct from *senatum legere* = to read over and revise the list of
senators (used of the censor). The head of the list was called
*princeps senatus.*

[2] *edicere, edictum*, technical terms ; *edicere* is used of the praetor
deciding how a case is to be tried, cf. Verr. 2. 1. 41 ; Flacc. 28. 67.
Then more generally of an order, declaration, proclamation. The
senate was convened by the *praeco* or by means of a notice posted in
some public place (*edictum*).

[3] A meeting of the senate opened by a declaration of the agenda
by the presiding magistrate, a consul, praetor, or tribune. This was
called *referre ad senatum.*

*quid censes ? quid tibi videtur ?*⎱
⎰ what is your opinion ?
*quid de ea re fieri placet ?*

*discessionem facere* (Sest. 34. 74)—to take the vote (by division).

*discedere (pedibus), ire in alicuius sententiam*[1] (Liv. 23. 10)— to vote for some one's motion.

*senatus decrevit (populusque iussit) ut*—the senate decreed (and the people ratified the decree) that . . .

*senatus consultum fit* (Att. 2. 24. 3)—a resolution of the senate (not opposed by a tribunicial veto) was made.

*senatus auctoritas*—the opinion of the senate in general.

*senatum alicui dare* (Q. Fr. 2. 11. 2)—to give a man audience before the senate.

*a senatu res ad populum reicitur*—a matter is referred (for decision) from the senate to the people.

*dicendi mora diem extrahere, eximere, tollere*—to pass the whole day in discussion.

*dimittere senatum*[1]—to dismiss the senate.

*nox senatum dirimit*—night breaks up the sitting.

---

[1] After the *rogatio sententiarum* came the voting, usually by division (*per discessionem, pedibus ire in sententiam*), but in cases of doubt each member was asked his opinion (*per singulorum sententias exquisitas*). The presiding officer then dismissed the meeting with the words *nihil vos moramur, patres conscripti,* "I need not detain you any longer." From this formula probably came the colloquial uses—(1) "I do not care for . . .," "I have no interest in . . ." (with the Acc.) ; (2) "I have nothing against . . .," "you have my consent to . . ." (with the Acc. and Inf. or *quominus*).

# XV. LAW AND JUSTICE

## 1. LAW IN GENERAL

*ius dicere* ⎫ to administer justice (said of the
*ius reddere* (Liv. 3. 33) ⎭ praetor).

*ius suum persequi*—to assert one's right.

*ius suum adipisci* (Liv. 1. 32. 10)—to obtain justice.

*ius suum tenere, obtinere*—to maintain one's right.

*de iure suo decedere* or *cedere*—to waive one's right.

*(ex) iure, lege agere cum aliquo*—to go to law with a person.

*summo iure agere cum aliquo* (cf. *summum ius, summa iniuria*)—to proceed against some one with the utmost rigour of the law ; to strain the law in one's favour.

*in ius, in iudicium vocare aliquem*—to summon some one before the court.

*diem dicere alicui*—to summon some one to appear on a given day ; to accuse a person.

*in iudicium venire, in iudicio adesse*—to appear in court.

*iudicia administrare*—to have charge of the administration of justice.

*iudicium exercere* (*vid.* p. 51, note)—to administer justice ; to judge (used of criminal cases before the praetor).

*iudicio praeesse*—to be president of a court.

*conventus agere* (B. G. 1. 54)—to convene the assizes (used of a provincial governor).

*quaestiones perpetuae* (Brut. 27. 106)—the standing commissions of inquiry.

*aliquem in integrum* (*vid.* p. 47, note) *restituere*—to reinstate a person in his right.

(1) *respondere* [1] (*de iure* or *ius*)—to give a legal opinion, decision on points of law.

(2) *cavere* (*in iure*) (Off. 2. 65)—to point out what precautions, what formal steps must be taken to insure immunity.

(3) *agere*—to be energetic in the conduct of the case; to plead before the judge.

*aequum iudicem se alicui praebere*—to judge some one equitably.

*ex aequo et bono* (Caecin. 23. 65)—justly and equitably.

*iudex incorruptus*—an impartial judge.

*ratio iudiciorum*—judicial organisation.

*aequa iuris descriptio* (Off. 2. 4. 15)—a sound judicial system.

*aequo iure vivere cum aliquo*—to live with some one on an equal footing.

*iustitium indicere, edicere* (Phil. 5. 12)—to proclaim that the courts are closed, a cessation of legal business.

*iustitium remittere*—to re-open the courts.

*ius ad artem redigere*—to reduce law to a system.

*ius nullum*—absence of justice.

*ius ac fas omne delere*  
*omnia iura pervertere* } to trample all law under foot.

*contra ius fasque*—against all law, human and divine.

*optimo iure*—with full right.

---

[1] In full *consulenti respondere*. From this consultation lawyers got the title *iuris* or *iure consulti*. In these three points, *respondere, cavere, agere,* consisted the practical duty of a jurist. Cicero, however (De Or. 1. 48), adds *scribere* = to draw up legal instruments such as wills, contracts, etc.

*ius praecipuum, beneficium, donum,* also *immunitas* [1] c. Gen.
—prerogative, privilege.

## 2. INQUIRY—TESTIMONY—TORTURE

*aliquid, causam cognoscere* } to hold an inquiry into a
*quaerere aliquid* or *de aliqua re* }   matter.

*quaestionem habere de aliquo, de aliqua re* or *in aliquem*—
to examine a person, a matter.

*quaestioni praeesse*—to preside over an inquiry.

*quaesītor*—the examining judge.

*incognita causa* (cf. p. 241, *indicta causa*)—without any
examination.

*in tabulas publicas referre aliquid*—to enter a thing in the
public records.

*deprehendere aliquem (in aliqua re)*—to catch a person,
find him out.

*deprehendere aliquem in manifesto scelere*—to take a person
in the act.

*testis gravis*—an important witness.

*testis locuples*—a witness worthy of all credit.

*testis incorruptus atque integer*—an impartial witness.

*aliquem testem alicuius rei (in aliquid) citare*—to cite a
person to give evidence on a matter.

*aliquem testem adhibere* }
*aliquo teste uti* } to use some one's evidence.

*aliquem testem dare, edere, pro-*
  *ferre* } to produce as a witness.
*aliquem testem producere* }

---

[1] *privilegium* in this sense is post-classical. In classical prose it
denotes a law passed for or against an individual (*privus*), e.g.
*privilegium ferre, irrogare de aliquo* (Cic.)

*testem prodire* (*in aliquem*)—to appear as witness against a person.

*testimonium dicere pro aliquo*—to give evidence on some one's behalf.

*pro testimonio dicere*—to state as evidence.

*testibus teneri, convictum esse*—to be convicted by some one's evidence.

*alicui admovere tormenta*
*quaerere tormentis de aliquo*⎫to have a person tortured.

*de servis quaerere* (*in dominum*)—to examine slaves by torture.

*cruciatūs tormentorum*—the pains of torture.

*aliquem a ceteris separare et in arcam conicere ne quis cum eo colloqui possit* (Mil. 22. 60)—to isolate a witness.

## 3. PROCESS—DEFENCE

*causa privata*—a civil case.

*causa publica* (Brut. 48. 178)—a criminal case.

*causam alicuius agere* (*apud iudicem*)—to conduct a person's case (said of an agent, solicitor).

*causam dicere, orare* (Brut. 12. 47)—to address the court (of the advocate).

*causam dicere*—to defend oneself before the judge (of the accused).

*causam dicere pro aliquo*—to defend a person.

*causam alicuius defendere*—to conduct some one's defence in a case.

*causam optimam habere* (Lig. 4. 10)—to have a good case.

*causam inferiorem dicendo reddere superiorem* (τὸν ἥττω λόγον κρείττω ποιεῖν) (Brut. 8. 30)—to gain a weak case by clever pleading.

*patronus*[1] (*causae*) (De Or. 2. 69)—counsel ; advocate.

*causam suscipere*
*ad causam aggredi* or *accedere* } to undertake a case.

*indicta causa* (opp. *cognita causa*)—without going to law.

*litem alicui intendere*—to go to law with, sue a person.

*adhuc sub iudice lis est* (Hor. A. P. 77)—the case is still undecided.

*lites componere* (Verg. Ecl. 3. 108)—to arrange a dispute (by arbitration).

*causam* or *litem obtinere*
*causā* or *iudicio vincere* } to win a case.

*causam* or *litem amittere, per-*
      *dere*
*causā* or *lite cadere* (owing to
      some informality) } to lose one's case.

*calumniae litium* (Mil. 27. 74)—chicanery (specially of wrongfully accusing an innocent man).

## 4. ACCUSATION—VERDICT—DECISION

*accusatio* (Cael. 3. 6)—a criminal accusation.

*actio, petitio*—a private, civil prosecution.

*nomen alicuius deferre* (*apud praetorem*) (Verr. 2. 38. 94)—to accuse, denounce a person.

*referre in reos aliquem*—to put some one on the list of the accused.

*eximere de reis aliquem*—to strike a person's name off the list of the accused.

*aliquis reus fit* (Fam. 13. 54)—some one is accused.

---

[1] They were not called *advocati* till under the Empire. In Augustan Latin *advocatus = amicus qui adest alicui* (*in iudicio*), i.e. a man who supported his friend by his presence and influence.

*iudices reicere* (Verr. 3. 11. 28)—to challenge, reject jury-
men.

*crimina diluere, dissolvere*—to refute charges.

*accusare aliquem rei capitalis (rerum capitalium)*—to charge
some one with a capital offence.

*caput alicuius agitur (vid.* p. 53)—a person's life is in
jeopardy.

*accusare aliquem peculatus, pecuniae publicae*—to accuse
some one of malversation, embezzlement of public
money.

*accusare aliquem falsarum tabularum* [1]—to accuse a person
of forging the archives.

*postulare aliquem repetundarum* [2] or *de repetundis*—to accuse
a person of extortion (to recover the sums extorted).

*accusare aliquem perduellionis*—to charge a person with
treason (hostile conduct against the state generally).

*accusare aliquem maiestatis*—to accuse a person of high
treason (more specific than the preceding).

*accusare aliquem ambitus, de ambitu*—to accuse some one
of illegal canvassing.

*accusare aliquem de vi, de veneficiis*—to accuse a person of
violence, poisoning.

*accusare aliquem inter sicarios* (Rosc. Am. 32. 90)—to
accuse a person of assassination.

*sententiae iudicum*—the finding of the jury.

*sententiam ferre, dicere* (Off. 3. 16. 66)—to give sentence
(of the judge, cf. p. 79, note).

---

[1] Cf. *tabulas publicas corrumpere* (Rosc. Am. 128) ; *commutare,* to
falsify public records.

[2] Extortion generally can be rendered by *violenta exactio pecuniarum,* or some verbal periphrasis (e.g. *per vim capere pecunias,*
etc.)

*iudicare causam* (*de aliqua re*)—to decide on the conduct
of the case.

*iudicium rescindere* ⎱ to rescind a de-
*res iudicatas rescindere* (Cic. Sull. 22. 63) ⎰ cision.

*lege Plautia damnari* (Sall. Cat. 31. 4)—to be condemned
under the Lex Plautia.

## 5. GUILT

*in culpa esse*—to be at fault ; to blame ; culpable.

*culpa alicuius rei est in aliquo*—some one is to blame in a
matter ; it is some one's fault.

*mea culpa est*—it is my fault.

*culpa carere, vacare* ⎫
*extra culpam esse* ⎬ to be free from blame.
*abesse a culpa* ⎭

*prope abesse a culpa* ⎫ to be almost culpable.
*affinem esse culpae* ⎭

*culpam in aliquem conferre, transferre, conicere*—to put the
blame on another.

*culpam alicui attribuere, assignare*—to attribute the fault to
some one.

*aliquid alicui crimini dare, vitio vertere* (Verr. 5. 50)—to
reproach, blame a person for . . .

*culpam committere, contrahere* ⎱ to commit some blame-
*facinus, culpam in se admittere* ⎰ worthy action.

*non committere, ut* . . .—to take care not to . . .

*culpam alicuius rei sustinere*—to bear the blame of a thing.

*culpam a se amovere* [1]—to exonerate oneself from blame.

*veniam dare alicui*—to pardon a person.

---

[1] Note *purgare aliquid*, to justify oneself in a matter ; *se alicui
purgare de aliqua re* (Fam. 12. 25) ; *alicui purgatum esse* (B. G.
1. 28).

## 6. PUNISHMENT—ACQUITTAL

*poena afficere aliquem* (Off. 2. 5. 18)⎫
*animadvertere in aliquem*         ⎬ to punish some one.
*punire aliquem*
*ulcisci aliquem* (*pro aliqua re*) ⎭

*poenas alicuius persequi* ⎫
*poenam petere, repetere ab aliquo* ⎪ to exact a penalty from
*poenas expetere ab aliquo*     ⎬   some one.
*supplicium sumere de aliquo* ⎭

*hanc poenam constituere in aliquem, ut* . . .—to ordain as
    punishment that . . .

*graviter consulere in aliquem* (Liv. 8. 13)—to deal severely
    with a person.

*poenas* (*graves*) *dare alicui*—to be (heavily) punished by
    some one.

*poenas alicui pendĕre* (*alicuius rei*)—to be punished by some
    one (on account of a thing).

*poenas dependĕre, expendĕre, sol-*⎫
  *vere, persolvere*           ⎬ to suffer punishment.
*poenam* (*alicuius rei*) *ferre, per-*⎪
  *ferre* ⎭

*poenam luere* (*alicuius rei*) (Sull. 27. 76)—to be punished
    for a thing, expiate it.

*luere*[1] *aliquid aliqua re* (De Sen. 20)—to atone for some-
    thing by . . .

*poenam subire*—to submit to a punishment.

*pecunia multare aliquem*—to condemn some one to a
    fine.

---

[1] To express the passive use *expiari*, e.g. *scelus supplicio expiatum est*.

*multam irrogare alicui* (Cic. dom. 17. 45)—to impose a
    fine (used of the prosecutor or the *tribunus plebis*
    proposing a fine to be ratified by the people).

*decem milibus aeris damnari*—to be fined 10,000 asses.

*in vincula (custodiam) dare aliquem* ⎫
*in vincula, in catenas conicere ali-* ⎬ to put some one in
*quem*     ⎭ irons, chains.

*in carcerem conicere aliquem*—to throw some one into prison.

*capitis* or *capite damnare aliquem*—to condemn some one
    to death.

*capitis absolvere aliquem* — to repeal a death-sentence
    passed on a person.

*supplicium alicui decernere, in aliquem constituere*—to decree
    the penalty of death.

*Solo capite sanxit, si quis* . . . (Att. 10. 1)—Solon made
    it a capital offence to . . .

*morte multare aliquem* (Catil. 1. 11. 28)—to punish any
    one with death.

*supplicium sumere de aliquo* — to execute the death-
    sentence on a person.

*supplicio (capitis) affici*—to suffer capital punishment.

*ad palum deligare* (Liv. 2. 5)—to bind to the stake.

*virgis caedere*—to beat with rods.

*securi percutere, ferire aliquem*—to execute a person, cut
    off his head.

*in crucem agere, tollere aliquem* ⎫
*cruci suffigere aliquem*     ⎬ to crucify.

*impune fecisse, tulisse aliquid*—to go unpunished.

*impunitum aliquem dimittere*—to let a person go scot-free.

*mortem* [1] *deprecari* (B. G. 7. 40. 6)—to beg for life.

---

[1] One can also say *vitam, salutem deprecari*, as *deprecari* means
(1) to obtain by supplication, (2) to avert by supplication.

# XVI. WAR

## 1. LEVIES—MILITARY OATH—ARMIES IN GENERAL

*aetas militaris*—military age.

*qui arma ferre possunt* or *iuventus*—men of military age.

*qui per aetatem arma ferre non possunt* or *aetate ad bellum inutiles*—men exempt from service owing to age.

*exercitum conficere* (Imp. Pomp. 21. 61)—to raise an army.

*milites (exercitum) scribere, conscribere*—to levy troops.

*dilectum habere*—to hold a levy.

*imperare milites civitatibus*—to compel communities to provide troops.

*nomen (nomina) dare, profiteri*—to enlist oneself.

*ad nomen non respondere* (Liv. 7. 4)—to fail to answer one's name.

*militiam* (only in the sing.) *capessere*—to take service in the army.

*militiam detrectare, subterfugere*—to try to avoid military service.

*excusare morbum, valetudinem*—to plead ill-health as an excuse for absence.

*militiae vacationem habere*—to be excused military duty.

*equo, pedibus merere* (Liv. 27. 11)—to serve in the cavalry, infantry.

*sacramentum (o) dicere* (*vid.* p. 179, note)—to take the military oath.

*milites sacramento rogare, adigere*—to make soldiers take the military oath.

*evocare undique copias*—to call up troops from all sides.

*evocati, voluntarii* (B. G. 5. 56)—the volunteers.

*omnes ad arma convocare*—to issue a general call to arms.

*efficere duas legiones*—to form two legions.

*complere legiones* (B. C. 1. 25)—to fill up the numbers of the legions.

*supplementum cogere, scribere, legere*—to levy recruits to fill up the strength.

*auxilia*[1] *arcessere*—to summon auxiliary troops.

*copias (arma) cum aliquo iungere* or *se cum aliquo iungere*— to join forces with some one.

*conducere, contrahere copias*—to concentrate troops.

*cogere omnes copias in unum locum*—to concentrate all the troops at one point.

*parare exercitum, copias*—to equip an army, troops.

*alere exercitum* (Off. 1. 8. 25)—to support an army.

*recensere, lustrare, recognoscere exercitum* (Liv. 42. 31)—to review an army.

*dimittere exercitum*—to disband an army.

*commeatum militibus dare* (opp. *petere*)—to give furlough, leave of absence to soldiers.

*magnae copiae* (not *multae*)—a large force, many troops.

*exiguae copiae* (Fam. 3. 3. 2)—a small force.

*ingens, maximus exercitus* (not *numerosus*)—a numerous army.

*robora peditum*—the flower of the infantry.

*milites levis armaturae*—light infantry.

---

[1] *auxilia* = auxiliary troops raised in the provinces, usually light cavalry. In Caesar's army the cavalry consisted of Gaulish, Spanish, and German auxiliaries. A thousand of these were attached to each legion and were usually commanded by a Roman officer.

*vetus miles, veteranus miles* ⎱veterans; experienced
*qui magnum in castris usum habent*⎰ troops.

*expeditus* (opp. *impeditus*) *miles*—a soldier lightly armed,
ready for battle.

*exercitatus in armis*—practised in arms.

*milites tumultuarii*[1] (opp. *exercitus iustus*) (Liv. 35. 2)—
soldiers collected in haste ; irregulars.

*tirones*—recruits.


## 2. PAY—SERVICE—COMMISSARIAT

*stipendium*[2] *dare, numerare, persolvere militibus*—to pay
the troops.

*stipendia facere, merere*—to serve.

*emeritis stipendiis* (Sall. Iug. 84. 2)—after having completed
one's service.

*militia functum, perfunctum esse*⎫
*rude donatum esse*[3] (Phil. 2. 29)⎭to retire from service.

*milites mercennarii* or *exercitus conducticius*—mercenary
troops.

*rem frumentariam comparare,*⎫
  *providere*                ⎪to look after the com-
*rei frumentariae prospicere* (B.⎬ missariat.
  G. 1. 23)                  ⎭

---

[1] *tumultus* is used of a sudden rising, rebellion, to repress which
all able-bodied men were called to arms. Such risings were particu-
larly common in Gaul, but cf. *tumultus servilis* (B. G. 1. 10);
*tumultus Istricus* (Liv. 41. 6. 1).

[2] *stipendium* first established in 406 B.C. ; it was paid at the end
of the campaign, hence *stipendia* often = campaigns, years of service.

[3] Used originally of gladiators, who on their retirement received
a staff or wooden sword (*rudis*), hence they were called *rudiarii*.
Cf. Ov. Tr. 4. 8. 24 *me quoque donari iam rude tempus erat.*

*frumentum providere exercitui*—to provide corn-supplies for the troops.

*frumenti vim maximam comparare*—to procure a very large supply of corn.

*intercludere commeatum*—to cut off the supplies, intercept them.

*intercludere, prohibere hostes commeatu* — to cut off all supplies of the enemy.

## 3. COMMAND—DISCIPLINE

*praeficere aliquem exercitui*—to place some one at the head of an army, give him the command.

*praeficere aliquem bello gerendo*—to charge some one with the conduct of a war.

*praeesse exercitui*—to be at the head of an army.

*magnum usum in re militari habere* (Sest. 5. 12)—to possess great experience in military matters.

*rei militaris rudem esse*—to have had no experience in war.

*vir fortissimus*—a hero.

*magnas res gerere*—to perform heroic exploits.

*res fortiter feliciterque gesta* ⎫ a success ; a glorious feat of
*res bene gesta* ⎭ arms.

*res gestae* [1]—exploits in war ; brilliant actions.

*summa belli, imperii* (B. G. 2. 4. 7)—the command-in-chief.

*cum imperio esse*—to hold a high command.

---

[1] Thus *magnae, memorabiles, praestantissimae res gestae*, and also *meae, tuae, suae*, etc. The phrase *rem gerere* can be used either of the combat (*proelium*) or the whole war (*bellum*), cf. B. G. 5. 44. 11 ; Off. 3. 108.

*imperii summam tenere* (Rep. 2. 28)⎫ to be commander-
*imperii summae praeesse* ⎭ in-chief.

*imperii summam deferre alicui* or *ad aliquem, tradere alicui*
—to appoint some one commander-in-chief.

*imperium transfertur ad aliquem* (not *transit*)—the command is transferred, passes to some one.

*imperium alicui abrogare* (Off. 3. 10)—to depose a person
from his command.

*modestia* [1] (opp. *immodestia*)—discipline (insubordina-
tion).

*dicto audientem esse alicui*—to obey a person's orders.

*milites disciplina coërcere* ⎫
*milites coërcere et in officio* ⎬ to keep good discipline
  *continere* (B. C. 1. 67. 4)⎭ amongst one's men.

## 4. WEAPONS

*arma capere, sumere*—to take up one's arms.

*arma expedire* (Tusc. 2. 16. 37)—to make ready for
battle.

*galeam induere*—to put on one's helmet.

*armis (castris) exuere aliquem*—to disarm a person.

*arma ponere* (not *deponere*)—to pile arms (cf. p. 189,
note).

*ab armis discedere* (Phil. 11. 33)—to lay down arms.

*in armis esse*—to be under arms.

*cum telo esse*—to be armed.

*extorquere arma e manibus*—to wrest weapons from some
one's hands.

---

[1] *modestia*, the character of the man who observes a mean (*qui
servat modum*), is used morally of self-restraint, moderation
(σωφροσύνη). In politics it means loyalty ; in the army, discipline.

*res ad arma venit*—matters have reached the fighting-stage.

*tela iacĕre, conicere, mittere*—to discharge missiles.

*extra teli iactum, coniectum esse*—to be out of range.

*ăd teli coniectum venire* (Liv. 2. 31)—to come within javelin-range.

*se obicere telis*—to expose oneself to missiles.

*eminus hastis, comminus gladiis uti*—to use javelins at a distance, swords at close quarters.

*gladium educere (e vagīna)*—to draw one's sword (from the scabbard).

*gladium in vaginam recondere*—to sheath one's sword.

*gladium stringere, destringere*—to draw one's sword.

*gladium alicui in pectus infigere*—to plunge one's sword in some one's breast.

*gladio aliquem per pectus transfigere* (Liv. 2. 46)—to transfix, pierce a man's breast with one's sword.

*sicam, cultrum in corde alicuius defigere*[1] (Liv. 1. 58)—to plunge a dagger, knife in some one's heart.

*decurrere (in armis)*—to manœuvre.

*vi et armis*—by force of arms.


## 5. WAR

*bellum parare*—to make preparations for war.

*apparatŭs* (rare in plur.) *belli*—preparations for war ; war-material.

*bellum indīcere, denuntiare*—to make formal declaration of war.

---

[1] *defigere* is also used metaphorically, e.g. *defigere omnes curas, cogitationes in rei publicae salute* (Phil. 14. 5. 13).

*res repetere* (*ab aliquo*) (Off. 1. 11. 36)—to demand satisfaction, restitution.

*res reddere* (*alicui*) (cf. p. 57)—to make restitution.

*bellum iustum* (*pium*)—a regular, formal war.

*bellum intestinum, domesticum* (opp. *bellum externum*)—a
civil war.

*bellum facere, movere, excitare*—to cause a war.

*bellum conflare* (Fam. 5. 2. 8)—to kindle a war.

*bellum moliri*—to meditate war.

*bellum incipere, belli initium facere* (B. G. 7. 1. 5)—to
commence hostilities.

*bello se interponere* (Liv. 35. 48)—to interfere in a war.

*bello implicari*—to be involved in a war.

*bellum cum aliquo inire*—to begin a war with some one.

*bellum impendet, imminet, instat*—a war is imminent.

*bellum oritur, exardescit*—war breaks out.

*omnia bello flagrant* or *ardent* (Fam. 4. 1. 2)—everywhere
the torch of war is flaming.

*bellum gerere cum aliquo*—to make war on a person.

*bellum coniungere* (Imp. Pomp. 9. 26)—to wage war in
conjunction with some one.

*bellum ducere, trahere, extrahere*—to protract, prolong a
war.

*omni studio in* (*ad*) *bellum incumbere*—to carry on a war
energetically.

*bellum inferre alicui* (Att. 9. 1. 3)—to invade.

*bellum* or *arma ultro inferre*—to be the aggressor in a
war ; to act on the offensive.

*bellum* (*inlatum*) *defendere*—to act on the defensive.

*proficisci ad bellum, in expeditionem* (Sall. Iug. 103)—to go
to war, commence a campaign.

*mittere ad bellum*—to send to the war.

*bellum administrare*—to have the control of the war.

*bello persequi aliquem, lacessere*—to harass with war.

*belli finem facere, bellum finire*—to put an end to a war.

*bellum conficere, perficere*—to terminate a war (by force of arms and defeat of one's opponents).

*bellum componere* (Fam. 10. 33)—to terminate a war (by a treaty, etc.)

*bellum transferre alio, in* . . .—to transfer the seat of war elsewhere.

*belli sedes* (Liv. 4. 31)—the seat of war, theatre of operations.

*rationem belli gerendi mutare* (Liv. 32. 31)—to change one's tactics.

## 6. THE ARMY ON THE MARCH

*agmen medium* (Liv. 10. 41)—the centre of the marching column.

*agmen primum*—the vanguard.

*agmen novissimum* (*extremum*)—the rearguard.

*agmen claudere, cogere*—to bring up the rear.

*signa* [1] *ferre, tollere* ⎫
*castra movere*      ⎬ to begin the march, break up the camp.
            ⎭

*agmen agere*—to set the army in motion.

---

[1] *signa* = standards of a maniple, cohort, or legion. Since Marius' time the *signum* of a legion was an eagle, those of the maniples different animals, wolf, horse, etc. In the camp the standards were fixed in the ground, in action they were carried in the front rank, hence several phrases—*signa convellere, tollere, efferre*, to break up camp ; *signa proferre, promovere*, to advance in battle-order ; *signa inferre*, to attack ; *signa conferre*, to come to close quarters ; *signa statuere*, to halt ; *signa convertere*, to change one's route ; *signa referre*, to retire ; *signa relinquere*, to desert, etc.

*procedere cum exercitu*—to advance with the army.

*magnis itineribus* (Sall. Iug. 37)—by forced marches.

*quam maximis itineribus* (*potest*)—by the longest possible forced marches.

*citatum agmen rapere*⎫ to lead the army with forced
*raptim agmen ducere* ⎭ marches.

*citato gradu incedere* (cf. p. 15)—to advance rapidly.

*loca, regiones, loci naturam explorare*—to reconnoitre the ground.

*iter facere*—to march.

*iter conficere* (B. C. 1. 70)—to traverse a route.

*iter maturare, accelerare*—to quicken the pace of marching.

*iter continuare* (B. C. 3. 11)—to march without interruption.

*iter non intermittere*—not to interrupt the march.

*iter flectere, convertere, avertere*⎫ to deviate, change the
*signa convertere* (B. G. 1. 25) ⎭ direction.

*averso itinere contendere in* . . .—to change one's route and march towards . . .

*iter tentare per vim* (cf. p. 11)—to force a way, a passage.

*agmen, exercitum demittere in* . . .—to march down on to . . .

*exercitum admovere, adducere ad* . . .—to advance on . . .

*signa sequi* (opp. *a signis discedere, signa relinquere*)—to follow the standards.

*ordines servare* (B. G. 4. 26)—to keep the ranks.

*confertis, solutis ordinibus*—with close ranks ; with ranks in disorder.

*raris ordinibus*—in open order.

*ordines turbare, perrumpere*—to break the ranks.

*agmine quadrato incedere, ire*—to march with closed ranks, in order of battle.

*agmine duplĭci, triplĭci*—in two, three columns.

*novissimos premere*—to press the rearguard.

*novissimos turbare*—to throw the rearguard into confusion.

*novissimos carpere*—to harass the rear.

*novissimis praesidio esse*—to protect the troops in the rear.

*opprimere hostes (imprudentes, incautos, inopinantes)*—to surprise and defeat the enemy.

*subsistere, consistere*
*gradum sistere* } to halt.

*capere, occupare locum*—to occupy a position (with troops).

*occupare loca superiora*—to occupy the high ground.

*praeoccupare locum* (Liv. 35. 27)—to occupy a place beforehand.

*tenere montem* (B. G. 1. 22)—to hold a mountain.

*consistere in monte*—to take up one's position on a mountain.

*considĕre sub monte (sub montis radicibus)*—to occupy the foot of a hill.

*praesidiis firmare urbem*
*praesidium collocare in urbe* } to garrison a town.

*praesidia, custodias disponere*—to station posts, pickets, at intervals.

*vigilias crebras ponere* (Sall. Iug. 45. 2)—to place a close line of sentry-posts.

## 7. THE CAMP

*castra stativa* (Sall. Iug. 44)—a permanent camp.

*castra hiberna, aestiva*—winter-quarters, summer-quarters.

*castra ponere, locare*—to encamp.

*idoneo, aequo, suo* (opp. *iniquo*) *loco*—in a favourable
  position.

*castra metari* (B. C. 3. 13)—to mark out a camp.

*milites in hibernis collocare, in hiberna deducere*—to take
  the troops to their winter-quarters.

*castra munire*—to make a fortified, entrenched camp.

*castra munire vallo* (*aggere*)—to fortify the camp with a
  rampart.

*fossam ducere*—to make a ditch, a fosse.

*vallum iacĕre, exstruere, facere*—to raise a rampart, earth-
  work.

*castra praesidiis firmare*—to strengthen the camp by
  outposts.

*praesidio castris milites relinquere*—to leave troops to
  guard the camp.

*castra coniungere, iungere* (B. C. 1. 63)—to make a camp
  in common.

*castra nudare* (B. G. 7. 70)—to leave the camp unde-
  fended.

*cohors, quae in statione est*—the cohort on guard-duty.

*vigilias agere in castris* (Verr. 4. 43)—to mount guard in
  the camp.

*custodias agere in vallo*—to keep watch on the rampart.

*stationes agere pro portis*—to be on duty before the gates.

*circumire vigilias* (Sall. Iug. 45. 2)—to make the round
  of the sentries.

*tesseram dare* (Liv. 28. 14)—to give the watchword,
  countersign.

*copias castris continere*—to keep the troops in camp.

*se* (*quietum*) *tenere castris*—to remain inactive in camp.

*excursionem in hostium agros facere*—to make an inroad
  into hostile territory.

*praedatum ire*—to go in search of plunder, booty.

*ferre atque agere* [1] *praedam*—to carry off booty.

*capere equos*—to capture horses.

*lignatum, aquatum ire*—to go to fetch wood, water.

*pabulatum, frumentatum ire*—to forage.

*pabulatione premi* (B. C. 1. 78)—to suffer from want of forage.

*omnia ferro ignique, ferro atque igni* or *ferro flammaque vastare*—to ravage with fire and sword.

*classicum* or *tuba canit ad praetorium*—the bugle, trumpet sounds before the general's tent.

*vasa conclamare* (B. C. 3. 37)—to give the signal for breaking up the camp, collecting baggage.

*vasa colligere* (Liv. 21. 47)—to pack the baggage (for marching).

*signa convellere* (*vid.* p. 253, note)—to pluck up the standards out of the ground (to begin the march).

*consilium habere, convocare*—to hold a council of war.

*rem ad consilium deferre*—to refer a matter to a council of war.


## 8. A SIEGE

*oppidum natura loci munitum* (B. G. 1. 38)—a town with a strong natural position.

*oppidum manu* (*opere*) *munitum*—a town artificially fortified.

*oppidum obsidere*
*oppidum obsidione claudere* } to besiege a city.

*oppidum in obsidione tenere*—to keep a town in a state of siege.

---

[1] *ferre* of things inanimate, *agere* of cattle.   Cf. φέρειν καὶ ἄγειν.

*oppidum fame domare*—to starve a town into surrender.

*oppidum oppugnare*—to storm a town.

*oppidum claudere operibus* (Nep. Milt. 7)—to invest a town with earthworks.

*oppidum cingere vallo et fossa*—to surround a town with a rampart and fosse.

*opera facere*—to raise siege-works.

*vineas agere* (B. G. 3. 21)—to advance pent-houses, mantlets.

*turres instituere, exstruere, excitare*—to raise towers.

*testudine facta moenia subire* (B. G. 2. 6)—to advance to the walls protected by a covering of shields.

*scalas admovere* (B. C. 3. 63)—to apply scaling-ladders.

*positis scalis muros ascendere*—to scale the walls by means of ladders.

*aries murum attingit, percutit*—the battering-ram strikes the wall.

*iter ruina patefactum*
*patentia ruinis* (*vid.* p. 185, note) } a breach. ·

*cuniculos agere* (B. G. 3. 21)—to make mines, subterraneous passages.

*oppidum tormentis verberare*—to rain missiles on a town, bombard it.

*tela ingerere, conicere*—to discharge showers of missiles.

*murum nudare defensoribus*—to drive the defenders from the walls.

*eruptionem facere ex oppido*
*crebras ex oppido excursiones*
*facere* (B. G. 2. 30) } to make a sally, sortie from the town.

*ignem inferre operibus* (B. C. 2. 14)—to set fire to the siege-works.

*subsidium alicui summittere*—to send relief to some one.

*munitiones perrumpere*—to break through the lines (and relieve a town).

*urbis obsidionem liberare* ⎱ to raise a siege (used of the
*oppidum obsidione liberare* ⎰ army of relief).

*obsidionem quattuor menses sustinere*—to hold out for four months.

*oppugnationem, obsidionem relinquere*—to give up an assault, a siege.

*portas obstruere* (B. G. 5. 50)—to barricade the gates.

*portas refringere* ⎱
*claustra portarum revellere* ⎰ to break down the gates.

*in oppidum irrumpere* ⎱
*in oppidum irruptionem facere* ⎰ to break into the town.

*oppidum capere, expugnare*—to take, storm a town.

*oppidum recipere*—to retake a town.

*oppidum incendere*—to fire a town.

*oppidum diripere*—to plunder a town.

*oppidum evertere, excīdere* — to completely destroy a town.

*oppidum solo aequare*—to raze a town to the ground.

*deditione facta* (Sall. Iug. 26)—after capitulation.

*arma tradere*—to surrender weapons.

*salutem petere a victore*—to beg for mercy from the conqueror.

*se suaque omnia dedere victori* ⎫ to give up one's person
*se suaque omnia permittere* ⎬ and all one's posses-
*victoris potestati* ⎭ sions to the conqueror.

*se permittere in fidem atque in potestatem alicuius* (B. G. 2. 3) —to surrender oneself to the discretion of some one.

*in fidem recipere aliquem* (Fam. 13. 16)—to deal mercifully with some one.

*libera corpora sub corona (hasta) veneunt* (B. G. 3. 16. 4)
　　—the free men are sold as slaves.

*cum uxoribus et liberis*—with wife and child.

*aliquem (incolumem) conservare*—to grant a man his life.

## 9. BEFORE THE FIGHT

*potestatem, copiam pugnandi hostibus facere*—to offer battle
　　to the enemy.

*potestatem sui facere (alicui)* (cf. p. 196, notes)—to accept
　　battle.

*proelio (ad pugnam) hostes lacessere, provocare*—to provoke
　　the enemy to battle.

*pugnam detrectare* (Liv. 3. 60)—to decline battle.

*supersedere proelio*—to refrain from fighting.

*hostem e manibus non dimittere*—to not let the enemy
　　escape.

*locum ad pugnam idoneum deligere*—to choose suitable
　　ground for an engagement.

*diem pugnae constituere* (B. G. 3. 24)—to fix a day for the
　　engagement.

*signum proelii (committendi) exposcere* (B. G. 7. 19)—to
　　demand loudly the signal to engage.

*signum proelii dare*—to give the signal to engage.

*vexillum proponere* (Liv. 22. 3)—to fix the ensign on the
　　general's tent (as a signal to commence the engage-
　　ment).

*ad arma concurrere*—to rush to arms.

*exercitum educere* or *producere in aciem*—to lead the army
　　to the fight.

*ad vim et arma descendere (vid.* p. 54, notes)—to have
　　recourse to force of arms.

*in certamen descendere*—to engage in the fight.

*in aciem descendere* (Liv. 8. 8)—to enter the field of battle.

*aciem* (*copias, exercitum*) *instruere* or *in acie constituere*—to draw up forces in battle-order.

*aciem triplĭcem instruere* (B. G. 1. 24) to draw up the army in three lines.

*aciem explicare* or *dilatare*—to extend the line of battle, deploy the battalions.

*media acies*—the centre.

*subsidia collocare*—to station reserve troops.

*equites ad latera disponere* (B. G. 6. 8)—to place the cavalry on the wings.

*contionari apud milites* (B. C. 1. 7)⎱to harangue the sol-
*contionem habere apud milites* ⎰ diers.

*ad virtutem excitare, cohortari* (or simply *adhortari, cohortari*) —to incite to valour.

*animos militum confirmare* (B. G. 5. 49)—to encourage, embolden the soldiery.

## 10. THE FIGHT

### (*a*) THE FIGHT IN GENERAL

*proelium committere*—(1) to begin the battle, (2) to give battle.

*proelium inire* (Liv. 2. 14)—to engage.

*proelium facere*—to give battle.

*proelio equestri contendere*⎱to give battle with a cavalry-
*proelium equestre facere* ⎰ division.

*proelium facere secundum*⎱
*proeliis secundis uti* ⎰to fight successfully.

*rem* (*bene, male*) *gerere* (*vid.* p. 187, note)—to win, lose a fight (of the commander).

*proelium intermittere*—to interrupt the battle.

*proelium dirimere* (B. C. 1. 40)—to break off the fight.

*proelium restituere*—to renew the battle with success.

*proelium renovare, redintegrare*—to begin the fight again.

*proelium deserere*—to give up the fight.

*proelio, armis decertare* (B. G. 1. 50)—to fight a decisive battle.

*acie (armis, ferro) decernere* ⎫
*in acie dimicare* ⎭ to fight a pitched battle.

*proelio interesse*—to take part in the engagement.

*ex equo pugnare*—to fight on horseback.

*certamen singulare*—single combat.

*provocare aliquem ad certamen singulare*—to challenge some one to single combat.

*proelium cruentum, atrox*—a bloody battle.

*proelium iustum* (opp. *tumultuarium*)—a pitched battle.

### (*b*) THE ATTACK

*classicum canit* (B. C. 3. 82)—the trumpet sounds for the attack.

*gradum inferre in hostem*—to march on the enemy.

*aggredi hostem* ⎫
*invadere, impetum* [1] *facere in hostem* ⎬ to attack the enemy.
*signa inferre in hostem* ⎭

*impetum sustinere* (B. G. 1. 26)—to resist the attack, onset.

*impetum excipere* [2] (Liv. 6. 12)—to parry the attack.

---

[1] *impetus* is not used in the dative sing. or in the plur. ; these cases are supplied by *incursio*.

[2] Caesar's method of attack was usually this : the troops drawn up on rising ground charged at the double (*concursus*); when within range came *emissio telorum* or *pilorum*. This was followed up by a hand-to-hand *mêlée* (*impetus gladiorum*).

*in medios hostes se inicere*—to rush into the midst of the foe.

*per medios hostes (mediam hostium aciem) perrumpere*—to break through the enemy's centre.

*manum (us) conserere cum hoste* ⎫
*signa conferre cum hoste* [1] ⎬ to come to close quarters.
        ⎭

*proelio concurritur* (Sall. Iug. 59)—the lines charge in battle one on another.

*adversis hostibus occurrere*—to attack the enemy in the front.

*aversos hostes aggredi* ⎫
*hostes a tergo adoriri* ⎬ to attack the enemy in the rear.

*iusto* (opp. *tumultuario*) *proelio confligere cum hoste* (Liv. 35. 4)—to fight a pitched, orderly battle with an enemy.

*acies inclīnat* or *inclīnatur* (Liv. 7. 33)—the line of battle gives way.

*proelium anceps est* ⎫
*ancipiti Marte pugnatur* ⎬ the issue of the battle is undecided.

*diu anceps stetit pugna*—the issue of the day was for a long time uncertain.

*res est in periculo, in summo discrimine*—the position is critical.

*res ad triarios* [2] *redit* (Liv. 8. 8)—the triarii must now fight (proverbially = we are reduced to extremities).

---

[1] *signa conferre cum aliquo* also sometimes means to join forces.

[2] The *triarii* were the veterans who made up the third line behind the *principes* and *hastati*. If these first two lines were beaten or in difficulties (*laborare*), the *triarii*, who were in a kneeling posture (*dextro genu innixi*, Liv. 8. 9), stood up (*consurgebant*, Liv. 8. 10) and continued the fight. Hence this proverb (*inde rem ad triarios redisse cum laboratur proverbio increbuit*). For the organisation of the legion in general *vid.* Liv. book 8.

## (c) CLOSE QUARTERS

*collatis signis (viribus) pugnare*—to fight hand-to-hand, at close quarters.

*tum pes cum pede collatus est* (Liv. 28. 2)—a hand-to-hand engagement ensued.

*collato pede* (Liv. 6. 12)—hand to hand.

*gladio comminus* (opp. *eminus*) *rem gerere*—to fight with swords at close quarters.

*omissis pilis gladiis rem gerere*—to throw down the javelins (*pila*) and fight with the sword.

*res ad gladios vēnit* ⎱ swords must now decide the
*res gladiis geri coepta est* ⎰ day.

*strictis gladiis in hostem ferri*—to throw oneself on the enemy with drawn sword.

*res ad manus venit*—the fighting is now at close quarters.

*laxatis* (opp. *confertis*) *ordinibus pugnare*—to fight in open order.

*ferarum* [1] *ritu pugnare*—to fight like lions.

*manu fortis*—personally brave.


## (d) TACTICS—REINFORCEMENTS

*in latus hostium incurrere* — to fall upon the enemy's flank.

*circumvenire hostem aversum* or *a tergo* (B. G. 2. 26)—to surround the enemy from the rear.

*multitudine hostium cingi* — to be surrounded by the superior force of the enemy.

---

[1] The Latin language uses the general term (*fera*) where we use the special (lion). Similarly *pecorum modo fugiunt* (Liv. 40. 27), where we translate "they flee like deer."

*equitatu superiorem esse* — to have 'the advantage in cavalry.

*parem* (opp. *impărem*) *esse hosti*—to be a match for the enemy.

*orbem* [1] *facere* (Sall. Iug. 97. 5)
*in orbem consistere* } to form a square.

*cuneum facere* (Liv. 22. 47)—to draw up troops in wedge-formation.

*phalangem facere* (B. G. 1. 24)—to form a phalanx.

*phalangem perfringere*—to break through the phalanx.

*subsidia summittere*—to send up reserves.

*integros defatigatis summittere*—to send fresh troops to take the place of those wearied with fighting.

*rari dispersique pugnare* (B. C. 1. 44)—to fight in skirmishing order.

*integri et recentes defatigatis succedunt*—fresh troops relieve the tired men.


(*e*) SUCCESSFUL ATTACK

*pellere hostem*—to repulse the enemy.

*acies hostium impellitur*—the enemy's line is repulsed.

*loco movere, depellere, deicere hostem* (B. G. 7. 51)—to drive the enemy from his position.

*summovere* or *reicere hostium equites*—to repel the attack of the enemy's cavalry.

*repellere, propulsare hostem*—to repulse an attack.

---

[1] *orbis* properly a circle, but corresponding almost exactly in its objects to our square-formation (*vid.* B. G. 4. 37, 5. 33; Sall. Iug. 97. 5). For a good account of Roman military formation see Kraner, *Uebersicht des Kriegwesens bei Caesar*, in his edition of the *Bellum Gallicum*.

*undique premi, urgeri* (B. G. 2. 26)—to be pressed on all sides.

*prosternere, profligare hostem*—to rout the enemy

## (*f*) Retreat—Flight—Pursuit

*signa receptui canunt*  
*receptui canitur* (B. G. 7. 47)} the retreat is sounded.

*pedem referre*—to retire (without turning one's back on the enemy).

*equitatus tutum receptum dat* — the cavalry covers the retreat.

*se recipere* (B. G. 7. 20)—to withdraw one's forces.

*loco excedere*—to abandon one's position.

*in fugam dare, conicere hostem*  
*fugare hostem* } to put the enemy to flight.

*fundere hostium copias*—to rout the enemy's forces.

*caedere et fundere hostem*  
*fundere et fugare hostem* } to utterly rout the enemy.

*prae se agere hostem*—to drive the enemy before one.

*fugam facere* (Sall. Iug. 53)—(1) to put to flight, (2) to take to flight.

*terga vertere* or *dare*—to flee, run away.

*terga dare hosti*—to run away from the enemy.

*fugae se mandare* (B. G. 2. 24)  
*fugam capessere, capere ·*  
*se dare in fugam, fugae*  
*se conicere, se conferre in fugam* } to take to flight.

*fuga salutem petere*—to seek safety in flight.

*fuga effusa, praeceps* (Liv. 30. 5)—headlong flight.

*pecorum modo fugere* (Liv. 40. 27) — to flee like deer, sheep.

*arma abicere*—to throw away one's arms.

*praecipitem se fugae mandare*—to flee headlong.

*ex (in) fuga dissipati* or *dispersi* (B. G. 2. 24)—soldiers routed and dispersed.

*hostes insequi, prosequi*—to pursue the enemy.

*hostes (fusos) persequi*—to follow up and harass the enemy when in flight.

*hostes assequi, consequi*—to overtake the enemy.

*fugientibus instare*—to press the fugitives.

*tergis hostium inhaerere*—to be on the heels of the enemy.

*fugam hostium reprimere* (B. G. 3. 14)—to bring the flying enemy to a stand.

*excipere aliquem fugientem*—to cut off some one's flight.

*magna caedes hostium fugientium facta est*—there was great slaughter of fugitives.

*capere aliquem vivum*—to take a person alive.

*effugere, elābi e manibus hostium* — to escape from the hands of the enemy

*dimittere e manibus hostes*—to let the enemy escape.

*eripere aliquem e manibus hostium*—to rescue some one from the hands of the enemy.

*se fuga recipere* (B. G. 1. 11)—to save oneself by flight.


## (g) Defeat—Massacre—Wounds—Losses

*proelio vinci, superari, inferiorem, victum discedere*—to be defeated in fight, lose the battle.

*cladem hostibus afferre, inferre*—to inflict a defeat on the enemy.

*cladem accipere*—to suffer a defeat.

*ingentem caedem edere* (Liv. 5. 13)—to cause great slaughter, carnage.

*stragem edere, facere*—to massacre.

*omnia strata sunt ferro*—all have perished by the sword.

*hostes, exercitum delere, concīdere*—to annihilate, cut up the
enemy, an army.

*hostes ad internecionem caedere,*
　*delere* (Liv. 9. 26)　　　 to absolutely annihilate
*hostium copias occidione occīdere*　the enemy.
　(Liv. 2. 51)

*vulnus infligere alicui*—to wound a person (also used
metaphorically).

*mortiferam plagam alicui infligere*—to inflict a mortal
wound on some one.

*vulnus (grave, mortiferum) accipere, excipere*—to be (seriously, mortally) wounded.

*multis et illatis et acceptis vulneribus* (B. G. 1. 50)—after
many had been wounded on both sides.

*vulneribus confectus*—weakened by wounds.

*vulnera (cicatrices) adversa* (opp.
　*aversa*)　　　　　　　　　　 wounds (scars) on the
*vulnera adverso corpore accepta*　breast.

*refricare*[1] *vulnus, cicatricem obductam*—to open an old
wound.

*ex vulnere mori* (Fam. 10. 33)—to die of wounds.

*magno cum detrimento*—with great loss.

*nostri circiter centum ceciderunt*—about a hundred of our
men fell.

*ad unum omnes*[2] *perierunt*—they perished to a man.

---

[1] *refricare* is also used metaphorically in the sense of renewing,
recalling, e.g. *dolorem* (De Or. 2. 48); *memoriam* (Phil. 3. 7. 18);
*desiderium* (Fam. 5. 17. 4).

[2] The phrase *ad unum omnes*, to a man, without exception, occurs
De Am. 23. 86; Fam. 12. 14; Liv. 2. 55; and without *omnes*, Fam.
10. 16; B. C. 3. 14.

## 11. VICTORY—TRIUMPH

*exercitus victor*—the victorious army.

*superiorem* (opp. *inferiorem*), *victorem* (*proelio, pugna*) *discedere*—to come off victorious.

*victoriam adipisci, parĕre*⎫
*victoriam ferre, referre*  ⎬to gain a victory, win a battle.
*proelio vincere*          ⎭

*victoriam reportare ab hoste*—to gain a victory over the enemy.

*victoriam praecipere* (*animo*) (Liv. 10. 26)—to consider one-self already victor.

*victoriam exploratam dimittere*—to let a sure victory slip through one's hands.

*sicut parta iam atque explorata victoria*—as if the victory were already won.

*victoriam conclamare* (B. G. 5. 37)—to raise a shout of victory.

*victoriam* or *de victoria gratulari alicui*—to congratulate a person on his victory.

*victoria multo sanguine ac vulneribus stetit* (Liv. 23. 30)—the victory cost much blood and many wounds, was very dearly bought.

*triumphare de aliquo* (*ex bellis*)⎫
*triumphum*[1] *agere de* or *ex ali-*⎪
   *quo* or c. Gen. (*victoriae,*⎬to triumph over some one.
   *pugnae*)                    ⎪
                              ⎭

*per triumphum* (*in triumpho*) *aliquem ducere*—to lead some one in triumph.

[1] E.g. *triumphum agere Boiorum* (Liv.) ; *Pharsaliae pugnae* (Cic.); *de Liguribus* (Liv.); *ex Aequis* (Liv.) For other phrases cf. *triumphum postulare, imperare ; triumphum tertium deportare ; triumphum consulis celebrare.*

*triumphum senatus Africano decernit* (Fin. 4. 9. 22)—the
senate decrees to Africanus the honours of a
triumph.

## 12. TRUCE—PEACE—TREATIES—ALLIANCE

*indutias facere* (Phil. 8. 7)—to make a truce.
*indutias violare*—to break a truce.
*ius gentium violare*—to violate the law of nations.
*agere cum aliquo de pace*—to treat with some one about
peace.
*pacem conciliare* (Fam. 10. 27)—to bring about a peace.
*pacem facere cum aliquo* — to make peace with some
one.
*pacem dirimere, frangere*—to break the peace.
*his condicionibus*—on these terms.
*pacis condiciones ferre* (not *proponere*)—to propose terms
of peace.
*pacis condiciones dare, dicere alicui* (Liv. 29. 12)—to dictate
the terms of peace to some one.
*pacis condiciones accipere, subire* (opp. *repudiare, respuere*)
—to accept the terms of the peace.
*pax convĕnit in eam condicionem, ut* . . .—peace is con-
cluded on condition that . . .
*summa pax*—deep peace.
*captivos permutare, commutare*—to exchange prisoners.
*captivos redimere* (Off. 2. 18)—to ransom prisoners.
*captivos sine pretio reddere*—to restore prisoners without
ransom.
*obsides dare*—to give hostages.
*obsides civitatibus imperare*—to compel communities to
provide hostages.

*pactionem facere cum aliquo* (Sall. Iug. 40)—to conclude a
    treaty with some one.

*ex pacto, ex fœdere*—according to treaty.

*fœdus facere (cum aliquo), icere, ferire*—to conclude a
    treaty, an alliance.

*fœdus frangere, rumpere, violare*—to violate a treaty,
    terms of alliance.

*socium aliquem asciscere* (B. G. 1. 5)—to make some one
    one's ally.

*in amicitia populi Romani esse* (Liv. 22. 37)—to be on
    friendly terms with the Roman people.

*a senatu amicus* [1] *appellatus est* (B. G. 1. 3)—he received
    from the senate the title of friend.


## 13. CONQUEST—SUBMISSION

*terra potiri*—to conquer a country.

*terram suae dicionis facere*  
*populum in potestatem suam re-*  
   *digere* (B. G. 2. 34)     to reduce a country to  
*populum in deditionem venire*      subjection to oneself.  
   *cogere*

*populum in deditionem accipere*—to accept the submission
    of a people.

*populum perdomare, subigere*—to subjugate a nation.

*populum, terram suo imperio, suae potestati subicere* (not *sibi*
    by itself)—to make oneself master of a people,
    country.

[1] *amicus*, the friend of the Roman people, distinct from *socius*, an
ally ; a *socius* was always *amicus*, but not necessarily *vice versa*.
The title *amicus populi Romani* was granted by the senate to
foreign princes in recognition of some signal service.

*se imperio alicuius subicere* (not
　　*alicui*) } 
*in deditionem venire* (without *alicui*)　} to make one's sub-
*in alicuius potestatem se permittere* } mission to some
　　　　　　　　　　　　　　　　　　　　one.

*sub imperio et dicione alicuius esse*
*subiectum esse, obnoxium esse im-*
　　*perio* or *dicioni alicuius* (not　} to be subject to some
　　simply *alicui*)　　　　　　　　　　} one, under some one's
*in potestate, in dicione alicuius*　} dominion.
　　*esse*

*qui imperio subiecti sunt*—subjects.

*aliquem ad officium* (cf. p. 172, note) *reducere* (Nep. Dat.
　　2. 3)—to reduce a people to their former obedience.

*aliquem in officio continere*—to keep some one in subjection.

*in officio manere, permanere*—to remain in subjection.

*Asiam in provinciae formam* (*in provinciam*) *redigere* (B. G.
　　1. 45)—to make Asia into a Roman province.

*Asia populi Romani facta est*—Asia was made subject to
　　Rome.

*gentem ad internecionem redigere* or *adducere* (B. G. 2. 28)
　　—to completely annihilate a nation.


# XVII.  SHIPPING

## 1. NAVAL AFFAIRS IN GENERAL

*navis actuaria*—a cutter.

*navis longa*—a man-of-war.

*navis oneraria*—a transport or cargo-boat.

*navis mercatoria*—a merchantman.

*oppidum maritimum*—a seaport town.

*navibus plurimum posse*
*rebus maritimis multum valere* } to have a powerful navy.

*navem, classem aedificare, facere, efficere, instituere*—to build a ship, a fleet.

*navem (classem) armare, ornare, instruere*—to equip a boat, a fleet.

*navem deducere (vid.* p. 186, note)—to launch a boat.

*navem subducere (in aridum)*—to haul up a boat.

*navem reficere*—to repair a boat.

*navem conscendere, ascendere*—to embark.

*exercitum in naves imponere* (Liv. 22. 19)—to embark an army.

*milites in terram, in terra exponere*—to disembark troops.

*classiarii*[1] (B. C. 3. 100)—marines.

*nautae, remiges*—sailors, rowers.

*vectores* (Phil. 7. 9. 27)—passengers.

*naves annotinae*—ships of last year.


## 2. VOYAGE—SHIPWRECK—LANDING

*solvere* (B. G. 4. 28)
*navem (naves) solvere* } to weigh anchor, sail.
*ancoram (ancoras) tollere*

*naves ex portu solvunt*—the ships sail from the harbour

*malacia et tranquillitas* (B. G. 3. 15)—a dead calm.

*vela in altum dare* (Liv. 25. 27)—to put to sea.

*ventum (tempestatem) nancti idoneum ex portu exeunt*—the ships sail out on a fair wind.

---

[1] Also *classici milites, classica legio* (Liv. 21. 41 ; 22. 19). The marines were recruited from the lowest classes (*capite censi*) and from the *liberti*. The rowers were slaves ; the ordinary sailors were *socii navales*.

*vela facere, pandere*⎫
*vela dare*      ⎬to set the sails.

*vela contrahere* (also metaph.)—to furl the sails.

*oram legere* (Liv. 21. 51)—to hug the coast.

*superare insulam, promunturium*—to double an island, cape.

*ventis reflantibus* (Tusc. 1. 49)—with the wind against one.

*cursum dirigere aliquo*—to set one's course for a place.

*cursum tenere* (opp. *commutare* and *deferri*)—to hold on one's course.

*cursum conficere* (Att. 5. 12. 1)—to finish one's voyage.

*gubernaculum tractare*⎫
*clavum tenere*     ⎬to steer.

*navem remis agere* or *propellere*—to row.

*remis contendere*          ⎫
*navem remis concitare, incitare*⎬to row hard.

*sustinere, inhibere remos* (De Or. 1. 33)—to stop rowing; to easy.

*navem retro inhibere* (Att. 13. 21)—to back water.

*naufragium facere*—to be shipwrecked.

*navis ad scopulos alliditur* (B. C. 3. 27)—the ship strikes on the rocks.

*vento se dare*—to run before the wind.

*in litus eici* (B. G. 5. 10)—to be stranded.

*deferri, deici aliquo*⎫ to be driven out of one's course; to
*tempestate abrĭpi*   ⎬ drift.

*procella (tempestas) aliquem ex alto ad ignotas terras (oras) defert*—the storm drives some one on an unknown coast.

*naufragium colligere* (Sest. 6. 15)—to collect the wreckage.

*appellere navem (ad terram, litus)*—to land (of people).

*appelli (ad oram)* (Att. 13. 21)—to land (of ships).

*ancoras iacere*—to drop anchor.

*ancoras tollere*—to weigh anchor.

*naves ad ancoras deligare* (B. G. 4. 29)

*naves (classem) constituere (in alto)*

} to make fast boats to anchors.

*ad ancoram consistere*

*ad ancoras deligari*

*in ancoris esse, stare, consistere*

} to ride at anchor.

*exire ex, de navi*

*egredi (ex) navi*

*exire, egredi in terram*

*escensionem facere* (of troops)

} to land, disembark.

*portu, terra prohiberi* (B. C. 3. 15)—to be unable to land.

*litora ac portus custodia clausos tenere*—to keep the coast and harbours in a state of blockade.

*deperire*—to founder, go down.

*aestu incitato*—at high tide.


## 3. A NAVAL BATTLE

*navis praetoria* (Liv. 21. 49)—the admiral's ship; the flagship.

*pugnam navalem facere*[1]—to fight a battle at sea.

*navem expedire*—to clear for action.

*navem rostro percutere*—to charge, ram a boat.

*navem expugnare*—to board and capture a boat.

*navem, classem deprimere, mergere*—to sink a ship, a fleet.

*classes concurrunt* (Liv. 26. 39)—the fleets charge.

---

[1] For a description of a sea-fight *vid.* B. G. iii. 13-16.

*copulas, manus ferreas (in navem)* ⎫
    *inicere* ⎬ to throw grappling-irons on board; to board.
*in navem (hostium) transcendere* ⎭

*navem capere, intercipere, deprehendere*—to capture a boat.

*vela armamentaque*—sails and rigging.

*ex eo navium concursu magnum incommodum est acceptum*
    —much damage was done by this collision.

*navigia speculatoria*—reconnoitring-vessels.

# APPENDIX

*ut ait Cicero* (always in this order)—as Cicero says.

*ut Ciceronis verbis utar*—to use Cicero's expression ; to say with Cicero (not *ut cum Cicerone loquar*).

*ut ita dicam*—so to speak (used to modify a figurative expression).

*ut non* (*nihil*) *dicam de* . . .—not to mention . . .

*ut plura non dicam*—to say nothing further on : . .

*ne dicam*—not to say . . . (used in avoiding a stronger expression).

*ne* (*quid*) *gravius dicam*—to say the least . . .

*ut breviter dicam*—to put it briefly.

*denique*
*ne multa, quid plura ? sed quid*
  *opus est plura ?*
*ut paucis* (*rem*) *absolvam*
*ut paucis* (*brevi, breviter*) *com-*
  *plectar*  }  in short ; to be brief.
*ut brevi comprehendam*
*ut brevi praecīdam*

*ut eorum, quae dixi, summam faciam*—to sum up . . .

*ne longum sit*
*ne longus, multus sim*  }  not to be prolix.
*ne diutius vos demŏrer*

*ne in re nota et pervulgata multus sim*—not to be diffuse on such a well-known subject.

*ut levissime dicam* (opp. *ut gravissimo verbo utar*)—to use the mildest expression.

*ut planius dicam*—to express myself more plainly.

*ut verius dicam*—to put it more exactly.

*ut semel* or *in perpetuum dicam*—to say once for all.

*ut in eodem simili verser*—to use the same simile, illustration.

*ut hoc utar* or *afferam*—to use this example.

*dicam quod sentio*—I will give you my true opinion.

*tantum* or *unum illud* or *hoc dico*—I will only say this much . . .

*non nego, non infitior*—I do not deny.

*hoc dici potest de aliqua re*
*hoc cadit in aliquid* } this can be said of . . .,
*hoc transferri potest in aliquid* } applies to . . .

*dixi quasi praeteriens* or *in transitu*—I said *en passant*, by the way.

*sexcenties, millies dixi*—I have said it a thousand times.

*ut supra* (opp. *infra*) *diximus, dictum est*—as I said above.

*dici vix* (*non*) *potest* or *vix potest dici* (*vix* like *non* always before *potest*)—I cannot find words for . . .

*incredibile dictu est*—it sounds incredible.

*supersedeo oratione* (not *dicere*)
*omitto dicere* } I avoid mentioning . . . ; I prefer not to touch upon . . .

*haec habeo dicere* or *habeo quae dicam*—this I have to say.

*haec (fere) dixit*—he spoke (very much) as follows.

*hanc in sententiam dixit*—the tenor of his speech was this . . .

*mihi quaedam dicenda sunt de hac re*—I have a few words to say on this.

*quod vere praedicare possum*—without wishing to boast, yet . . .

*quod non arroganter dixerim*—which I can say without offence, arrogance.

*pace tua dixerim* or *dicere liceat*  
*bona (cum) venia tua dixerim* } allow me to say . . .

*non est huius loci* c. Inf.  
*non est hic locus, ut . . .* } this is not the place to . . .

*sed de hoc alias pluribus*—more of this another time.

*atque* or *sed haec (quidem)*  
   *hactenus*     } so much for this subject . . . ;  
*atque haec quidem de . . .*   enough has been said  
*ac (sed) de . . . satis dixi,*   on . . .  
   *dictum est*

*haec (quidem) ille*—this much he said.

*haec Ciceronis fere*—this is very much what Cicero said.

*atque etiam hoc animadvertendum est*—there is this also to notice.

*ad reliqua pergamus, progrediamur*—to pass on.

*hic (ille) locus obscurus est*—this passage is obscure.

*hoc in medio relinquamus*—let us leave that undecided.

*sed lābor longius*—but that takes us too far.

*non id ad vivum reseco* (Lael. 5. 8)—I do not take that too strictly.

*nonnulla praedīcam*—I wish to say a few words in preface.

*ut omittam* c. Accus.  
*cum discessi, -eris, -eritis ab* } putting aside, except.  
*praeter* c. Accus.

*ut praetermittam* c. Acc. c. Inf. } to except the fact  
*praeterquam quod* or *nisi quod* } that . . .

*hoc in promptu est* ⎫
*hoc in aperto est* ⎰ it is clear, evident.

*hoc est luce (sole ipso) clarius*—this is as clear as daylight.

*hoc facile intellegi potest* ⎫
*hoc per se intellegitur* ⎬ that is self-evident, goes without
*hoc sua sponte appāret* ⎭ saying.

*ex quo intellegitur* or *intellegi*
  *potest, debet* ⎫
*ex quo perspicuum est* ⎬ from this it appears, is
*inde patet, appāret* ⎭ apparent.

*apparet et exstat* ⎫
*exstat atque eminet* ⎰ it is quite manifest.

*si quaeris, si verum quaerimus*—to put it exactly.

*id quod maximum, gravissimum*
  *est* ⎫
⎬ the main point.
*quod caput est* ⎭

*quod maius est*—what is more important.

*testis est, testatur, declarat* ⎫
*documento, indicio est* (without ⎪
  demonstr. pron. but *cui rei* ⎬ this shows, proves . . .
  *documento, indicio est*) ⎭

*sed hoc nihil (sane) ad rem*—but this is not to the point.

*aliquid* (τι) *dicis* (opp. ⎫ there is something in what you
  *nihil dicis*) ⎬ say; you are more or less
*est istuc quidem aliquid* ⎭ right.

*audio, fateor*—I admit it, say on.

*ain tu ?*—do you think so? are you in earnest?

*nonne ?*—is it not so?

*quorsum haec (dicis)?*—what do you mean?

*male* (opp. *bene*) *narras (de)*—I am sorry to hear . . .

*monstra dicis, narras*—it is incredible.

*clarius loquere*—speak up, please.

*mihi crede* (not *crede mihi*)—believe me.

*per me licet*—I have no objection.

*rem acu tetigisti*—you have hit the nail on the head.

*ita prorsus existimo*—that is exactly what I think.

*ita res est*—it is so.

*res ita* (*aliter*) *se habet*—the matter stands so (otherwise).

*nec mirum, minime mirum* (*id quidem*), *quid mirum ?*—no wonder.

*neque id mirum est* or *videri debet*—there is nothing strange in that.

*et recte* (*iure, merito*)
*et recte* (*iure*) *quidem* ⎱quite rightly.
*recte, iure id quidem*

*neque immerito* (*iniuria*)
*neque id immerito* (*iniuria*) ⎱and rightly too.

*meo* (*tuo, suo*) *iure*
*iusto iure* ⎱with perfect right.

*iustissime, rectissime*
*optimo iure* (cf. *summo iure* ⎱legitimately ; with the fullest right.
  p. 237).

*macte virtute* (*esto* or *te esse iubeo*)—good luck to you.

*sed manum de tabula !*—but enough !

# INDEX

eripere spem, 154
erogare, 202, 218
errantes stellae, 7
error, 81
errores Ulixis, 12
eructare, 8
erudire, 96
eruditus, 93
erumpere, 35 (note)
eruptio, 8,
escendere, 122
esse (live), 32
esurire, 34
eventus, 44
evertere bonis, 188
   oppidum, 259
   rationem, 104
   rem publicam, 224
evincere, 105
evocare copias, 247
evocati, 247 (note)
evomere, 8, 163
exacta aetas, 33
exactio, 242 (note)
exaggerata oratio, 124
exalbescere, 149
exanclare, 50
exanimari, 31, 140
excedere dicimum annum, 33
   ex pueris, 32
   finibus, 10
   modum, 174
   vita, 39
excepti et expensi tabula, 204
excerpere, 142
excidere oppidum, 259
excipere hospitio, 193
   impetum, 262
   vulnus, 268
excitare a mortuis, 177
   ad spem, 154
   ad virtutem, 165, 261
   admirationem, 158
   animum, 151
   bellum, 252
   clamores, 118
   e somno, 38
   ignem, 5
   libidinem, 167

excitare motus, 145
   odium, 162
   turrim, 208
excolere, 95
excruciari, 174
excubare, 256
excultus, 95
excurrere, 10, 13
excursio, 256, 258
excusare, 37
excutere iugum, 228
   risum, 35
exedere, 51 (note)
exemplum, 99, 143
exercere artem, 114
   crudelitatem, 156
   imperium, 187
   inimicitias, 63
   iudicium, 51 (note)
   metalla, 51 (note)
   navem, 51 (note)
   vectigalia, 51
exercitatus in armis, 248
   in dicendo, 121
   in re publica, 213
exercitus, 247 *f.*
exhaurire, 40
exheredari, 199
exigere fabulam, 118
   nomina, 207
   pecuniam, 203
existimatio, 68, 69 (note), 220
existimator, 114
exitium, 52
exitus, 39, 44
expedire arma, 250
   navem, 275
   negotium, 72
   salutem, 54
expedita oratio, 124
expeditus ad, 121, 123
expellere ex urbe, 225
   regno, 227
expendere poenas, 244
experientia, 90 (note)
experiri, 90
expetere poenas, 163
expiare manes, 182
   scelus, 166

nudus, 251
numen, 177
numerare, 202
numeri, 117, 125
numerose cadere, 125
numerus, 117
nummus, 203 *f.*
nuncupare, 182
nundinae, 217
nuntius, 67, 198
nuptiae, 198
nutus, 1, 59

Ob, 44
obducere, 147
obdurescere, 147
obiectum esse, 52
obire, 39
obligare, 59
obliquum agmen, 254
obliquus, 16
obliterari, 90
oblivio, 89 *f.*
obnoxium esse, 272
obnuntiare, 184
obortis lacrimis, 35
obrepere, 33
obscurus, 214
obsecrare, 61 *f.* (note)
obsequi, 61, 173
obserare, 186
obsidere, 257
obsides, 270
obsidio, 257
obsignare, 144, 199
obsitus, 189
obsolescere, 200
obsoletus, 136, 189
obstare, 56
obstringere beneficio, 59
  fide, 160
  religione, 179
  scelere, 166
obstruere iter, 11
  luminibus, 208
  portas, 259
obterere, 28
obtinere dignitatem, 215 *f.*
  imperium, 226

obtinere ius, 237
  provinciam, 230
obtingere, 230
obtrectare, 68
obtundere, 24
obvenire, 230
obversari, 76
obviam, 14
obvolvere caput, 24
occaecari, 49, 167
occasio, 48
occasus solis, 6, 9
occidens, 9
occidentalis, 9 (note)
occidere, 39
occumbere, 39
occupare aliquem, 149
  locum, 255
  pecuniam, 203
  regnum, 226
occupatus, 73, 211
occurrere, 263
Oceanus, 5
oculus, 27, 126
odium, 161 *f.*
odor, 209, 224
offendere, 14, 168 *f.*
offensio, 168 *f.*, 220
officiosus, 172
officium, 172 *f.*
oleum, 71
Olympia (ludi), 120
omen, 184 *f.*
omittere occasionem, 48
  pila, 264
  timorem, 150
onerare, 168
onerarius, 272
opem ferre, 54 *f.*
opera, 71 *f.* (note)
opes, 55 *f.*, 220
opifex, 1
opinio, 79 *f.*
oppetere, 39
oppidum, 9, 257 *f.*
opponere, 108 *f.*
opportunitas loci, 9
oppressum esse, 38, 207
oppugnare, 258 *f.*

tritae aures, 24
triumphus, 269
trivio (in), 12
tuba, 257
tumultus, 224 (note)
tunicatus, 189 (note)
turbare mare, 5
 mentem, 145
 omnia, 224
 ordines, 254
turbator vulgi, 223
turpis, 164
turris, 208
tus, 182
tuto (in), 53
tyrannis, 226

UBERTAS, 125
ulcisci, 163 *f.*
ultimae terrae, 11
ultro citroque, 16
umbilicus, 3
umbracula, 98 (note)
umbratilis, 94 (note)
unguiculis (ab), 32
universitas rerum, 1
unus, 21 (note)
urbs patria, 31
urere, 8
usura, 203, 205
usus (experience), 90
 (utility), 56
uti aliquo, 62
 crudelitate, 84 (note)
 magistro, 96
 prudentia, 84 (note)
 solacio, 55
 suo consilio, 84
 suo iudicio, 83
 valetudine bona, 84 (note)
 verbis, 136
utilitas, 56
uxor, 198

VACARE, 72
vacatio, 247
vacillare, 88
vadum, 4
vagina, 251

vagus, 7
valedicere, 197 (note)
valere eloquentia, 121
 memoria, 88
valetudo, 36 (note)
vallum, 256, 258
valva, 186
varietas caeli, 6
vasa, 257
vastare, 257
vectigal, 51
vectores, 273
vehi, 14
velle alicuius causa, 58
 aliquem, 196
velum, 273
venalis, 59 (note)
vendere, 228
veneficia, 242
venenum, 40
veneo, 228 (note)
venerari, 177
venia, 156
venire ad gladium, 264
 in dubium, 81
 in mentem, 76
 in morem, 200
 in oblivionem, 89
 in proverbium, 139
 in sermonem, 67
 in vituperationem, 66
 obviam, 14
ventus, 5, 7
ver, 22
verba copulata, 139
 dare, 171
 facere, 122
verbi causa, 99 (note)
verbis alicuius, 136
verbum (ad), 136
vergere, 9
verisimilis, 80
veritas, 80 (note)
verno tempore, 22
versari ante oculos, 28
 in angustiis, 42
 in discrimine, 53
 in ore, 66
 in periculo, 53

# INDEX II